SAVAGE
EARTH

SAVAGE

ALWYN SCARTH

EARTH

TED SMART

In association with Granada Television

HarperCollins*Publishers*
77–85 Fulham Palace Road
London W6 8JB

This edition produced for:
The Book People Ltd.
Hall Wood Avenue
Haydock
St Helens WA11 9UL

02 01 00 99 98 97
10 9 8 7 6 5 4 3 2 1

I am very pleased to record my most sincere thanks (in alphabetical order) to Anthony Newton, Francine Ozanne, Katie Piper, Jean-Louis Renaud, Henri Rouvier and Jean-Claude Tanguy, for all their valuable help while I was preparing this book.

Alwyn Scarth was for 30 years a Lecturer in Geography at Dundee University. He is now based mainly in Paris where he continues his writing and research.

Adapted from the Granada Television series SAVAGE EARTH. The production team behind SAVAGE EARTH was: Series Producer: Bill Jones; Producers: Liz McLeod, Bill Lyons; Directors Chris Malone, Bill Lyons; Assistant Producers: Kate Coombes, Emma Hawley, Debra Prinselaar, Ann-Marie Burnham; Film Research: Maggi Cook; Production Co-ordinator: Del Bowen-Hayes; Production Finance: Tim Hynes; Cameras: Lawrence Jones, Tim Pollard; Sound: Mark Atkinson; Film Editors: David Creswell, Kim Horton; Music: Howard Davidson; Graphic Design: Paul Kearton.

ISBN 0 583 33421 0

Designed by Clare Baggaley

Colour reproduction by Colourscan, Singapore
Printed and bound by Graficas Estella, Spain

CONTENTS

1

2

3

4

the Earth in perspective

THE EARTH IS A DYNAMIC PLANET: IT IS CONSTANTLY CHANGING. THE IMMENSE ENERGY THAT LIES BENEATH THE SURFACE MOVES CONTINENTS, CREATES ISLANDS AND CAN OPEN UP GREAT CRACKS IN THE GROUND. FOR EXAMPLE, WHILE THE ATLANTIC OCEAN IS WIDENING AT ITS CENTRE, THE FLOOR OF THE PACIFIC OCEAN IS PLUNGING BENEATH THE SURROUNDING LAND MASSES, WHERE IT MELTS AND FORMS THE MOST SPECTACULAR SYSTEM OF VOLCANOES IN THE WORLD: THE 'RING OF FIRE'. EARTHQUAKES ACCOMPANY MANY OF THESE DYNAMIC CHANGES, AS WELL AS VOLCANIC ERUPTIONS, AND TOGETHER THEY COMPRISE THE MOST SPECTACULAR EXAMPLES OF THE EARTH'S POWER.

On a day-to-day basis, we are aware only of the catastrophic manifestations of the changes that are occurring beneath the Earth's crust, and as a result it has taken scientists many years to discover the reasons for these dramatic events. The true picture unfolds over millions of years with the movement of the plates that make up the land-masses and ocean floors at an average annual rate of around 10cm (4in). This, however, is fast enough to have opened up the whole Atlantic Ocean between Europe and North America within 180 million years. The Earth is 4,600 million years old – there has been plenty of time for slow changes to produce vast results.

From the human point of view, the powers unleashed when a movement takes place – perhaps a slip of just 5m (16½ft) in rocks 10km (6¼ miles) deep – can cause a devastating earthquake. Molten rock, rising through a narrow chimney in the crust, can explode and bury an entire city.

On 23 January 1973 Helgafell erupted on the island of Heimaey, off the coast of Iceland, threatening the town of Vestmannaeyjar

Volcanic activity produces volcanoes, hot springs and geysers, such as this one at Yellowstone National Park, United States

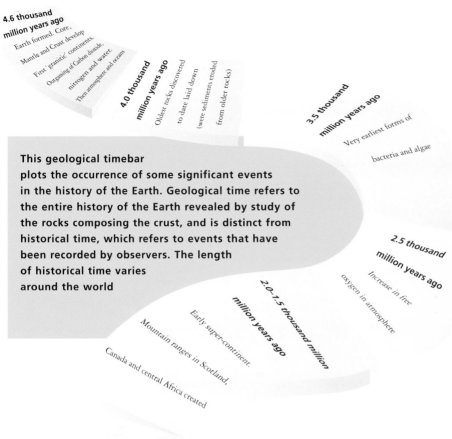

4.6 thousand million years ago
Earth formed. Core, Mantle and Crust develop. First 'granitic' continents. Outgassing of Carbon dioxide, nitrogen and water. Then atmosphere and oceans

4.0 thousand million years ago
Oldest rocks discovered to date laid down (were sediments eroded from older rocks)

3.5 thousand million years ago
Very earliest forms of bacteria and algae

This geological timebar plots the occurrence of some significant events in the history of the Earth. Geological time refers to the entire history of the Earth revealed by study of the rocks composing the crust, and is distinct from historical time, which refers to events that have been recorded by observers. The length of historical time varies around the world

2.5 thousand million years ago
Increase in free oxygen in atmosphere

2.0–1.5 thousand million years ago
Early super-continent. Mountain ranges in Scotland, Canada and central Africa created

700 million years ago
Early multicellular life

570 million years ago
Super-continent breaks up. Organisms with shells; fossils

500 million years ago
Early fish

450 million years ago

350 million years ago

300 million years ago

225 million years ago

180 million years ago

140 million years ago

65 million years ago

50 million years ago
Early horses

350 million years ago
Early trees. Main coal measures. 'Hercynian' mountains in central France, central Germany, Poland

225 million years ago
Super-continent splits in two: 'Laurasia' in north; 'Gondwanaland' in south

140 million years ago
Early flowering plants
Andean mountains begin to form

10,000 years ago
'Modern' Man

450 million years ago
Early land plants. 'Caledonian' mountains in Scotland, Norway, eastern United States

300 million years ago
New super-continent 'Pangaea' Early reptiles

180 million years ago
Laurasia splits; Atlantic Ocean starts opening Gondwanaland splits; Indian Ocean starts opening Early birds and mammals

65 million years ago
Extinction of dinosaurs
Early primates
Rocky Mountains begin to form

40–50 million years ago
India starts to collide with Asia; Himalayan mountains begin to form
Africa colliding with Europe; Pyrenees and Alps begin to form

15 million years ago
Arabia separates from Africa; Red Sea opens

11 million years ago
Mediterranean Sea closed at Straits of Gibraltar, dries up for a time

100,000 years ago
Neanderthal Man

1.8 million years ago
Start of widespread glaciations

c.3 million years ago
Stone tools used by human-like beings

the Earth's surface

THE DIFFERENT WAYS IN WHICH SECTIONS OF THE EARTH'S CRUST BEHAVE ARE ESSENTIAL TO AN UNDERSTANDING OF EARTHQUAKES AND VOLCANOES. HERE WE OUTLINE THE DIFFERENT TYPES OF INTERACTION BETWEEN THE CRUSTAL PLATES THAT COMPRISE THE OCEAN FLOORS AND THE CONTINENTS ON WHICH WE LIVE, AND WHAT IS HAPPENING BENEATH THE EARTH'S SURFACE.

Subduction: where one oceanic plate plunges underneath another, volcanic islands such as the Aleutian Islands, off the coast of Alaska, may form; also produces earthquakes

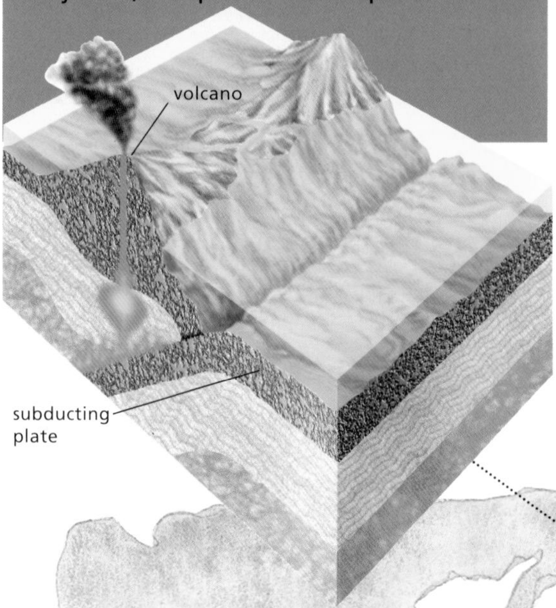

volcano

subducting plate

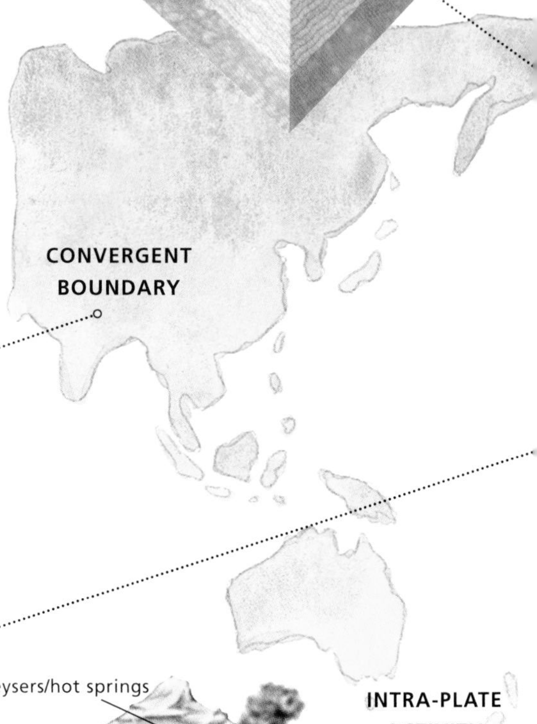

CONVERGENT BOUNDARY

Collision: where one continental plate plunges underneath another. This process forms ranges of high, folded mountains such as the Himalayas. Continuing pressures cause frequent earthquakes along cracks or faults in the rocks

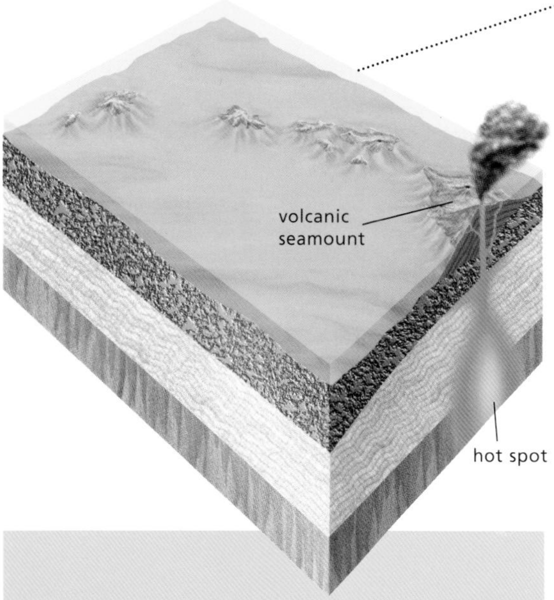

geysers/hot springs

INTRA-PLATE ACTIVITY

volcanic seamount

hot spot

hot spot

Oceanic hotspot: where volcanic activity in the form of hotspots creates volcanic seamounts that may build up above sea-level as in Hawaii

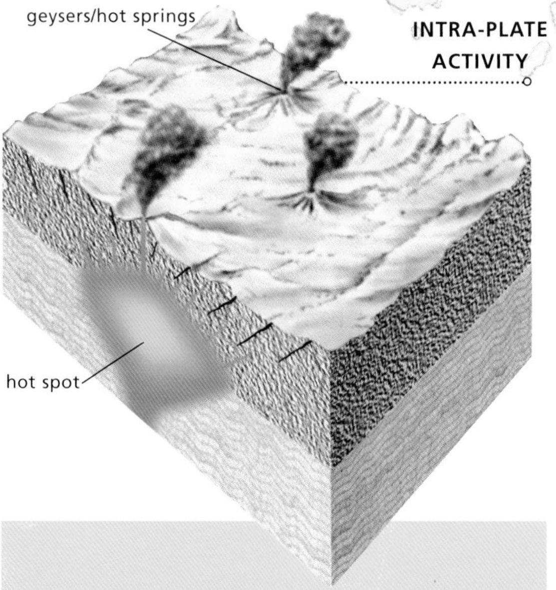

Continental hotspot: where volcanic activity producess hot springs, geysers and other forms of mild volcanic activity, as seen on North Island, New Zealand

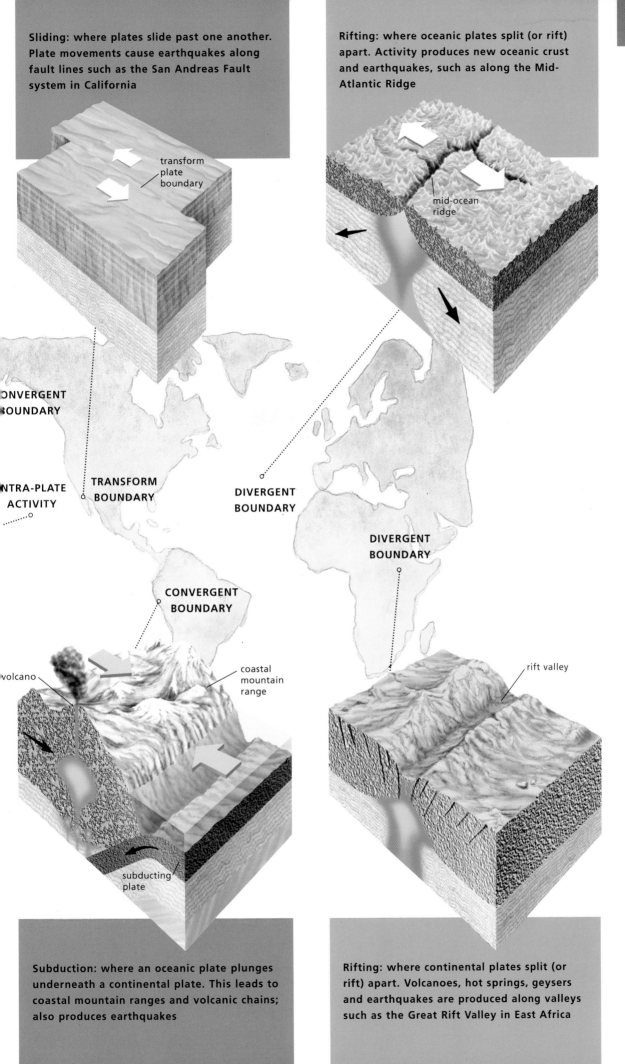

Sliding: where plates slide past one another. Plate movements cause earthquakes along fault lines such as the San Andreas Fault system in California

transform plate boundary

Rifting: where oceanic plates split (or rift) apart. Activity produces new oceanic crust and earthquakes, such as along the Mid-Atlantic Ridge

mid-ocean ridge

ONVERGENT
BOUNDARY

NTRA-PLATE
ACTIVITY

TRANSFORM
BOUNDARY

DIVERGENT
BOUNDARY

DIVERGENT
BOUNDARY

CONVERGENT
BOUNDARY

volcano

coastal mountain range

rift valley

subducting plate

Subduction: where an oceanic plate plunges underneath a continental plate. This leads to coastal mountain ranges and volcanic chains; also produces earthquakes

Rifting: where continental plates split (or rift) apart. Volcanoes, hot springs, geysers and earthquakes are produced along valleys such as the Great Rift Valley in East Africa

summary

THE AIM OF THIS BOOK IS TO EXAMINE ALL ASPECTS OF EARTHQUAKES AND VOLCANIC ERUPTIONS IN TERMS OF THE SIX QUESTIONS ESSENTIAL TO ANY INVESTIGATION: WHY? HOW? WHERE? WHAT? WHO? AND WHEN?

Why?
The answer to this question is dependent on the nature of the Earth's interior.

How?
Here we need to look at the results of the movements of the crustal plates.

A bleak view showing the aftermath of the 1906 earthquake in San Francisco, California

Where?
The location of earthquake and volcanic activity is directly linked to the growth, conflict and destruction of these plates.

What?
This is the question that receives the closest attention in this book. Earthquakes vary in magnitude and in their destructive intensity. Volcanic eruptions display over a dozen different styles, producing anything from hot water to molten lava and the finest ash. Both earthquakes and eruptions generate important secondary effects, which can be just as calamitous: huge sea-waves or tsunamis, mudflows, landslides, fires, famines, diseases and vast destruction.

Who?
Here we must focus attention on the victims of these natural disasters. The numbers involved depend on a range of factors including the density of population, the style of building, and the extent of awareness and emergency training.

When?
Since the Earth behaves with a certain consistency, careful study of the past encourages scientists to forecast its future behaviour. It is possible to make long-term forecasts in terms of say, ten or 100 or 1,000 years, especially after an area has been closely monitored. But the Earth functions in long time-spans, and short-term predictions are extremely difficult to make for both eruptions and earthquakes. The millions of people living in the dangerous belts of the Earth's surface, however, desperately need to know exactly when the next eruption or earthquake will happen. There has been significant progress, but until such time that accurate predictions can be made, we will have to rely on the speedy communication of information, advances in building technology and populations that are well-equipped to deal with disasters when they strike.

Trees flattened by the blast produced by the eruption of Mount St Helens in 1980

Old Faithful, a geyser at Yellowstone National Park, United States, erupts about once every 67 minutes and its timetable is posted daily for visitors. Other geysers may erupt much less regularly

the composition
of the Earth

THE REASONS THAT EARTHQUAKES AND VOLCANIC ERUPTIONS TAKE PLACE DEPEND ON THE
NATURE OF THE EARTH'S INTERIOR. THE DIAGRAM (RIGHT) SHOWS HOW THE DIFFERENT
ELEMENTS THAT COMPRISE OUR PLANET ARE ARRANGED, AND THE INDIVIDUAL
SECTIONS OF THE STRUCTURE OF THE EARTH ARE DESCRIBED BELOW.

The core

The globe is made up of a core surrounded by concentric shells. The core itself comprises nearly one third of the global mass. The inner core, 5,100–6,400km (3,169–3,977 miles) deep has a temperature of about 4,300°C. It is apparently composed of iron, kept solid in spite of its heat by the tremendous pressures confining it.

The outer core

The surrounding outer core, 2,885–5,100km (1,793–3,170 miles) deep is also composed largely of iron, but with some nickel and a few lighter elements. This outer core is fluid and convection currents keep it in slow but constant motion. These currents and the rotation of the globe make the outer core a self-exciting dynamo that has developed the Earth's magnetic field.

The Earth is a dipole, ie. it has two magnetic poles, North and South. During the planet's history, however, the poles have, at different times, become reversed. These magnetic reversals have been used to date rocks and have proved to be vitally important in demonstrating the movement of crustal plates (see pp.18–19).

The mantle

The outer core is enveloped by the mantle which comprises the lower mantle and the upper mantle. The lower mantle is 2,235km (1,390 miles) thick and 650–2,885km (404–1,793 miles) deep. It is solid, hot and held under great pressure. Nevertheless, stresses and strains and convection currents and creep have developed within it. Surrounding the lower mantle is a shell about 500km (311 miles) thick, lying between 60–150km (37–93 miles) and 650km (404 miles) deep. This shell is composed of a transition zone and the more plastic layers of the upper mantle. Together, they form the asthenosphere (from the Greek *asthenos* meaning 'weak') which reacts to stresses and strains in a fluid way, although it is only partly molten. Convection currents keep the asthenosphere in slow, but continuous, motion and they are thus probably a major driving force behind the movement of the plates across the Earth's surface.

An eruption on Stromboli, an island off the coast of Sicily in the Mediterranean

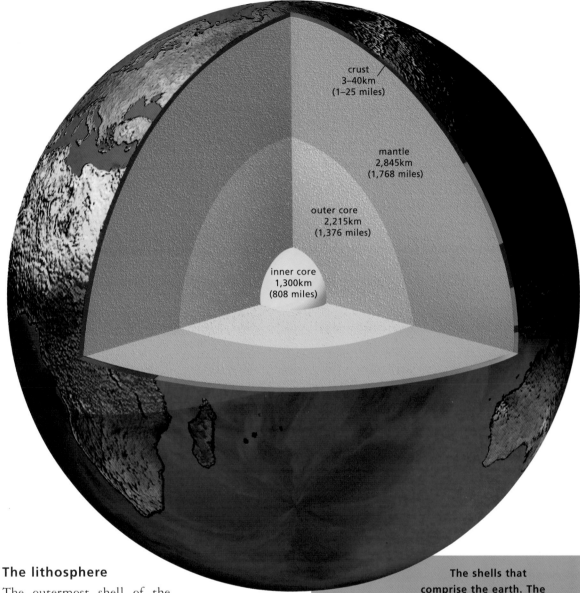

crust
3–40km
(1–25 miles)

mantle
2,845km
(1,768 miles)

outer core
2,215km
(1,376 miles)

inner core
1,300km
(808 miles)

The lithosphere

The outermost shell of the globe is the lithosphere (from the Greek *lithos* meaning 'stone'), which can be as little as 60km (37 miles) thick below the oceans, but can reach as much as 150km (93 miles) thick beneath the continents. Like the other shells, the lithosphere is divided into two layers: the lower layer is the solid upper mantle; the upper, outermost layer is the Earth's crust. The thickness of the crust varies from about 70km (43½ miles) under the main mountain ranges to only 3km (1¾ miles) along the crests of the mid-ocean ridges. It is an average of 40km (25 miles) thick on the continents, where it is pale in colour, generally granitic in character, with a low density. Under the oceans, on the other hand, it is dense, dark-coloured and basaltic, and averages no more than 6km (3¾ miles) in

The shells that comprise the earth. The upper part of the mantle comprises the plastic asthenosphere, 150–650km (93–404 miles) deep, and the cooler, more solid lithosphere, 60–150km (37–93 miles) thick. The thickness of the outermost layer, the crust, has been exaggerated on this diagram

thickness. This crust that seems so firm to us is thin, brittle and fragile. It accounts for just one thousandth of the volume of the globe.

There is a constant interchange and interaction between the global shells – and especially between the outermost layers. The main results are the growth, movement and consumption of the global plates; and their most obvious manifestations are earthquakes and volcanic eruptions.

chapter 1

PLATE
TECTONICS

plate growth at the mid-ocean ridges

THE GROWTH, MOVEMENT, COLLISION AND CONSUMPTION OF THE PLATES THAT COMPRISE
THE EARTH'S CRUST ARE THE BASIC CAUSES OF EARTHQUAKES AND VOLCANIC ERUPTIONS.
HERE WE LOOK AT THE DIFFERENT WAYS IN WHICH PLATES INTERACT, A STUDY KNOWN AS
PLATE TECTONICS. THE FIRST OF THESE IS PLATE GROWTH.

The best example of plate growth can be seen along the Mid-Atlantic Ridge. Although it rises about 4,000m (13,000ft) above the oceanic plains, most of the ridge is submerged. The crest of the ridge only rises above sea-level in Iceland, but volcanic islands also emerge from its flanks in Jan Mayen, the Azores, Ascension Island, and Tristan da Cunha. The ridge rises to two parallel crests that face each other across a long central depression. This is the point at which the plates are growing and diverging. Here the Atlantic Ocean is actively widening at an average rate of just a few centimetres a year. Thus New York is moving further away from London.

upwelling under
ocean creates a
spreading ridge

mid-ocean
ridge

The Mid-Atlantic Ridge is a submerged mountain range rising about 4,000m (13,000ft) above the ocean floor and only emerges above sea-level in a few places along its length

It seems that the plates are being pulled apart along the mid-ocean ridge by diverging convection currents operating in the asthenosphere and upper mantle. This process is also known as rifting. The divergence causes the solid basaltic plates to split open along many parallel cracks or fissures that trend along the ridge. The cracks can be as little as 1m (3¼ft) or as long as 1km (⅔ mile). Whatever their lengths, they have the same effects. They cause mild earthquakes and mild eruptions. The earthquakes rarely exceed magnitude 6.0 but have shallow sources around 5km (3 miles) deep. So little land is exposed on or near the mid-ocean ridge that the earthquakes usually pass unnoticed, but the earthquake that shook the Azores on 1

hotspot

convergent zone:
downwelling
subducts dense
oceanic crust
into the
mantle

descending ocean plate

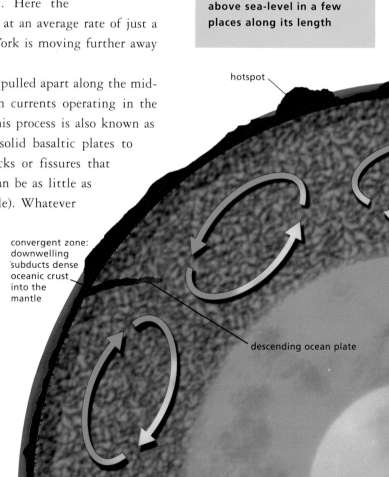

January 1980 was intense enough to cause serious damage in Angra do Heroísmo in Terceira.

Once the plates have cracked and rifted apart, the pressures on the zone directly below are immediately reduced. The asthenosphere is only 3km (1¾ miles) beneath the crest of the ridge and the lower pressure allows some of the minerals within it to melt out. Together these minerals form what is often called primary basalt, which is less dense than the materials of the asthenosphere as a whole. Thus, the primary basalt rises into cracks as they develop and become available and makes its way towards the surface of the ridge. This activity is enormously important in the Earth's dynamic growth. It accounts for three-quarters of the annual production of volcanic rock on Earth. Every year 3km³ (¾ cubic mile) of new volcanic rock is added to the diverging plate margins. Most of it solidifies in the cracks en route and becomes welded

Lava erupted underwater forms characteristic 'pillow lavas' as it cools

to one or other of the diverging plates. The primary basalt that succeeds in reaching the surface is changed a little on the way into a form of basalt lava. From diving machines, it can be seen emerging as pillow-like lumps that glow red-hot in the murky water. The cold water quickly quenches them into their characteristic shapes as they ooze out, one after the other, and pile up in masses of solidified 'pillow lavas' on the surface of each diverging plate. The pressure of the water also ensures that there are no explosions. The growth of oceanic plates is marked therefore, by mild, continued activity, rather than savage outbursts.

Earth scientists have noted that as each crack in the ocean floor becomes choked with solidified basalt lava, new cracks rift open alongside them. Piles of basalt congeal on the edges of each plate as they move

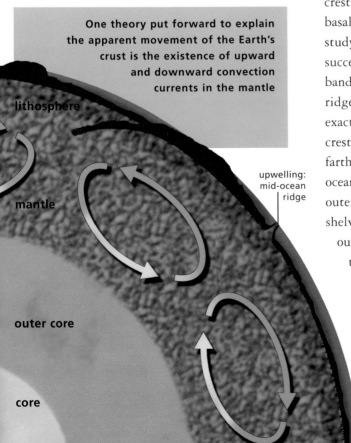

One theory put forward to explain the apparent movement of the Earth's crust is the existence of upward and downward convection currents in the mantle

lithosphere

mantle

outer core

core

upwelling: mid-ocean ridge

apart. The newest basalts, therefore, occupy the crests of the ridges while increasingly older basalts form the flanks of the ridge. Scientists studying Paleomagnetism (see pp.18–19) have succeeded in dating and identifying different bands of basalt on either side of the diverging ridge. It shows that the bands alternate in exactly the same way on either side of the ridge crest, and the older the bands of basalts, the farther away they were from the crest of the mid-ocean ridge. The oldest bands occurred on the outer fringes of the ocean, near the continental shelves. Thus the ocean floor must have spread out from the mid-ocean ridges. In addition, as the basalts cooled, they become denser. Therefore, where the basalts are new and hot they are high, and form a mid-ocean ridge. As they cool, become denser, and move further from the mid-ocean ridge, they sink. Thus the mid-ocean ridges are flanked by abyssal plains over 4,000m (13,000ft) deep.

paleomagnetism

THE EXISTENCE OF PLATE GROWTH AT OCEAN RIDGES AND THEREBY THE CREATION OF THE
ATLANTIC OCEAN OVER THE PAST 180 MILLION YEARS HAVE BEEN CONFIRMED BY AN AREA OF
STUDY KNOWN AS PALEOMAGNETISM (MEANING 'FOSSIL MAGNETISM').

The Earth acts like a giant magnet with poles at points to the north and south. Although these
correspond roughly with the geographical poles (the top and bottom of the imaginary axis of the
rotation of the Earth), they do not occur at exactly the same points. At present the magnetic north pole
is 1,900km (1,180 miles) from the North Pole; the magnetic south pole is about 2,600km (1,615 miles)
from the South Pole. The magnetic poles move slowly around the geographical poles, and over several
thousands of years their *mean* positions coincide. In accordance with our normal polarity (ie. the
magnetism that exists at present), a freely swinging compass needle points to the magnetic north pole,
and as it is moved it will dip at different angles according to its latitude.

Over time, the poles have, at irregular intervals, and for different lengths of time, become reversed
(known as 'reverse polarity'). When rocks form, eg. as sediments or cooled solidified volcanic rocks, they
often contain minerals that become magnetized and
will point, like compass needles, to the magnetic
pole of the day. Analysis of carefully-chosen,
uncontaminated rock specimens, shows their
latitude and position in relation to the
magnetic pole that existed when they were
formed. A pattern of magnetic reversals has
now been worked out for the last several
hundred million years.

These tests have been vital in
establishing how plates grow and move.
For example, when the results are plotted
on maps of mid-ocean ridges, a simple
general pattern emerges: stripes of normal
magnetism alternate with stripes of
reverse magnetism. This pattern is
mirrored on either side of the ridge, with
the stripes of rock increasing in age, the
further they are away from the ridge crest on
both plates. This discovery, made in the 1960s,
formed one of the foundations of the theory of
plate tectonics, because it showed how plates
grow at the mid-ocean ridges.

Paleomagnetic studies from rocks on the
continental crust also demonstrate the way in
which the plates have moved to reach their
present positions. If magnetism is not lost or
changed once it is attained, rocks magnetized at
the same time should point to the same

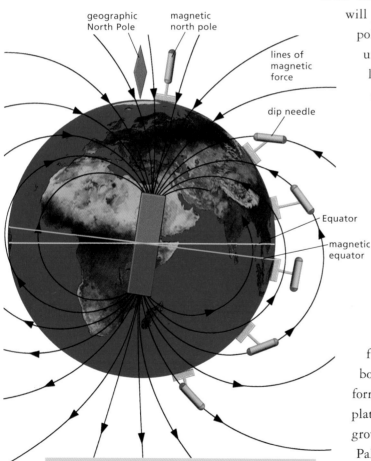

geographic
North Pole

magnetic
north pole

lines of
magnetic
force

dip needle

Equator

magnetic
equator

The angle of a dip needle (a compass in a
vertical plane) determines lines of latitude as
it moves through the Earth's magnetic field. It
can thus indicate the position of rocks at the
time they became magnetized, helping us to
track the movement of the continents

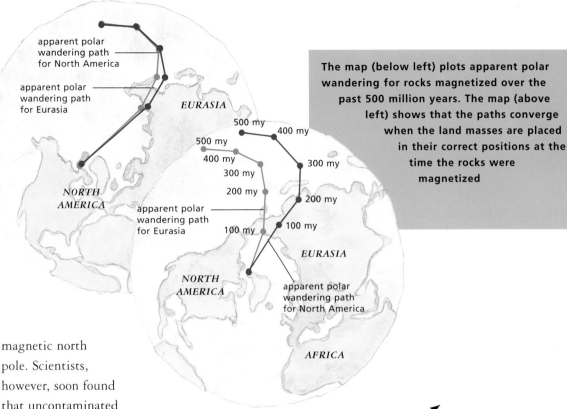

apparent polar wandering path for North America

apparent polar wandering path for Eurasia

EURASIA

500 my
400 my
500 my
400 my
300 my
300 my
200 my
200 my
apparent polar wandering path for Eurasia
100 my
100 my

NORTH AMERICA

NORTH AMERICA

EURASIA

apparent polar wandering path for North America

AFRICA

The map (below left) plots apparent polar wandering for rocks magnetized over the past 500 million years. The map (above left) shows that the paths converge when the land masses are placed in their correct positions at the time the rocks were magnetized

magnetic north pole. Scientists, however, soon found that uncontaminated magnetized rocks of exactly the same age in different continents did not point to the same north pole. Similarly, magnetized rocks of different ages on the same continent also pointed to different north poles.

Scientists plotted and mapped the poles to which the various magnetized rocks on different continents seemed to be pointing. In general, specimens from the most recent rocks pointed most closely to the present north pole. The older the specimens the more they diverged – suggesting that the continents and the plates carrying them must have moved in relation to the pole. Some plates had moved more than others and in different directions. Also, when continents had been joined together (as India and Asia are today), the plots of their apparent poles ran parallel. And, when continents split apart (as North America separated from Europe), the divergence increased.

By conducting worldwide tests, it became a relatively simple matter to discover where the various rocks (and their continents) had been situated when they were magnetized: place the specimens of the same age in their correct original location and they all point to the same magnetic pole. Soon it becomes apparent that the outlines of the continental masses resemble pieces of a jigsaw that were once locked together.

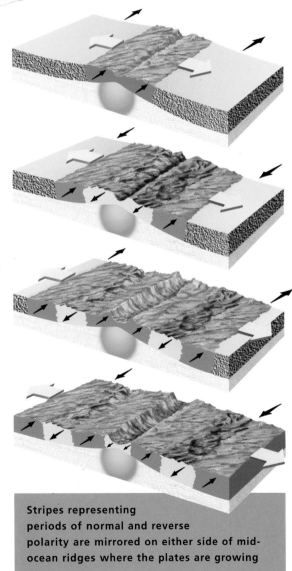

Stripes representing periods of normal and reverse polarity are mirrored on either side of mid-ocean ridges where the plates are growing

continental movement

EARTH SCIENTISTS HAVE SHOWN THAT FEATURES FOUND ON MANY SEPARATE CONTINENTS ORIGINALLY LAY NEXT TO EACH OTHER. THROUGHOUT HISTORY AND PRE-HISTORY CONTINENTS HAVE JOINED AND SEPARATED AS THE GLOBAL PLATES HAVE CARRIED THEM ACROSS THE FACE OF THE EARTH.

The last time the continents were all joined was about 300 million years ago in the super-continent called 'Pangaea'. About 225 million years ago, it split into a southern continent 'Gondwanaland', and a northern continent, 'Laurasia'. Soon afterwards both these large continents began to split into the continents that are recognizable today. Take the present continents (and their shelves) and put them in their positions of 225 million years ago. Many independent features then match closely. In old Laurasia, the outlines of the edge of the continental shelves, about 1,000m (3,280ft) deep, fit neatly together in the Atlantic Ocean. Eastern Canada, southern Greenland and Ireland lie together. Brazil fits equally well into the Gulf of Guinea, off Africa. The continents of old 'Gondwanaland' group around Antarctica. South America, South Africa, Madagascar and India fit to one side of Antarctica. Australia and New Zealand joined Antarctica too along the Great Australian Bight.

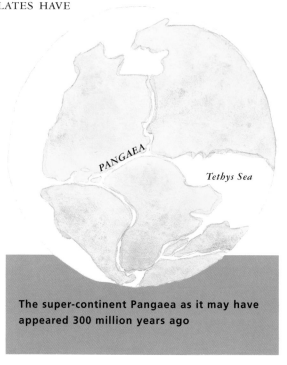

The super-continent Pangaea as it may have appeared 300 million years ago

The fit of the southern continents and India around Antarctica 225 million years ago

This movement is illustrated by many of today's geological features. A physical map of the world shows how structures and rock types run from one continent to another, although they are now widely separated.

Thus, the old Caledonian Mountains of Scotland continue both to Norway and Greenland and the Appalachians in the United States. The present ocean floor between these fragments is comprised of younger basalts formed when the plates carried the continental masses apart (see pp.18–19).

The world's coal and oil deposits were formed in a humid tropical climate. Now, they are not only widely scattered across the globe, but they almost all lie far from the latitudes of their origin. Similarly, when 'Laurasia' had a tropical climate, 'Gondwanaland' was experiencing a period of glaciation. All the southern continents,

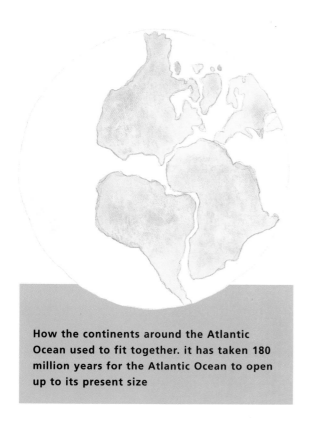

How the continents around the Atlantic Ocean used to fit together. it has taken 180 million years for the Atlantic Ocean to open up to its present size

together with the Indian sub-continent, must have been near the ice-covered South Pole at that time. Since that period, India, however, has crossed the equator and crashed into Asia.

The continental movements can thus be demonstrated by matching geological structures, rock types, fossil remains of flora and fauna, as well as the fit of many continental shelf outlines. Paleomagnetic evidence corroborates the matching fits and their subsequent separation.

Volcanic hotspots also reveal the movement of the plates. They are caused by convectional plumes of hot material that burn through the mantle like blowtorches, breaking through the lithosphere and forming large volcanoes. These plumes seem to be stationary. If the plates above them were also stationary then each plume would have formed one enormous volcano. As it is, hotspot volcanoes, such as those in Réunion in the Indian Ocean and the Hawaiian Islands in the Pacific Ocean, are amongst the world's largest volcanoes. But these active hotspot volcanoes lie at the end of a line of extinct volcanoes, the oldest of which lie furthest from those that are presently active: those at the far north-western end of the Hawaiian line, are 75 million years old. Thus, the Hawaiian Islands stand at the south-eastern end of submerged volcanoes forming the Hawaiian and Emperor lines of seamounts. Even within the Hawaiian Islands, activity is concentrated on their south-eastern parts at Mauna Loa and Kilauea on Hawaii. This process is continuing at this moment as a new volcanic island, Loihi, is building up to the south-east beneath the surface of the Pacific Ocean.

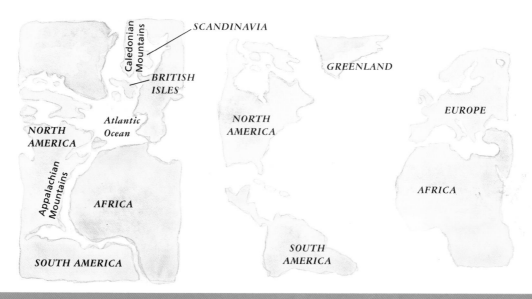

Mountains of comparable age and structure are found in North America, the British Isles and Scandinavia. When the landmasses are reassembled they show the mountains as a continuous range that was formed around 300 million years ago

plate consumption at the subduction zones

Subduction occurs when one plate slides underneath another, and the areas in which it occurs are extremely unstable. Most of the Earth's subduction takes place around the Pacific Ocean, the floor of which comprises several different crustal plates. The Pacific Plate is by far the largest, and is moving north-westwards and plunging beneath both the North American Plate and the Eurasian Plate. It also interacts with the Philippine Plate and the Indian-Australian Plate.

Subduction zones form volcanic chains on land and arcs of volcanic islands in the sea. This pattern is particularly clear along the subduction zones that surround the Pacific Ocean, and gives it its name, the 'Ring of Fire'

Elsewhere in the eastern Pacific the Nazca Plate is sinking below the South American Plate, the Cocos Plate is plunging under Central America and the small Juan de Jura Plate has been almost completely overridden by the North American Plate. Where the Indian-Australian Plate is composed of oceanic crust it plunges beneath the Eurasian Plate alongside Indonesia, but where it carries the Indian continental mass, it is thrust under the Eurasian continental mass in Tibet. The main topographical results of subduction are dramatic: highly folded mountains, chains of large volcanoes on land, and arcs of volcanic islands in the ocean. Thus the Andes and Cascade Range in the Americas, and Japan, Indonesia and the Aleutian Islands all have the

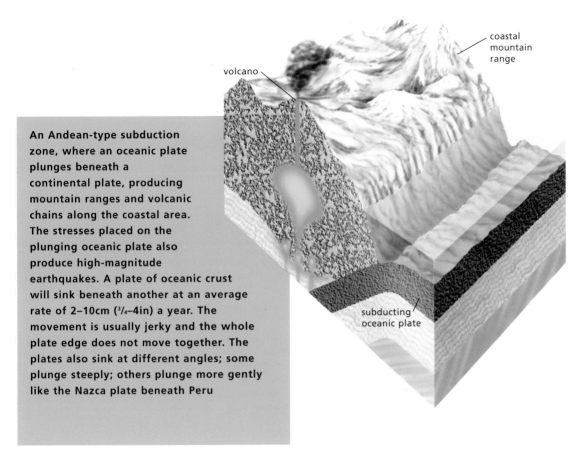

volcano

coastal
mountain
range

subducting
oceanic plate

An Andean-type subduction
zone, where an oceanic plate
plunges beneath a
continental plate, producing
mountain ranges and volcanic
chains along the coastal area.
The stresses placed on the
plunging oceanic plate also
produce high-magnitude
earthquakes. A plate of oceanic crust
will sink beneath another at an average
rate of 2–10cm (³/₄–4in) a year. The
movement is usually jerky and the whole
plate edge does not move together. The
plates also sink at different angles; some
plunge steeply; others plunge more gently
like the Nazca plate beneath Peru

same fundamental cause. These narrow bands contain some of the most active and unstable ground on Earth.

Subduction

A plate of oceanic crust sinks beneath another plate at an average rate of 2–10cm (³/₄–4in) a year. The movement is usually jerky and the whole plate edge does not move together. The plates also sink at different angles; some plunge steeply like the Marianas subduction zone, others plunge more gently like the Nazca plate beneath Peru.

Subduction starts at the ocean trenches which range from 5,000–11,000m (16,400–36,100ft) deep. The subducted plate forms one wall of the trench, the outer edge of the overriding plate forms the opposite wall. As the plate is subducted, the edge of the overriding plate scrapes the sediments from it and they are added, folded and smashed, into the overriding plate. Such movements mean that these areas are prone to severe earthquakes. The stresses and strains on the plunging oceanic plate are even

greater: energy accumulates until the plate jerks downward again and generates a high magnitude earthquake.

The Benioff Zone

Most of these earthquakes are shallow and occur in the first 20–30km (12¹/₂–18¹/₂ miles) of the plunging plate. However, research carried out by the American scientist H. Benioff had shown that intermediate and deep focus earthquakes also occurred quite frequently. These sometimes reached a depth of 700km (435 miles) but no more. Benioff had also discovered that these earthquakes were not arranged vertically below the trench, but sloped down at an angle under the overriding plate. The deepest earthquakes were furthest from the trench. In fact Benioff made his discovery before subduction became a recognized feature of global dynamics. Indeed the distribution of these earthquakes played a major role in first formulating ideas about plate subduction. For this reason the plunging band of earthquakes on the subducting plate is called the Benioff Zone.

THE FORMATION OF VOLCANOES IN SUBDUCTION ZONES

When it sinks, the subducing plate which has a coating of wet sediments, disturbs the hot asthenosphere of the mantle. At a depth of about 80km (50 miles), the once-solid plate starts to melt, and this releases water from the hydrous minerals within the oceanic plate. The water rises into the asthenosphere in the wedge between the sinking and the overriding plate. The addition of water is one of the main factors

volcano

subducting
oceanic plate

Volcanic island arcs are generated were two oceanic plates converge. This type of subduction has produced the Aleutian Islands off the coast of Alaska

that cause some of the minerals to melt from the asthenosphere. As the plate sinks further it is subject to greater pressures. Other minerals melt from it, and join the asthenosphere, and also produce more water. Other changes take place until the subducted plate melts completely and becomes assimilated into the asthenosphere at a depth of about 700km (435 miles). It is for this reason that there are no earthquakes on the

Benioff Zone at a depth greater than 700km (435 miles).

The freshly melted minerals derived from the asthenosphere, and probably also from the subducting plate, are less dense than the surrounding asthenosphere. The melt is therefore more buoyant and slowly begins to rise, but before it reaches the surface, it undergoes many changes and may spend centuries underground. The melted minerals in the asthenosphere are often called primary magma, which, at first, is very similar to the primary basalts that rise up in the mid-ocean ridges (see pp.16–17). But in subduction zones, the thickness of the overriding crustal plate blocks easy access to the landsurface, and the molten rocks therefore rise much more slowly. The magma is also often trapped either just under or within the overriding plate where it collects in a magma reservoir. These reservoirs are often 25–50km (15½–31 miles) deep and could hold up to 20km^3 (4¾ cubic miles) of magma. Smaller reservoirs sometimes even form above them, closer to the surface.

The temperature of the primary magma entering the reservoir is probably approaching 1400°C. It soon starts to cool and some of the minerals begin to crystallize out. Those with the highest melting (or solidification) points are the first to do so. These also happen to be denser than the primary magma and settle towards the bottom of the reservoir. The proportion of silica-rich minerals increases in the upper part of the reservoir because they have lower melting points. The upper parts of the reservoir also retain their gases and water. This partial crystallization means that distinct layers develop in the reservoir: the dense basic magma containing few gases lies at the bottom, with silicious magma containing more gas and water occupying the top. The lower layers are more fluid, whereas the upper layers are viscous. The hot magma may also melt some of the cool plate forming the walls of the reservoir. If the plate contains continental rocks, they are usually broadly granitic (and therefore silicic) in character. Thus when the walls melt they contaminate the magma and can increase further the silicic content of the reservoir's upper layers.

ash cloud

column of gas and finer fragments

explosion

strato volcano

Benioff Zone

subduction of plate

crustal melting

magma reservoir

new magma injection

partial melting

water release

The formation of subduction volcanoes. Magma produced as the subducting plate descends rises up through the mantle towards the surface where it may become trapped in a magma reservoir before erupting on the surface

The final important change is the dilation or expansion of the magma, which may be enough to set the magma on its journey to the surface. Many experts, however, now believe that the eruption process is precipitated when a further batch of primary magma is injected into the reservoir from below. This appears to be true of the eruptions of Pinatubo in the Philippines in

1991 and Mount St Helens in 1980. The injection of new magma causes the old magma to force its way out of the reservoir, usually in a narrow chimney or vent that pierces the crust. As the magma rises up the vent the pressures upon it from the surrounding rock are reduced, but the rising magma itself builds up considerable pressure, expanding fractures, pushes rock aside and generating thousands of shallow, low magnitude earthquakes.

The next critical point is about 2km (1¼ miles) below the surface, a point that occurs just below small volcanoes, but that is well within the body of their larger counterparts. At this depth the confining pressures are now so low that gas and water bubbles start to separate out from the magma and begin to rise, and these in turn push the magma upwards. Its uppermost layers become a frothy foaming liquid which quickly approaches the top of the vent. Suddenly the water and gas bubbles overcome the viscosity of the magma, the bubbles explode, and the volcano erupts. The magma is smashed into fine dust, ash or pumice that can tower 30km (18½ miles) into the air and can plunge a 200km (124 mile) area into total darkness. The upper, silicic layers of magma evacuate the reservoir, and the denser, more basic layers may follow them in more docile lava flows. About 500 volcanoes have erupted from subduction zones within the past 10,000 years.

There are of course, many complications to this scenario, but the basic outline of subduction zones is remarkably simple. They are made up of parallel bands comprising an ocean trench, a plunging plate with shallow, intermediate and deep earthquakes, and a volcanic chain or island arc, rising parallel to the trench and 150–200km (93–124 miles) away.

when continents collide

INDIA, AFRICA, AUSTRALIA AND ANTARCTICA WERE JOINED TOGETHER IN THE SOUTHERN CONTINENTAL MASS OF GONDWANALAND ABOUT 225 MILLION YEARS AGO. WHEN GONDWANALAND BEGAN TO DISINTEGRATE, INDIA BEGAN ITS NORTHWARD JOURNEY, TRAVELLING AT A RATE OF 5–10CM (2–4IN) PER YEAR. THE INDIAN CONTINENTAL MASS FIRST CRASHED INTO THE TIBETAN EDGE OF SOUTHERN ASIA ABOUT 50 MILLION YEARS AGO. BUT THE PLATE HAS CONTINUED TO MOVE NORTH, CRUMPLING THE SEDIMENTS SCRAPED FROM THE SEA-FLOOR INTO ENORMOUS FOLDS, THRUSTING THE EDGE OF THE INDIAN CONTINENT UNDER THE SHATTERED AND SLICED SOUTHERN EDGES OF ASIA. A FEW MILLION YEARS LATER THE RESULT WAS THE HIMALAYAS.

The Asian collision zone

The Himalayan range of mountains is 8,000m (26,250ft) high, 300km (186 miles) wide and 4,000km (2,490 miles) long, and stretches from Afghanistan in the east to Myanmar (Burma) in the west. Sections of India became rammed under Tibet, practically doubling the normal thickness of continental crust, and making Tibet, at over 3,000m (9,840 ft), the highest and largest plateau in the world. The collision has compressed the continental crust by about 2,000km (1,243 miles). In response to this assault the Asian continent simply cracked under the strain. Great blocks of Mongolia, China and south-east Asia were forced to slip sideways, chiefly towards the South China Sea. Tibet, for instance, is being pushed south-eastwards at a rate of about 2–3cm (1in) per year. Huge blocks of Asia are sliding past each other along cracks, or major faults, such as the 2,000km (1,243 mile) long Altyn Tagh fault in north Tibet, and the Red River fault in Vietnam. Vietnam has slipped at least 600km (373 miles) south-east on this fault at a rate of between 3cm and 5cm (1¼–2in) a year. But in fact there are many thousands of such faults, most of which seem to

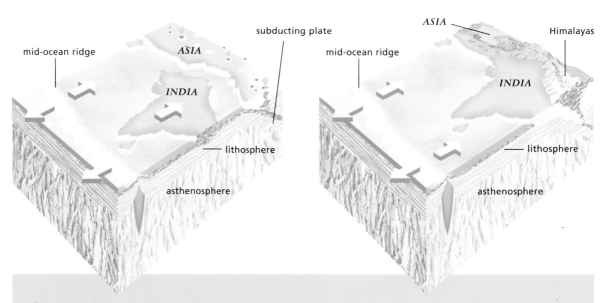

When the Indian sub-continent first broke free from Gondwanaland it travelled northwards at 5–10cm (2–4in) per year. About 50 million years ago it collided with southern Asia forming the Himalayas. This movement continues today as the Indo-Australian plate pushes northwards at a rate of about 5cm (2in) a year

slip sideways, but many also move up and down.

One of the chief results of this tremendous collision has been violent and frequent earthquakes. The cracks, or faults, might stay locked together for centuries, but eventually the pressures exerted on them cause them to give way. One slight movement is enough to shake the ground for a minute or two over 500km (311 miles) or more. In a highly-populated area like China, this could cause the deaths of 100,000 people. The pressure thrusting India under the Himalayas also generates powerful earthquakes there. Fortunately, most happen in sparsely-populated areas and only a few, such as those at Quetta in 1935 and Assam in 1896, have caused large numbers of deaths.

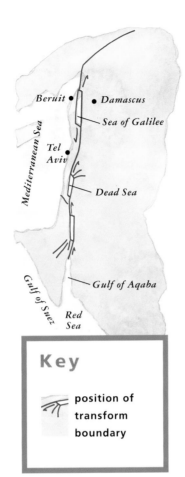

Key

position of transform boundary

The Middle East collision zone

A few million years after India began its contest with Asia, the Red Sea and the Gulf of Aden opened up. A small plate carrying Arabia, gradually drifted away from Egypt and Somalia, areas that stayed with the rest of the African plate. The Arabian continental mass has acted much like India, but on a smaller scale, crumpling mountain ranges in Iran, the Caucasus, and Turkey.

As it advanced northwards, it slid past Palestine, Israel and western Syria, along a great lateral fault-crack marked by the River Jordan valley. Arabia has also pushed Turkey westwards towards Greece, along one of its main cracks, the North Anatolian fault. In this area too, frequent, violent, and lethal earthquakes are caused by thrusting, crumpling, or sliding, and have caused extensive damage in Iran, north-eastern Turkey, and Armenia at different times over the past few decades.

The Himalayas began to form when the Indian plate collided with, and dipped underneath, the Asian plate. The resulting thickness of the continental crust accounts for the great height of the mountains

The Mediterranean collision zone

The predominant legacy of the collision zones described above has been earthquakes. Volcanic eruptions do occur, notably Hassan Dag in central Turkey, but they usually play a subordinate role. Volcanoes are much more important, however, in the Mediterranean collision zone.

When the African plate split from Gondwanaland, it began travelling northwards more slowly than the Indian-Australian plate. Nevertheless, it soon also began to crush the floor of the ocean between old Gondwanaland to the south and old Laurasia to the north. The part of this ocean lying between Europe and Africa may be regarded as an early prototype of the Mediterranean Sea. Eventually the northward push of Arabia against Asia blocked off the eastern exit of this ocean. About 70 million years ago, the African Plate began crushing its oceanic crust up against the Eurasian Plate. The story is made complicated because both plates were broken into smaller microplates, one of which lies under the Aegean Sea, another under Apulia and the Adriatic Sea east of Italy, and a third in northern Morocco. In addition, Africa and Europe did not always close up together in the same direction. The final major complication is that the Bay of Biscay swung open, detached Spain from Brittany and turned it south-eastwards between Africa and Europe. In addition, Turkey is being squeezed westwards towards Greece as Arabia is pushed northwards.

In the past 70 million years these movements have produced an extremely complicated pattern of crumpled, folded mountains and intermittent subduction zones. This provides some explanation for the way that the mountain ranges around the Mediterranean curve across the map. The Pyrenees run west-east. The Sierra Nevada in Spain curves around the edges of a microplate almost to join the Atlas Mountains in North Africa. They, in turn, are relayed by the Pelitorani Mountains of northern Sicily into Calabria and follow the edge of the Adriatic microplate up the Apennines. They join the Alps curving around the Adriatic plate and then turn eastwards into the Carpathians and also bend southwards into a mass of smaller ranges in the Balkans extending into Greece. Then the mountains broaden into their wider bands; as they cross Turkey, one follows the south coast, the other the north coast. And off they continue into Iran to join the Himalayas.

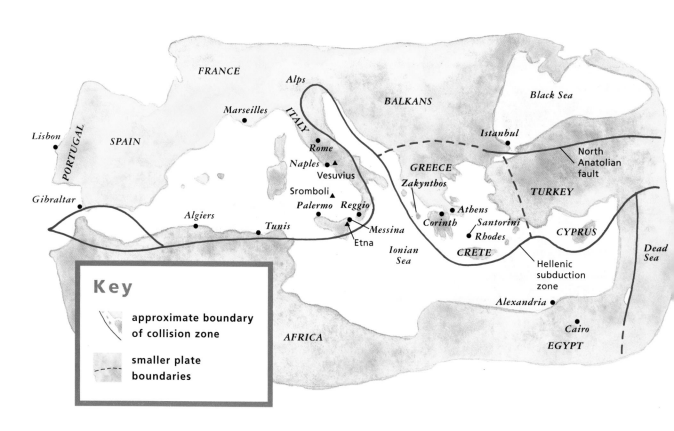

Key

approximate boundary of collision zone

smaller plate boundaries

Lava-flows on Etna, one of many volcanoes that have grown up within the complex pattern of plate boundaries in the Mediterranean

In all this area, there is only one subduction zone approaching the clarity of those in the Pacific Ocean. This is the Hellenic Arc, where the African Plate plunges beneath the Aegean Plate, and the last chains of the Balkan Mountains. It causes the main active volcanoes of the Aegean Sea: Santorini, Nisyros, Milos and Kos in particular. In Italy, the Aeolian Islands, north of Sicily, are probably also related to subduction of the African plate east of Sicily. Vesuvius and the volcanoes around Naples may be a result of subduction where the African plate and the Adriatic microplate plunge below Europe. Etna, however, appears to rise on deep secondary cracks in the crust caused by the impact of the two major plates. Other volcanoes have arisen along cracks within the Atlas Mountains of Morocco, whereas active volcanoes only occur in Catalonia in the Iberian Peninsula. The very irregularity of the volcanic pattern is a symptom of the almost chaotic history of this region. A few examples pin-point their extraordinary story. Southern Sicily belongs to the African plate, as does the top of the Matterhorn in the Alps. Its base, however, belongs to the European plate. The collision has also forced rocks up from the upper mantle, so that they now form the Troodos Mountains in Cyprus. The rocks of most of the mountain ranges around the Mediterranean Sea are crumpled, folded and thrust over each other in great slices, but the crust is also stretching in parts of the Apennines, in the Aegean Sea and in the Vienna Basin. The Gulf of Corinth is widening and Sicily is moving further from Calabria.

All these complicated contortions produce one simple result: the area around the Mediterranean is riddled with earthquakes that are small manifestations of these movements. But, even here, their distribution is not entirely straightforward. Peninsular Greece has by far the most earthquakes every year. On the other hand, southern Italy, especially Calabria and Eastern Sicily, has perhaps the highest incidence of severe earthquakes in the world for such a small area. The Balkans and north Africa experience severe earthquakes quite often, but there have relatively few in the Alps in recorded history, and the Iberian Peninsula has had even fewer.

plate sliding and rifting

The plates that comprise the Earth's surface are not always in direct confrontation, they may also slide past each other, or rift and split apart. These are not benign processes, however, as the people of Los Angeles and San Francisco in the United States, and the Great Rift Valley in East Africa can testify.

Plate sliding

In some cases certain plates meet each other at an oblique angle thus avoiding subduction or collision altogether, such as San Andreas Fault system in southern California (see right), and the River Jordan-Dead Sea Fault system in the Middle East (see p.27). In such conditions there is little chance for volcanic eruptions to develop. But the plates do not glide past each other as if they had been well-oiled. As on all other fault-cracks, the dislocation is jerky. Each horizontal slip can cause earthquakes just as powerful as their counterparts in subduction zones.

Plate splitting

The Atlantic Ocean developed when the North and South American plates split from Eurasia and Africa respectively. Plates probably start to split when conditions in the mantle change. For example, an alteration in the convection currents could start stretching a new zone of oceanic or continental crust in a new zone.

As the crust stretches, it gets thinner and eventually cracks under the strain into a long furrow. Both edges of the furrow also crack and form blocks of crust that drop down like steps towards the central trough. These cracks are faults, which cut through the whole crust. Thus, when the crust is pulled apart and becomes thinner, the result is downward vertical displacements in a long band. Because of the depth of the faults, molten rock can sometimes rise and form volcanoes at the surface. Each displacement on the faults also causes an earthquake. This process is called rifting and is how the Atlantic Ocean first started to open up. As the Atlantic Ocean rifted open, volcanic rocks spewed out, and their remains form the

lavas of Skye and Mull and other Hebridean Islands. In the Great Rift Valley system of East Africa massive eruptions have formed great volcanic piles.

In north-eastern Africa, the extension and rifting has been even greater: the Arabian plate has already split off. On land, great piles of volcanic rocks have erupted in the Afar Triangle near Djibouti. The Red Sea and the Gulf of Aden have opened up as rifting has allowed erup-tions to create new oceanic crust. In the future, the eastern fringe of the African plate (Somalia, Tanzania and Kenya) could also split off.

Once a mid-ocean ridge develops and the ocean crust begins to spread outwards from it, the separation of the two diverging plates is complete. The Atlantic Ocean has long been in this position. The faulted step-like blocks that bordered its original trough are a long way apart. Thick sediments eroded from both the American and European continents now bury most of them along the Atlantic fringe. But these old faults are not wholly dead. They can still quake: on 31 August 1886, an earthquake damaged Charleston, South Carolina, when one of these ancient buried blocks slipped again. The edges of the 300 million year-old rift forming the Midland Valley in Scotland still also produce a flurry of tremors every year.

California

Hayward fault
Calaveras fault
San Francisco
San Andreas fault
Garlock fault
Los Angeles

A view to the west showing Asia in the foreground and Africa in the background as photographed by the crew of the Space

Shuttle Columbia. The Red Sea is widening, as rifting produces new oceanic crust, pushing Saudi Arabia further from Africa

LEFT Aerial view along the San Andreas fault, California. ABOVE A geyser at Lake Bogoria, Kenya, part of the Great Rift Valley of East Africa

chapter**2**

EARTHQUAKES

earthquakes in history

A major earthquake is one of the most sudden, unpredictable and terrifying events on Earth, shattering our assumption that we live on 'solid ground'. Earthquakes are lethal because they happen without warning, and while long-term forecasts can be made, accurate short-term prediction is extremely difficult. Thus earthquakes have claimed over 1.5 million victims since 1900 – including an estimated 600,000–850,000 in Tangshan, China, in 1976. A further 3,000,000 people were killed as a result of earthquakes between 1600 and 1900.

It is little wonder that such catastrophes have been recorded for centuries. Archives in China date back to 2300 BC while Japanese records start from AD 416. In contrast, North American reports only began in the early 19th Century. Thus on the world scale, records are incomplete and sporadic, and have often become distorted by exaggeration. The most active area in Europe, the area around the Mediterranean Sea, has preserved the longest records, going back – albeit incompletely – for 2,500 years.

Greece experiences the most earthquakes in Europe. On average, a small earthquake happens there once every three days, but not many are as devastating as the one that hit Argostoli in the Ionian Islands in 1953. In Ancient Greece the cities of Corinth and Sparta, for instance, were destroyed, and rebuilt several times. The people associated the torments of earthquakes with their god Poseidon, the 'Earth-shaker'. However, Ancient Greece also provides a rare example of some benefit resulting from earthquakes. When an earthquake occurred during their frequent inter-city wars, the armies declared a truce, and returned home until the following summer!

In Italy, earthquakes tend to be less frequent, but are sometimes stronger and usually more devastating than in Greece. The toe of Italy, Calabria, and eastern Sicily (see above), have had some of the most savage earthquakes recorded in Europe – notably in 1783 and 1908. These big earthquakes seem to happen once every 90–125 years, but in between, other earthquakes have also cost hundreds of lives. The last major earthquake in the area devastated Messina in Sicily and Reggio in Calabria on 28 December 1908 – the Feast of the Massacre of the Innocents – when about 160,000 people died, and many towns were left in ruins.

The Romans suffered earthquakes too. On 5 February AD 62 an earthquake severely damaged Pompeii; repairs were not complete by the time Vesuvius erupted in AD 79. In Naples, an earthquake rocked the theatre where the Emperor Nero was making his stage debut as a musician, thereby bringing his performance to an abrupt end. Typically, Nero was upset by the Gods' apparent slight to his talents.

The Greek god of the sea Poseidon, the 'Earth-shaker', was believed to control earthquakes. He was also depicted as a charging bull because of the power he was able to unleash

the earthquake at Lisbon

1 November 1755

SPAIN AND PORTUGAL ARE AMONG THE MOST SEISMICALLY STABLE COUNTRIES IN SOUTHERN EUROPE, BUT THE EARTHQUAKE THAT DESTROYED LISBON IN 1755 WAS PROBABLY THE MOST POWERFUL RECORDED IN THE LAST 2,000 YEARS. AT 10.00 ON 1 NOVEMBER, ALL SAINTS' DAY, THE GROUND SHOOK VIOLENTLY FOR SEVEN TERRIFYING MINUTES. ALL OF PORTUGAL, MOST OF SPAIN AND MUCH OF MOROCCO VIBRATED. FURTHER AFIELD, CHANDELIERS IN THE CASTLES AND CHATEAUX OF WESTERN EUROPE STARTED TO SWING, CHURCH BELLS BEGAN TO PEAL, WAVES APPEARED ON THE SURFACE OF LOCH NESS IN SCOTLAND, AND BOATS WERE RIPPED FROM THEIR MOORINGS IN THE CANALS OF AMSTERDAM.

Key

⟋ River Tagus

Although well-documented, it is quite difficult to piece together exactly what happened, as reports range from the exaggerated to the understated. Probably well over 100,000 people were killed. Even King José Manuel and his family had a narrow escape, leaving their palace in Belem, outside Lisbon, just before it collapsed.

A British surgeon in Lisbon, Richard Wolsall, described his experiences in a letter to the Royal Society of London. In his detailed account, he wrote that the first shock seemed to last:

'about the tenth part of a minute, and then came down every church and convent in town, together with the King's palace and the magnificent opera-house … there was not a large building in town that escaped … The shocking sight of the dead bodies, together with the shrieks of those who were half-buried in the ruins … far exceeds all description … the most resolute person durst not stay a moment to remove a few stones off the friend he loved most, though many might have been saved by so doing: but nothing was thought of but self-preservation; getting into open places, and into the middle of streets, was the most probable security'.

Then, about noon, fires broke out, 'occasioned from the goods and the kitchen fires being all jumbled together.' There must have been an immense 'firestorm.' Mr Wolsall reported that a gale

An artist's impression of the view of Lisbon from the sea seen before the earthquake of 1755

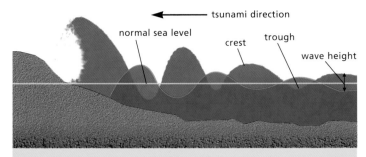

normal sea level

tsunami direction

crest

trough

wave height

Soon after the earthquake the sea surged up into a huge 12m (39½ft) tsunami that flooded lower Lisbon

suddenly blew up on what had previously been a perfectly calm day, and 'made the fire rage with such fury, that, at the end of three days, all the city was reduced to cinders'. Thus many of those who had survived the falling masonry were burnt to death a few hours later. In spite of this terrible loss of life the cremation of the dead bodies was a source of some relief to the surgeon because, at least, it stopped the spread of disease.

The earthquake also produced a huge wave or tsunami. 'Every element seemed to conspire to our destruction.' Soon after the devastating shock, the sea surged up 12m (39½ft) and flooded lower Lisbon. Thousands of people who had assembled for safety on the vast quays alongside the River Tagus were drowned and sucked out into the Atlantic Ocean when the wave subsided. The victims included the Spanish Ambassador and 35 of his servants. Less than an hour later, the tsunami crashed over the walls of the Spanish port of Cádiz and swept on to Gibraltar, the Moroccan coast, and Madeira.

By the evening of All Saints' Day, Lisbon was a heap of burning rubble. Three-quarters of the buildings were damaged beyond repair. In the centre of the city, it was impossible to make out the old pattern of the streets. Many people fled the city, but for those that remained, there were additional hazards: food was scarce, there were powerful aftershocks, and the bewildered inhabitants were easy prey for thieves.

The terrible news sent shock-waves throughout Europe's intellectual community, that had longer-lasting effects than those generated by the earthquake. Prompted by these events the French philosopher Voltaire began his most famous book, *Candide*, published in 1759. The work analyzed the idea of divine justice, and questioned the prevailing notion of the time, that Man was living in 'the best of all possible worlds'. Thanks to Voltaire, the Lisbon earthquake changed the intellectual climate, helping to pave the way for a new revolutionary age.

Following the Lisbon earthquake, three-quarters of the city's buildings were thrown to the ground, or destroyed by fire

earthquake features

AN EARTHQUAKE IS A SUDDEN AND VIOLENT MOVEMENT OF THE EARTH'S SURFACE CAUSED BY THE SLOW MOVEMENTS OF THE CRUSTAL PLATES EXERTING A VARIETY OF FORCES ON THE ROCKS ABOVE.

The rocks themselves are elastic and can store mechanical energy in the same way as a compressed spring. When the stresses and strains are exerted slowly, over long periods of time, the rocks bend and crumple to accommodate them, forming enormous, complicated folds. These folds form the basic features of the rocks in the world's younger mountain ranges such as the Alps and the Himalayas, and the remnants of older ranges such as the Appalachians.

FAULTS

When forces are applied more strongly, or if they finally exceed the strength of the weakest part of the solid rock, then the rock gives way and cracks. The strain energy is relieved and the forces are accommodated by a sudden dislocation of the rocks on either side of the crack. This is called 'elastic rebound'. The movement may be over in a few seconds at its source, but the vast amount of energy released travels through the rocks of the crust in earthquake (seismic) waves, that travel outwards for a distance of up to 1,000km (621 miles), and can be registered on sensitive earthquake-measuring equipment (seismographs), all over the world. The crack marking the dislocation is called a fault. Following an earthquake the rocks on either side of the fault come to rest in new positions. The degree of displacement varies but occasionally can be visible on the land surface as a fault scarp.

The rock masses on either side of the fault soon become locked together in new positions due to forces exerted upon them from the crust: friction is perhaps the most important of these. The stresses and strains that caused the original dislocation continue, and eventually break the 'frictional lock', causing another earthquake.

Faults rarely exist in isolation, but tend to cluster in parallel sheaves. Within this arrangement one fault may be dislocated while the others stay locked. In addition displacements do not necessarily occur along the whole length

> When rocks crack in response to the strain along a fault, energy is released producing a dislocation. This is called 'elastic rebound'

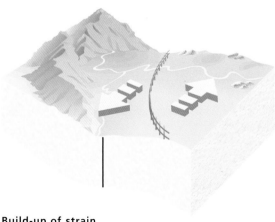

fence

fault

Original position of rocks

Build-up of strain

of a given fault. Most faults are apparently divided into segments; one or more segments may jolt, whilst others remain still. Eventually, it seems, those segments that have been locked for a long time will move and 'catch up' with their neighbours. The San Andreas fault system in California provides probably the most famous example of different movements along different

Dislocation produced by the Californian earthquake at San Fernando in 1971 is visible in this picture

segments. The southern segment of the fault has not dislocated since 1857, whereas one of the central segments (see right) moves every 20 or 30 years. Such varied displacements are valuable because they can provide a basis for the difficult task of predicting earthquakes. Segments along active faults that have not generated earthquakes for an abnormal length of time in relation to the fault as a whole, often attract particular attention, and are known as 'seismic gaps'.

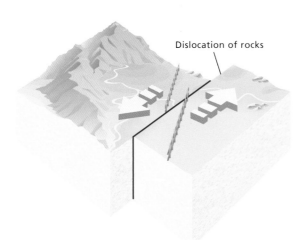

Dislocation of rocks

Strain released

Allan Lindh

Geologist with the United States Geological Survey, Allan Lindh is one member of the team responsible for establishing the Parkfield Experiment (see also pp.168–169). In their centre at Menlo Park, just outside San Francisco, California, they are aiming to solve the mystery of earthquake prediction by constantly analyzing seismic activity, deformation of the earth's surface, water levels and magnetic fields.

'Parkfield is unique in a lot of ways ... the reason we are here is that in the past it has produced magnitude 6 earthquakes ... every 20–30 years.'

He explains seismic gap theory as follows:

'As people noticed around the world that there were other places where earthquakes seemed to be regular they developed something called seismic gap theory. The idea is since the plates are moving all the time at a steady rate and since that is what causes the earthquakes, you look at one place, look at how fast the plates are moving, look when the earthquake last occurred, and see, given how fast the plates are moving, how soon it can happen again.'

Parkfield lies between two major sections of the San Andreas fault. The northern part is constantly slipping and does not produce large earthquakes. The southern part, however, produces powerful earthquakes. The 'transitional' area around Parkfield experiences relatively regular magnitude 6 earthquakes, although at the time of writing, it has been just over 30 years since the last one. Allan is fairly confident that the next one will come within the next five years.

types of fault

THERE ARE THREE BROAD GROUPS OF FAULTS THAT ARE ALL BASICALLY RELATED TO THE CRUSTAL MOVEMENTS WHICH PREDOMINATED DURING THEIR FORMATION. NORMAL FAULTS ARE CAUSED WHEN THE CRUST IS STRETCHED; REVERSE FAULTS ARE CAUSED WHEN IT IS COMPRESSED; WRENCH FAULTS FORM BETWEEN BLOCKS THAT SLIDE HORIZONTALLY PAST EACH OTHER. MOVEMENTS ALONG ALL THREE TYPES OF FAULTS ARE LIKELY TO PRODUCE SEVERE EARTHQUAKES.

Faults cut through the solid rocks of the crust at different angles known as the dip of the fault-plane. Successive movements along the fault-plane can polish the rocks in such a way that they will glisten if erosion exposes them on the Earth's surface. At other times, the friction caused by the dislocation crushes and shatters the rocks along the fault-plane, so that they form lines of weakness called shear-zones, that might be exploited by surface streams and carved into valleys.

Normal faults

When the crust is stretched, the rocks are gradually pulled apart until they fracture and form a 'normal fault'. Here a rock mass moves relatively downwards, down the dip of the fault-plane. The surface area of the land is slightly increased as a result. The Wasatch Front near Salt Lake City in Utah is an example of a normal fault.

Reverse faults

When the crust is compressed as two rock masses are forced together, then a 'reverse fault' can develop. Here a rock mass moves up the dip of the fault-plane. In this case the area of the land surface is slightly reduced. The El Asnam fault in Algeria is an example of this type of fault. When the angle of such a fault-plane is very low, the resulting feature is often called a

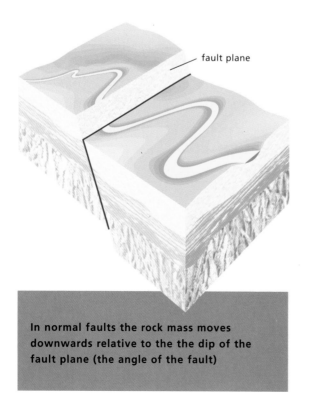

fault plane

In normal faults the rock mass moves downwards relative to the the dip of the fault plane (the angle of the fault)

fault plane

In reverse faults the rock mass moves upwards relative to the dip of the fault plane

'thrust fault', where one block has been thrust over another. These reverse and thrust faults are typical of mountain ranges which are, of course, predominantly zones of collision and compression.

Horizontal faults

When the crust is subjected to horizontal or lateral forces the faults dislocate the rock masses sideways. Faults produced in this way have been given many names, including 'wrench faults' and 'lateral faults'. These are no less destructive than other types of faults, and they have caused a great deal of damage in California, China and Turkey within the last 25 years. The effects of the lateral wrenching can be seen in displaced fences, culverts or even streams, for instance, along the San Andreas Fault in California. These horizontal displacements are described as 'dextral', or right-lateral, when they move to the right in relation to the observer, and 'sinistral', or left-lateral, when they move to the left. For example, when an observer faces the San Andreas Fault, the land beyond the fault-line appears to have moved to the right. Thus it is a dextral wrench fault. There is no stretching or compression directly associated with wrench faults although they may contain certain segments that move up or down.

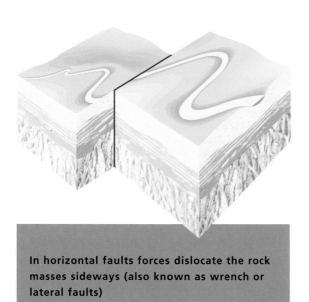

In horizontal faults forces dislocate the rock masses sideways (also known as wrench or lateral faults)

This aerial view north-west along the San Andreas fault shows scarps formed by displacements along the fault. An uplifted block on the right gives way to a similarly uplifted block on the left in the distance

earthquake waves

THE SOURCE OF EARTHQUAKE WAVES IS KNOWN AS THE FOCUS AND REPRESENTS THE EXACT POINT WITHIN THE EARTH'S CRUST WHERE DISLOCATION BEGINS. THE FOCUS OF MOST EARTHQUAKES IS LESS THAN 30KM (18½ MILES) DEEP. ON THE SURFACE, DIRECTLY ABOVE THE FOCUS, IS THE EPICENTRE OF THE EARTHQUAKE. THIS IS WHERE THE GREATEST DAMAGE USUALLY OCCURS.

fault scarp

epicentre

focus

fault

The focus of an earthquake is the point within the Earth's crust where dislocation begins. The epicentre is the point on the Earth's crust directly above the focus

Waves produced by the earthquake spread through the Earth. Initially, they cause powerful vibrations but they grow weaker as they spread out from the focus. There are two groups of earthquake waves, body waves and surface waves, each travelling at different speeds and causing different types of vibration. In general terms, body waves travel faster than surface waves, but surface waves cause greater damage.

Body waves

Body waves are so-called because they travel through the body of the Earth. There are two types of body waves: primary waves and secondary waves.

Primary, or 'P-waves', can pass through both solids and liquids, including water and molten rocks, in the Earth's interior. They travel fastest of all, and give the first indication on earthquake-registering seismographs, as well as in the streets, that an earthquake is imminent. They are longitudinal, or compressional waves, and cause the rocks to vibrate forwards and backwards in the direction of the wave movement. As the P-wave passes, the rock particles are squeezed together. Then, once the wave has passed through, the rock particles return more or less to their original state. P-waves travel at about 6km (3¾ miles) per second through continental crust, and at about 8km (5 miles) per second through oceanic crust. Sometimes P-waves can be transmitted into the atmosphere as booming sound waves.

Secondary, or 'S-waves' only travel at about half the speed of P-waves – 3.6km (2¼ miles) per second through continental crust and about 4.7km (3 miles) per second through oceanic crust. Secondary waves cannot pass through

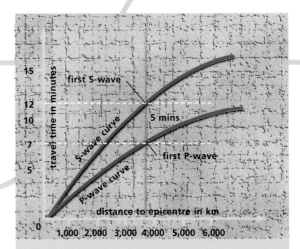

The difference in the speeds of P- and S-waves can be used to plot the distance of seismic stations from earthquake epicentres

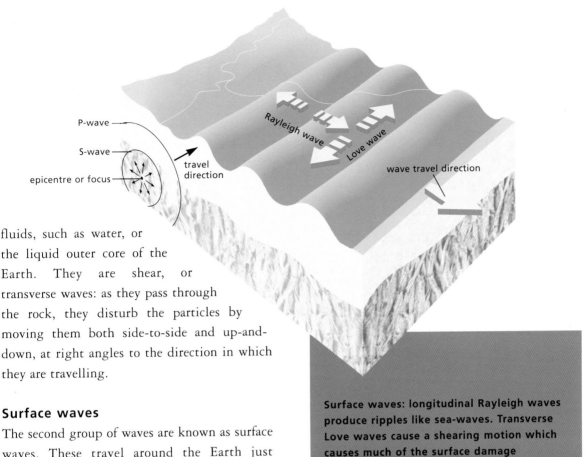

P-wave

S-wave

epicentre or focus

travel direction

Rayleigh wave

Love wave

wave travel direction

fluids, such as water, or the liquid outer core of the Earth. They are shear, or transverse waves: as they pass through the rock, they disturb the particles by moving them both side-to-side and up-and-down, at right angles to the direction in which they are travelling.

Surface waves

The second group of waves are known as surface waves. These travel around the Earth just underneath the surface. Within this group there are two different types, Love waves and Rayleigh waves, named after the scientists who first described them.

Surface waves arrive shortly after the body waves. They can cause extensive damage in built-up areas, in part because they take longer to pass through a given spot. They are, of course, restricted to the crust close to the Earth's surface. Love waves travel faster than Rayleigh waves. Love waves push the rocks horizontally sideways at right angles to the direction in which they are travelling. They shear buildings rather like secondary body waves, but unlike S-waves, Love waves cause no vertical motion. Rayleigh waves are the slowest moving earthquake waves. Rather like water travelling in an ocean wave, Rayleigh waves push the rock particles upwards and backwards as they advance. The particles move in a vertical plane following an elliptical path as the wave passes by.

In practice there are some complications to these intricate patterns. Waves can be bent, or refracted when they pass from one rock type to

Surface waves: longitudinal Rayleigh waves produce ripples like sea-waves. Transverse Love waves cause a shearing motion which causes much of the surface damage

another, or from one shell of the globe to another. Also, when body waves reach the Earth's surface much of their energy is reflected back down into the ground. This can vastly increase the amount of vibration that takes place near the landsurface. Thus, miners working deep in the solid rock beneath Tangshan in July 1976 survived whilst violent shaking destroyed much of the city above them.

The type of underlying rock is an important factor in the amount of damage caused by an earthquake. Good, solid granite and massive layers of sandstone, for instance, vibrate much less than silty, sandy alluvium that occurs alongside rivers and in coastal areas. Thus, in 1908, the beautiful waterfront built on alluvium at Messina in Sicily was wrecked, whilst buildings on the solid rock west of the city survived. A similar pattern was revealed at San Francisco in 1906, Tokyo in 1923, and at Kobe in 1995.

measuring earthquakes

THERE ARE TWO DIFFERENT WAYS OF MEASURING AN EARTHQUAKE. THE FIRST IS A CALCULATION OF ITS MAGNITUDE OR STRENGTH. THE SECOND IS A JUDGEMENT OF INTENSITY MADE BY EVALUATION OF REPORTS OF THE EXTENT OF SURFACE DAMAGE.

earthquakes

44

Seismographs

The great earthquake that devastated Lisbon in 1755 (see pp.36–37) caused chandeliers to swing in many of the great houses of western Europe. This effect, produced when a free mass (in this case the chandelier) remains at rest, while a fixed object (the house) moves in response to the ground's vibrations, forms the basis of the way in which modern seismographs work. If the movements of the chandelier could have been traced on the floor of the room in which it was situated it could have recorded the vibrations of the earthquake. Modern seismographs record both horizontal and vertical vibrations. These are registered on a paper trace over a drum, calibrated to a clock, which rotates with the passage of time. Thus seismographs register the size, or amplitude, of the vibrations caused by the shock waves, and the time at which they occur.

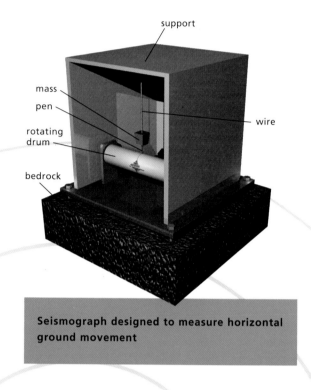

Seismograph designed to measure horizontal ground movement

A seismograph consists of a freely-pivoting horizontal strut, fixed to an upright support, that is firmly anchored to the ground. The horizontal strut has a heavy mass at the far end, to which a pen is attached. The pen traces a continuous line onto the paper, which is wrapped around a rotating drum lying on its side on a horizontal axle, which is also anchored to the ground like the upright support. If no ground movements take place the pen would trace a straight line. When the earthquake shock waves arrive the pen swings up and down. This is because the waves vibrate the vertical support and the drum that are both fixed to the ground. The horizontal strut vibrates much less due to the inertia of the heavy mass at its far end. Thus the paper on the drum shifts backwards and forwards under the pen, tracing the movement on the paper. The rotation of the drum is calibrated to a clock so that these vibrations can be timed accurately. To record all horizontal movements caused by waves

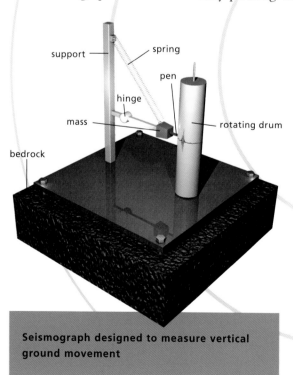

Seismograph designed to measure vertical ground movement

two seismographs are used; one to record waves travelling north or south; the other east or west.

A third seismograph registers vertical movements. In this case, a solid horizontal support is fixed firmly in place and the drum rotates about a vertical axle. The heavy mass and the pen are suspended vertically by a fine spring from the well-anchored horizontal support.

Seismographs throughout the world

The number of seismographs in operation has vastly increased since the World-wide Standardized Seismographic Network, (WWSSN), was first established in 1962. The earthquake waves reach many stations in less than ten minutes. The network transmits the data to central computers and the focus, epicentre and size of the earthquake are known well within the hour. Many more earthquakes are registered than ever make the headlines – about one million earthquakes happen every year – fortunately major earthquakes are rare.

Books were shaken from the shelves of this book shop in Los Gatos, California, during the Loma Prieta earthquake in 1989

earthquake scales

ALTHOUGH THE MAJORITY OF EARTHQUAKES PASS VIRTUALLY UNNOTICED, SEVERAL TIMES A DECADE, VIOLENT EARTHQUAKES DEVASTATE ENTIRE AREAS. THERE IS, HOWEVER, NO SINGLE WAY OF MEASURING THESE LARGE VARIATIONS IN EARTHQUAKES AND THEIR EFFECTS. THE TWO MOST COMMON WAYS OF MEASURING AND ANALYZING EARTHQUAKES ARE IN TERMS OF THEIR MAGNITUDE AND INTENSITY.

The magnitude and intensity scales were devised in an attempt to establish an absolute scale of earthquake values. Both have since been modified to take into account modern technological advances. The magnitude scale is based on calculations of the vigour of earthquakes at their source. The intensity scale describes informed, but subjective, assessments of the varying effects of earthquakes on the landsurface.

Magnitude

The scale of earthquake magnitudes was devised by the American seismologist Charles Richter in 1935. At first, his aim was simply to compare earthquakes in different areas of California, but his method soon spread all over the world. Consequently it is now usually known as the Richter Scale of magnitude. It is based on the size, or amplitude, of the waves traced by the pen on the seismograph, and on the distance between the instrument, and the focus of the earthquake. The seismographs had to be standardized so that waves of equal length traced out lines of equal size on all the instruments. The waves weaken as they spread out from the focus of the earthquake and Richter therefore had to make allowance for the distance between the focus and the instrument. This distance could be calculated by measuring the time interval between the arrivals of the P-waves and S-waves. Adjustments could then also be made to standardize for the effect of distance – as if all the instruments were 100km (62 miles) from the focus.

The magnitude 8.1 earthquake that struck Mexico City in 1985 destroyed hundreds of buildings, and damaged many more

Richter devised a formula using the maximum vibration actually measured on the seismograph standardized for the effect of its distance from the focus. The size and strength of any earthquake could then be calculated in absolute terms as its magnitude. The values were then placed on a logarithmic scale. While it is generally held that earthquake magnitudes of between 1.0 and 10.0 can be measured on the Richter Scale, in fact the scale is open-ended, and a very large earthquake could, in theory, exceed magnitude 10.0. To compare, the Messina earthquake of 1908 measured 7.5, the Anchorage (Alaska) earthquake in 1964 measured 8.4, while the Moroccan earthquake that destroyed the town of Agadir in 1960 reached only 5.8. The Lisbon earthquake of 1755 could have exceeded 9.0.

The Richter Scale is logarithmic, thus a rise of one unit of magnitude represents a ten-fold increase in the measurement of earthquake waves on the seismograph: a magnitude 5.0 earthquake is ten times greater than one of magnitude 4.0. The differences in the energy released are much greater. For each unit of magnitude, the energy released at the focus increases by 30–32 times.

Magnitude tells us little about the effect of earthquakes on human lives, and does not necessarily correlate with intensity (see pp. 48–49), even near the epicentre. The Anchorage earthquake (magnitude 8.4) killed a relatively small number of people (131) in part because the area was sparsely populated. The Agadir earthquake (magnitude 5.8) claimed 12,000–14,000 lives mainly because the focus of the earthquake was particularly shallow – just 2–3km (1¼–1¾ miles) deep – and was situated directly beneath the town.

the Richter scale of magnitude

Magnitude	Qualitative Description	Average number per year	Approx. intensity equivalent near epicentre (Mercalli scale)	
0–1.9	-	700,000	I–V	Recorded but not felt
2–2.9	-	300,000	I–V	Recorded but not felt
3–3.9	Minor	40,000	I–V	Felt by some
4–4.9	Light	6,200	I–V	Felt by many
5–5.9	Moderate	800	VI–VII	Slight damage
6–6.9	Strong	120	VIII	Damaging
7–7.9	Major	18	IX–XI	Destructive
8–8.9	Great	1 every 10–20 years	XII	Widely devastating

Note. Recent advances in earthquake studies have brought modifications to the original scale, and seismologists use more refined methods of comparing earthquakes, although the principles of operation remain much the same.

This bridge, destroyed during the Alaska earthquake of 1964, lay a short distance from the epicentre. The Alaskan earthquake measured 8.4 on the Richter scale

intensity

IN GENERAL, THE MOST SEVERE EFFECTS OF AN EARTHQUAKE OCCUR AT AND AROUND THE EPICENTRE, WITH THE SHOCK WAVES BECOMING WEAKER AS THEY SPREAD OUT FROM THAT POINT. AS NOTED EARLIER (SEE PP.36–37), WHILE THE LISBON EARTHQUAKE OF 1755 DEVASTATED THE CITY, IT WAS FELT AS A MILD SHUDDER ON THE STREETS OF BORDEAUX, AND CAUSED RIPPLES ON THE WATER AT LOCH NESS, SCOTLAND, 1,750KM (1,090 MILES) AWAY. ALL EARTHQUAKES HAVE VARIABLE EFFECTS, AND DIFFERENT TYPES OF UNDERLYING ROCK RESPOND IN DIFFERENT WAYS TO THE SHOCK WAVES PASSING THROUGH THEM. IT IS THESE VARYING EFFECTS THAT THE SCALE OF EARTHQUAKE INTENSITY TRIES TO EVALUATE.

The intensity of an earthquake is assessed by subjective, qualitative observations of its effects on the landscape; unlike the Richter scale it is not based on mathematical calculations. The degree of damage in built-up areas and changes in the natural landscape have been put in a scale ranging from I–XII. The scale then allows the effects of new earthquakes to be quickly placed in the appropriate category. It is also possible to assess the intensity of earthquakes that happened before the development of seismographs.

Intensity has been evaluated ever since the Calabrian earthquakes in Italy in 1783 caused such widespread and variable devastation. The basis of the present scale was devised by the Italian geologist, Mercalli, in 1902 and modified versions are still in use. A modified Mercalli Scale, developed in 1931, is used in the United States; slightly different versions are used in Japan and Europe. In Europe the MSK Intensity Scale is used, named after the scientists who derived it: Medvedev, Sponheuer and Karnik. Their aim was to quantify degrees of damage to structures, and classify the types of building affected, more clearly.

The basis of intensity evaluation is what witnesses saw or felt, as well as reports, and responses to questionnaires in each area affected. The timing and, especially, the site of these descriptions is significant primarily because the intensity of an earthquake can vary within a small area. Nowadays, after an earthquake in the United States, for example, the National Earthquake Information Centre sends out questionnaires to government officials, police officers, fire officers and other volunteers. Thus, the variable pattern of damage and earthquake intensity is built up and mapped, and this serves not merely an historical record, but also to evaluate earthquake risk for the future.

For instance, the pattern of intensity during the San Francisco earthquake of 1906 varied from VI–X, even within the city itself. The most intensely affected areas were built on coastal silts, and those least affected on compact hard rocks. Eighty-three years later, the most serious damage caused by the the Loma Prieta earthquake also occurred around the coast and on recent land-fill sites in the Bay area.

Occasionally the most intense damage can happen a long way from the epicentre. For example, during the Michoacán earthquake in Mexico in 1985, some of the greatest – and certainly the most lethal – damage happened 360km (224 miles) away in Mexico City. The Mexican capital is built partly on silt on the drained floor of Lake Texcoco. These silts amplified the ground motion by 75 times. The result was losses of US$4 billion and up to 35,000 lives. Intensity assessments thus have a practical and vital application that magnitude evaluations cannot match. A further advantage of an intensity scale is that it provides a ready summary of what earthquakes can do.

ABOVE The mansions on Nob Hill were devastated by fire following the 1906 San Francisco earthquake. Here a stone fireplace and chimney are all that remain standing BELOW Forward ground movement during the earthquake caused this railway track to buckle

modified Mercalli Intensity Scale of 1931

I Felt only rarely. Sometimes dizziness or nausea; birds and animals uneasy; trees, structures, liquids, doors sway.

II Felt indoors by a few, especially on upper floors. Same other effects as I, but more noticeably; delicately suspended objects may swing.

III Felt indoors, especially on upper floors, by several people. Usually rapid vibration, as if lightly loaded lorries passing. Hanging objects and standing motor cars rock slightly.

IV Felt indoors by many, outside by few. Some awakened, no-one usually frightened. Sensation of heavy object striking building. Vibration as of heavy lorries passing. Crockery, windows and doors rattle; walls and frames creak; hanging objects and standing motor cars sway.

The Loma Prieta earthquake 1989 damaged many roads. This is a collapsed section of the San Francisco-Oakland Bay Bridge

V Felt indoors by almost everyone, outdoors by most people. Many awakened, a few frightened and run outdoors. Buildings tremble, crockery and windows sometimes break and some vases fall. Pictures and doors clatter, small objects move. Some liquids spilt; clocks stopped; trees shaken; animals anxious.

This 21-storey steel apartment building collapsed during the Mexico earthquake in 1985

VI Felt by all indoors and outdoors. Many frightened and some alarmed. All awakened. People, trees and bushes shaken. Liquids set in motion; small bells set ringing. Crockery broken; plaster cracks and falls; books, vases fall over. Some furniture moved. Domestic animals try to escape. Minor landslides on steep slopes.

VII All frightened, run outdoors, general alarm. Some people thrown to ground. Trees shaken quite strongly; waves and mud stirred up in lakes; sandbanks collapse. Large bells ring. Suspended objects quiver. Much damage in badly-built buildings, old walls; slight in well-built buildings. Chimneys crack, much plaster, tiles and loose bricks fall. Heavy furniture overturned. Concrete ditches damaged.

VIII Alarm approached panic. Vehicle drivers disturbed. Trees shaken and broken. Sand and mud spurt from ground, marked changes in springs and wells. Much damage to ordinary and older buildings; walls, chimneys, pillars, towers, statues and gravestones crack or fall. Very heavy furniture overturned.

IX General panic. Ground cracked open 10cm (4in). Much damage to structures built to withstand earthquakes. Frequent partial or total collapse in other buildings, and reservoirs, underground pipes broken; buildings dislodged from foundations. Rockfalls.

X Widely-cracked ground, fissures up to 1m (3¼ft) wide. Frequent river-bank and coastal landslides and shifted sands. Water-levels change; water thrown onto riversides, etc. Serious damage to dams, embankments, bridges. Severe damage to well-built wooden structures, masonry structures destroyed along with their foundations. Rails bent; open cracks and waves on roads. Pipes torn apart.

XI Widespread serious ground disturbance, broad fissures, landslips and landslides. Muddy water spurts upward. Tsunamis develop. Severe damage to all wooden structures, great damage to dams. Few masonry structures remain upright, pillars of bridges and viaducts wrecked. All pipelines wrecked. Rails badly bent. Main roads impassable.

XII Total damage to all constructions, great disturbance to ground with many shearing cracks. Many large landslides on slopes, rockfalls common, rock masses dislocated, water channels altered and dammed. Ground surface waves like water and remains undulating. Objects thrown into the air.

In 1976 a magnitude 7.9 earthquake devastated the town of Joyabaj, Guatemala

earthquake report

This earthquake report questionnaire is sent out by the US Geological Survey to those affected by earthquakes, and helps to map the intensity of the earthquake, by asking people what they saw and felt. It is also a way of assessing the types of damage sustained by different types and ages of building. It asks people to describe damage to their own homes as well as to other buildings in their area.

the effects
of earthquakes

PEOPLE, ANIMALS AND MAN-MADE STRUCTURES ARE THE MOST VULNERABLE TO
EARTHQUAKES; WIDE OPEN SPACES ARE MUCH LESS VULNERABLE. THE DIRECT EFFECTS OF
EARTHQUAKES ARE ALSO OFTEN FAR LESS DEVASTATING AND LIFE-THREATENING THAN THE
SECONDARY CATASTROPHES THAT THEY CAUSE: FIRES, TSUNAMIS, LANDSLIDES, FAMINES AND
EPIDEMICS. IT IS THEREFORE MUCH MORE DANGEROUS TO BE IN A CITY THAN IN THE
SURROUNDING COUNTRYSIDE BOTH DURING AND AFTER AN EARTHQUAKE.

PRIMARY EFFECTS

In open country, the shocks can form small
scarps, about 1m (3¼ft) high, for distances of
3km (1¾ miles) or more. The Armenian
earthquake of 1988 formed a fine example.
Where great fault-scarps have already formed,
further uplift of the block can take place,

forming a fresh scarp along the base of the slope.
This is common on active faults in Utah and
Nevada. Elsewhere the ground cracks, throwing
down trees or precipitating landslides. Thus the
1906 San Francisco earthquake felled some
redwood trees in northern California. The Calabrian earthquake of 1783, and the earthquakes

The magnitude 7.8 Peruvian earthquake of 1970 caused the beach sediments underneath this road, along
the bay in western Chimbote, to slump and fissure

at Anchorage in 1964 and Loma Prieta in 1989, all caused massive landslides.

Historical reports of earthquakes often claimed that the ground had cracked open and swallowed up entire buildings or settlements. A more logical explanation, however, is that landslides or rock falls were responsible. Even in open country, some places are clearly safer than others. The foot of a sandy sea-cliff is no place to seek refuge from an earthquake: even if there is no landslide the earthquake may well cause a tsunami. Solid, hard rock such as granite is more stable than the sandy-clays of a damp alluvial plain where liquefaction may occur.

When you stamp repeatedly on a patch of wet sand on a beach, it immediately becomes wet, loses its cohesion, and the area around the point of impact becomes a miniature quicksand: the sand has liquefied in response to the vibrations caused by the stamping. Shock waves produced by earthquakes cause liquefaction on a grand scale – with spectacular effects on buildings. Elsewhere, different grain-sizes or different types of shock wave vibration can cause sand and water to spurt out in little cones called 'sand boils' that look like little volcanoes and may reach up to 30cm (12in) high.

In relatively rare cases streams can be diverted. The El Asnam earthquake in Algeria in 1980 pushed back a small lake when land was jerked upwards across a stream. In California many streams crossing the San Andreas Fault system bend to the right as a result of its right-lateral displacement.

The general nature of the underlying rocks may also play a role in the area over which earthquakes are felt. The effects of the San Francisco earthquake in 1906 were restricted to a relatively narrow belt of California, 200km (124 miles) wide, possibly because the notably faulted rocks to the east quickly weakened the shock waves. In contrast, the New Madrid earthquakes in Missouri occurred in broad, gently sloping, less fractured rocks. Consequently shocks were clearly felt 1,200km (746 miles) away from the epicentre.

During urban earthquakes the vibrations of the shock waves often dislodge cornices,

Following the 1989 Loma Prieta earthquake many homeowners in the area buttressed their foundations to prevent further damage from aftershocks

decorative statues, concrete panels, or cause floors or façades or whole buildings to collapse. Pillars supporting bridges and roads are often sheared at their base or where they join the superstructure.

These effects can also be exacerbated by the type of soil underlying the buildings in a city. In damp alluvium, shaking increases the underground water pressure and water invades all the interstices in the sandy silt. The whole mass shudders and liquefies. The ground liquefied during the earthquake at Niigata in Japan in 1964. Several blocks of flats stayed intact but keeled over at a steep angle and sank about 5m (16½ft): some grateful inhabitants escaped from their homes by walking down the outside walls of the blocks. During the Alaskan earthquake, also in 1964, liquefaction of frost-ridden ground at Turnagain Heights in Anchorage sent suburban homes sliding sideways. A relatively small number of people were killed in these two earthquakes, but in general, liquefaction is probably one of the main direct causes of earthquake fatalities: it was a major contributor to the numbers of lives lost in San Francisco in 1906, Messina and Reggio di Calabria in 1908, Tokyo in 1923 and Kobe in 1995.

SECONDARY EFFECTS

The main secondary effects of earthquakes are fire, tsunamis, landslides, epidemics, famine, changes in the level of the land, and their cost in human lives.

Fire

Historically, movements produced by earthquakes knocked inflammable material into open hearths, causing fires to break out within a few minutes. Poor quality housing and wooden buildings were soon destroyed. When earthquakes wrecked the Cretan Palaces about 1750 BC, excavations have revealed ample evidence of the fires that followed. More recently it was fire, starting in the slums, spreading to Chinatown and onto the wealthier areas of the city, that caused most of the damage to San Francisco in 1906. Fire devastated the wooden homes of Tokyo after the Kanto earthquake in 1923: 25–30 per cent of the 143,000 victims met their deaths as a result of fire.

In modern cities, earthquakes compound the effects of fire by cutting gas and water pipes. The former adds to the combustion and explosions, while the latter removes the most effective means of stopping it. When the water

The Sherman Glacier as it appeared before the 1964 earthquake. The picture (right) shows the glacier partially covered by a rockslide caused by the earthquake

Sand boils, such as this caused by the Peruvian earthquake in 1970, can reach up to 30cm (12in) in height

supply was cut in San Francisco, whole streets were blown up to stop the fire consuming the whole city. Similarly, severed electric cables can be very dangerous. In Kobe, in 1995, for example, cables dangled, sparkling in the narrow streets for days afterwards.

Disease

Burst water pipes provide a further hazard, especially where the water can become infected. Diseases such as cholera and typhoid fever can become rife. There is always the danger that disease can reach epidemic proportions in a devastated city because communications and medical supplies may be cut off by damaged roads, railways or bridges.

Landslides

Earthquakes often cause landslides, especially in steep river valleys, and coastal cliffs. In weak sands or clays, in particular, the slightest vibration can bring down a whole slope. In Calabria in 1783, continual shocks swept through the country from 5 February until the end of May. This earthquake probably caused more physical damage to open country than any recorded in Europe. There was a landslide in practically every ravine in western Calabria, and it was common for entire fields to be transported over 500m (1,640ft) downslope.

A magnitude 7.8 earthquake 70km (43½ miles) off the coast of Peru on 31 May 1970, caused the most spectacular landslide of modern times, high up in the Andes, causing at least 20,000 of the 66,000 recorded fatalities. The earthquake itself killed about 25,000 people in the Andean town of Huaraz, and destroyed most of the houses in the Rio Santa Valley. Severe vibrations disturbed the steep, glacier-covered flanks of Huascaran (6,768m, 22,205ft), dislodging about 1 million m³ (35 million ft³) of ice from its summit, which fell onto a mass of rock and ice 800m (2,625ft) below. Shortly afterwards 50 million m³ (1,766 million ft³) of rock and melting ice began to move down the Rio Santa Valley at nearly 350km/h (217mph).

About 14km (8¾ miles) from Huascaran, the earthquake had devastated the small town of Yungay. Two survivors saw the landslide advancing. They ran to the cemetery knoll and, moments later, they watched a flow of rock, ice and mud, 3m (9¾ft) high, swamp the ruins of Yungay and seal the fate of 20,000 people.

The 1923 earthquake and the fires that followed caused devastation in Tokyo. This photograph was taken from the top of the Imperial Hotel, one of the few buildings to survive the earthquake

The peak of a mountain to the right of the picture collapsed to form this rockslide

tsunamis

THE MOST WIDESPREAD OF THE SECONDARY EFFECTS OF EARTHQUAKES ARE HUGE, AND FREQUENTLY DEVASTATING, SEA-WAVES OR TSUNAMIS. THE WORD COMES FROM THE JAPANESE 'TSU', MEANING HARBOUR, AND 'NAMI' MEANING WAVE; 'A WAVE BREAKING INTO A HARBOUR'. IN FACT THEY ARE SO POWERFUL THAT THEY CAN CROSS THE PACIFIC OCEAN WITH EASE.

When an earthquake epicentre is on the sea-floor, or very near the coast, the faulting can cause the Earth's crust to sag and generate large submarine landslides. The water falls into the subsidence, so that the sea often retreats soon after the earthquake. About 10–15 minutes later the water returns as a huge wave that crashes onto the shore. Meanwhile, the tsunami spreads very quickly out to sea but is virtually undetectable until it reaches shallow coastal waters again. The great Chilean earthquake on 21–22 May 1960 generated three tsunamis that reached Japan, 16,000km (9,950 miles) away, 22 hours later. Over 3,000 houses and 250 bridges were destroyed, 2,500 ships damaged and 165 people killed. During its journey, the tsunami toppled the huge statues on Easter Island, drowned 50 people and caused US$50 million worth of damage in Hawaii. Ships on the open sea, however, were not affected.

The basic reason for this apparent anomaly is that in deep water, the wave length (the distance between the wave crests) of the tsunamis can be over 500km (311 miles), but the amplitude (height from crest to trough) may be less than 10m (33ft). The waves thus have imperceptible slopes. However, they do move fast, up to 800km/h (497mph), where the waters are 5,000m (16,400ft) deep over the abyssal plains

The tsunamis that followed the Alaskan earthquake of 1964 wrecked the sea front at Kodiak as seen here

of the oceans. As they approach shallow water, the friction of the sea-floor slows down the wave but increases its height. The tsunami can then form walls of water 30m (98ft) high that break and then crash upon the shore at speeds of about 80km/h (50mph). Narrowing, funnel-shaped, bays increase wave height even further which helps explain why devastation has often been very severe on heavily indented coasts such as Japan, Chile and Alaska. The highest recorded tsunami was caused by the Japanese earthquake of 24 April 1771. It reached a height of 85m (280ft) and caused 9,313 deaths in Japan alone.

Most tsunamis do most of their damage near

sea level   displacement

their source and only about 10 per cent devastate areas more than 8,000km (4,970 miles) away. Nevertheless, at such a distance they are still much more destructive than earthquake shock waves. Earthquakes cause most tsunamis; volcanic eruptions account for only 5 per cent.

The Pacific Ocean accounts for about 75 per cent of damaging tsunamis, with 12 per cent in

Ships and debris were also washed up along the shore at the port of Seward

the Mediterranean. Both areas experience violent earthquakes (and eruptions). Less seismically active areas produce fewer tsunamis: the Atlantic Ocean 9 per cent, the Indian Ocean 3 per cent.

The Lisbon earthquake of 1755 caused possibly the largest recorded European tsunami, reaching 15m (49ft) high in Portugal, Spain and Morocco. Following the Calabrian earthquake of 1783, tsunamis swept up and down the Straits of Messina. The Prince of Scilla and 2,473 of his people were swept out to sea. There was one survivor: a woman, 'four months gone with child' was rescued after nine hours. Miraculously both mother and child were unharmed.

Tsunamis, Simoda Bay, Japan, 23 December 1854. Extracts from the log of Russian frigate *Diana*

'The first earthquake shock was at 9.15 [am] and lasted 2–3 minutes. At 10.00 [am] a huge wave entered the bay and swamped the whole town and its houses and temples in a few minutes. Masses of debris started to float about ... Then the water began to rise up and boil ... and crashed onto the town ... There were innumerable whirlpools that turned the frigate round and round ... She was buffeted so much that the cannons were dislodged and one man was killed and several injured.'

'At 10.30 [am] a junk was thrown up against the frigate. It smashed open and sank. Only two men were saved because they had been thrown ropes. The rest were drowned down below where they had sought refuge. At 11.15 [am] the frigate lost two anchors and was sent twirling round again. By then the whole town was a flattened, empty space. Only 17 houses out of about 1,000 were still upright ... The waters kept on rising and falling until noon and the sea-level varied from minus 8¾ft [2.65m] to plus 39½ft [12m].'

'At 2.00 [pm] the sea-floor rose up again so violently that it threw the frigate onto its side several times. When calm returned, it took four whole hours to disentangle the ... mess of the ship's ropes and anchor-chains ... the bay was no more than a mass of ruins.'

increasing wave height

decreasing water depth

changing land levels and human cost

THE FINAL SECONDARY EFFECTS OF EARTHQUAKES ARE THEIR TERRIBLE COST IN HUMAN LIVES AND CHANGES IN THE LEVEL OF THE LAND.

Changing land levels

Usually the least devastating secondary effect of earthquakes is that the level of the land can rise or fall over a wide area. Such displacements are small and are most clearly visible in coastal areas. Darwin reported that the Chilean earthquake on 20 February 1835 raised the land by about 1m (3¼ft) around the Bay of Concepción. Captain Fitzroy, the commander of the Beagle 'found beds of putrid mussel-shells, still adhering to the rocks' some 3m (9¾ft) above the high-water mark, whereas before the earthquake they had always lived below low water. Older seashells were scattered over the land to a height of 200m (656ft), which showed that the uplift of 1835 was only the last of many during the preceding centuries. The Alaskan earthquake in 1964 displaced about 160,000km² (61,776 square miles) of land. In and around Prince William Sound, a long hump was upraised – in places by over 10m (33ft). Alongside it ran a trough marked by some 2m (6½ft) of subsidence. Both ran from north-east to south-west parallel to the fault-line that had generated the earthquake. Lines of dead barnacles underlined the old raised coastline all around Prince William Sound and the Kenai Peninsula nearby.

Mexico 1985. Many buildings were left as heaps of rubble

Human cost

The final secondary effect of earthquakes is loss of human life. As has already been discussed, earthquakes themselves pose very little threat. Serious injury or death is caused mainly by the collapse of buildings or other man-made structures, such as roads and bridges, or when the earthquakes provoke other catastrophic events already outlined. The death-toll resulting from an earthquake bears little direct relationship to its magnitude, but is more closely related to its intensity, because this is in part a measure of damage caused by the shock-waves. Other factors include the density of population, the style of building that predominates in the area affected and the time of day when the shock occurs.

Chance was one of the reasons for the difference in death-toll between the earthquakes in Tokyo in 1923 and Anchorage in 1964. In Anchorage it was Good Friday, and public buildings were empty. Moreover the area was, and still is, much less densely populated. The earthquake that badly damaged Kalamata in Greece in 1986, fortunately occurred in the early evening, when everyone was outside. Similarly many people were outside enjoying the sunny holiday weather on 1 January 1980, when an earthquake struck Terceira in the Azores, damaging the beautiful city of Angra do Heroísmo. The empty apartments and other buildings meant there were few casualties.

It is usually better to be inside a wooden hut than an old, hurriedly-built block of flats, during an earthquake. Survival, however, is frequently a matter of chance. There was a remarkable example of lucky escape during the Calabrian earthquake in 1783. At Terra Nuova, the first shock on 5 February buried the priest

As many as 35,000 people could have been killed by the Mexico earthquake although the official figure is 9,500. 30,000 people were injured and 100,000 left homeless

with some of his flock alive under a huge pile of rubble. The second 'shock' came just in time. It disturbed the ruins, and they scrambled to safety. During the Mexican earthquake in 1985, a young French couple were on their honeymoon in an hotel in the centre of Mexico. The hotel was wrecked. In bed at the time the earthquake struck, the floor of the couple's room collapsed and, together with their bed, they fell nine storeys. The couple were later rescued, astonished, but otherwise unharmed.

Sir William Hamilton – husband of Admiral Lord Nelson's mistress Emma Hamilton – who provided a report of the Calabrian disaster, described apparent differences in the positions of bodies found when the rubble was cleared away. The men, he claimed, tended to be found in an attitude of struggle. In contrast the women often had their hands clasped over their heads, as if they had given up in despair. Mothers, however, always had their arms clutched tightly around their children.

Amongst those who are trapped, rates of survival vary greatly according to how seriously they are injured, the time taken for them to be rescued and how determined the individual is to survive. The age of the victim is also another important factor: older people tend to be weaker and lack the strength necessary to survive for long periods without food or water, or to dig their way out. Babies, however, seem to be remarkably robust and can survive even after being trapped for several days. In addition, the fact that babies are unaware of the dangers they face, means that they do not suffer from shock or stress.

For those who survive relatively unscathed, additional stress is caused by the frantic search for friends and family, something that is seen in all television footage following such disasters. Shock, panic, fear, hunger, illness, bereavement and even robbery may be suffered by many, if not all, survivors before normality can be restored. The statistics of death-tolls from earthquakes, therefore, cover a wide range of calamities.

Statistics themselves cannot always be taken at face value. Death-tolls figures must be regarded as estimates and, in some cases, they can only be guesses. Until the last century, there were no accurate census returns. The population before and after an earthquake, and thus the total death-toll, could only be an estimate. Even today, after the earthquakes in Tangshan, China in 1976 and in Mexico City in 1985, for example, some estimates of fatalities were four or five times greater than others. This may be due to the availability of accurate census information, different ways of interpreting information, or other, financial or politically motivated reasons.

Uplifted sea floor at Cape Cleare, Montague Island, Prince William Sound following the 1964 Alaska earthquake

some important
earthquakes

Date	Magnitude	Site	Est. deaths
464 BC		Sparta, Greece	20,000
AD 342		Antioch, Turkey	40,000
565		Antioch, Turkey	30,000
856 Dec		Corinth, Greece	45,000
893		Armenia	20,000
1038 9 Jan		Shansi, China	23,000
1057		Chihli, China	25,000
1169		Sicily, Italy	25,000
1183		Syria-Lebanon	20,000
1201		Aegean Sea	100,000
1268		Silicia, Asia Minor	60,000
1290 27 Sept		Chihli, China	100,000
1293 20 May		Kamekura, Japan	30,000
1456 5 Dec		Naples, Italy	30–60,000
1531 26 Jan		Lisbon, Portugal	30,000
1556 23 Jan	8.3?	Shansi, China	830,000
1641 5 Feb		Tabriz, Persia	30,000
1653 23 Feb		Smyrna, Turkey	15,000
1667 Nov		Shemaka, Caucasus	80,000
1693 9–11 Jan		Catania, Italy	60,000
1715 May		Algeria	20,000
1727 18 Nov		Tabriz, Persia	77,000
1731		Peking, China	100,000
1737 11 Oct		Calcutta, India	300,000
1755 7 June		Kashan, Persia	40,000
1755 1 Nov	9.0?	Lisbon, Portugal	100,000+
1759 30 Oct		Jordan Valley	20,000
1783 5 Feb		Calabria, Italy	80,000
1797 4 Feb		Quito, Ecuador	41,000
1822 5 Sept		Aleppo, Syria	22,000
1828		Echigo, Japan	30,000
1835 20 Feb	8.5	Concepcion, Chile	35
1847 8 May		Zenkoji, Japan	12–34,000
1853 21 April		Shiraz, Persia	12,000
1853 11 July		Ispahan, Persia	10,000
1857 9 Jan	8.3	Fort Tejon, California	1

1857 16 Dec	6.5	Italy	12,000
1861 21 Mar		Mendoza, Argentina	18,000
1868 13 Aug		Peru-Ecuador	25,000
1868 16 Aug		Ecuador-Colombia	70,000
1896 15 June		Sanriku, Japan	27,000
1897 12 June	8.7	Assam, India	1,500
1905 4 April	8.6	Kangra, India	19,000
1906 18 April	8.25	San Francisco, USA	700
1906 17 Aug	8.6	Valparaiso, Chile	20,000
1907 21 Oct	7.7	Afghanistan	12,000
1908 28 Dec	7.5	Messina-Calabria, Italy	160,000
1915 13 Jan	7.0	Avezzano, Italy	32,000
1920 16 Dec	8.6	Kansu, China	200,000
1923 1 Sept	8.3	Tokyo, Japan	143,000
1927 22 May	8.3	Nan-Shan, China	200,000
1932 26 Dec	8.5	Kansu, China	70,000
1934 15 Jan	8.4	Bihar India-Nepal	10,700
1935 30 May	7.5	Quetta, India (Pakistan)	35–60,000
1939 25 Jan	8.3	Chillan, Chile	28,000
1939 26 Dec	7.9	Erzincan, Turkey	30,000
1948 5 Oct		Soviet-Iranian border	19,800
1949 5 Aug	6.8	Ambato-Ecuador	6,000
1954 9 Sept	6.8	Orleansville (El Asnam), Algeria	1,500
1960 29 Feb	5.8	Agadir, Morocco	14,000
1960 21–30 May	9.5 (3.5)	Southern Chile	5,700
1962 1 Sept	6.9	Qazvin, Iran	12,000
1963 26 July	6.0	Skopje, Yugoslavia	1,200
1964 27 Mar	8.4	Anchorage, Alaska	131
1968 31 Aug	7.3	Dashye Bayaz, Iran	12,000
1970 31 May	7.8	Ancash, Peru	66,000
1972 23 Dec	6.2	Managua, Nicaragua	5,000
1975 4 Feb	7.5	Haicheng, China	1,328
1976 4 Feb	7.9	Guatemala	22,000
1976 6 May	6.5	Friuli, Italy	1,000
1976 28 July	7.9	Tangshan, China	850,000
1978 16 Sept	7.4	Iran	15,000
1980 10 Oct	7.2	El Asnam, Algeria	20,000
1980 23 Nov	7.0	Irpinia, Italy	4,000
1985 19 Sept	8.1	Michoacan, Mexico	20,000
1988 7 Dec	6.8	Armenia	25,000
1989 17 Oct	7.1	Loma Prieta, California	62
1990 21 June	7.7	North-west Iran	50,000
1993 30 Sept		Maharashtra, India	15,000
1995 17 Jan	7.2	Kobe, Japan	5,500
1997 May	7.1	E. Iran	1,560

earthquake distribution

ONE OF THE FEW BENEFITS RESULTING FROM THE COLD WAR PERIOD WAS THAT THE ACCURATE INFORMATION ABOUT THE WORLD DISTRIBUTION OF EARTHQUAKES WAS AVAILABLE FOR THE FIRST TIME. THE TEST BAN TREATY, AGREED BETWEEN THE NUCLEAR POWERS IN THE EARLY 1960S, LIMITED OPEN-AIR NUCLEAR TESTS, BUT UNDERGROUND TRIALS CONTINUED. UNDERGROUND NUCLEAR EXPLOSIONS GENERATE SMALL EARTHQUAKES THAT CAN BE MONITORED USING SEISMOGRAPHS. ALMOST OVERNIGHT, WESTERN GOVERNMENTS RELEASED FUNDS TO ESTABLISH A WORLD-WIDE NETWORK OF 120 SEISMOLOGICAL STATIONS, EACH EQUIPPED WITH THREE STANDARDIZED SEISMOGRAPHS. THERE ARE NOW OVER 1,000.

The seismographs not only record any earthquake, but they also reveal the place where it happened, whether it was generated by the Earth itself, or by a bomb. The vibrations are timed on the seismographs with the shock waves taking longer to reach the more distant stations. P-waves travel faster than S-waves (see pp.42–43), therefore, the further a station is from the source of the earthquake, the greater will be the time delay between the arrival of the P-waves and the arrival of the S-waves. Because the general speed of both kinds of waves is known, it is possible to calculate the distance between the seismograph and the source of the earthquake. For example, if the calculated distance was 1,000km (621 miles), then the earthquake could have occurred anywhere on a circle with a radius of 1,000km (621 miles). If several stations have registered the shocks, and scientists have calculated their own distances from the source of the earthquake, the radii of these circles, when drawn on a map, should all intersect at one point. This point represents the epicentre of the earthquake or nuclear explosion.

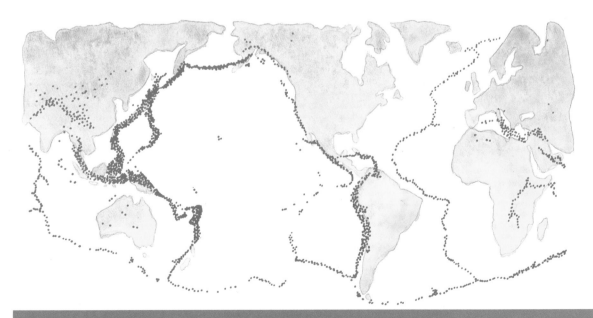

This map illustrates the distribution of earthquakes with magnitudes greater than or equal to 5 recorded 1980–1990

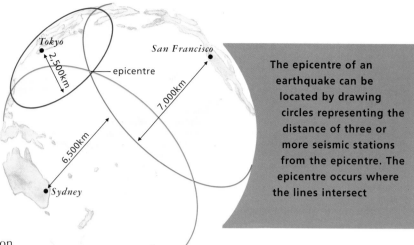

Tokyo

2,500km

epicentre

San Francisco

7,000km

6,500km

Sydney

The epicentre of an earthquake can be located by drawing circles representing the distance of three or more seismic stations from the epicentre. The epicentre occurs where the lines intersect

In fact, as with triangulation surveys used for land-mapping, measurements from only three different stations are needed to plot the epicentre of an earthquake accurately.

Once it was possible to calculate earthquake epicentres quickly they could then be mapped. A standardized map of the main earthquakes during the previous few years was published in 1967. Their distribution was even more strikingly limited to long narrow zones than had ever been imagined. The lines formed by plotting the locations of earthquake epicentres were to give a major clue to the existence of the plates that make up the Earth's crust. The sites of the earthquakes virtually marked out the plate boundaries. Thereafter, earthquakes were seen in their true light as an important manifestation of the way in which the Earth works.

The earthquakes occurred in three main lines: first, around the Pacific Ocean (on the subduction zones); second, in a broad, complex belt stretching from the Azores and Gibraltar, via the Alps, the Mediterranean Sea and the Himalayas, to south-east Asia, (where the plates with continents upon them are colliding); and third, on the ridges in the Atlantic, Indian and Pacific Oceans. In these mid-ocean ridges, where the plates are separating, the earthquakes tend to be relatively small. But, in the areas of subduction and collision, they are often extremely violent. Subduction and collision zones account for 90 per cent of earthquakes.

The foci of most earthquakes are shallow. About 70 per cent of earthquakes begin at depths of less than 70km (43½ miles) – and most of those start in the brittle rocks less than about 30km (18½ miles) deep. About 25 per cent of earthquakes have foci between 70km (43½ miles) and 300km (186 miles) deep. These are called 'intermediate'. The remaining five per cent of earthquakes are called 'deep focus' and they occur at depths between 300km (186 miles) and 700km (435 miles). All earthquakes occurring below 70km (43½ miles), in fact, have their source on crustal slabs undergoing subduction. No earthquakes are generated below a depth of 700km (435 miles) because the crustal slabs have then become 'assimilated' into the plastic asthenosphere. But, even in the subduction zones, deep earthquakes are uncommon: relatively shallow earthquake foci are the norm all over the world.

In general terms, subduction zones and collision zones have the most frequent high magnitude and high intensity earthquakes; these are linked in turn to high death-tolls in heavily-populated areas. Earthquakes caused by lateral displacements such as those in China, southern California and northern Turkey tend to have similar characteristics. Earthquakes on mid-ocean ridges are lower in magnitude and less intense. In addition only small areas of the ridges actually rise above sea-level. There is also a category of earthquakes that are associated with the rise of molten rock that is usually the prelude to volcanic eruptions (see pp.90–93). These tend to be weak and very shallow.

However, whatever their location, most earthquakes of similar magnitudes and intensities that occur in similar human environments have roughly similar physical effects.

the San Francisco earthquake

18 April 1906

THE SAN ANDREAS FAULT ON CALIFORNIA MUST BE THE MOST FAMOUS AND MOST CAREFULLY-STUDIED IN THE WORLD BECAUSE ITS EARTHQUAKES THREATEN MILLIONS OF PEOPLE IN ONE OF THE WORLD'S WEALTHIEST AREAS. THE 'BIG ONE', A HIGH-MAGNITUDE EARTHQUAKE, IS BUILDING UP SOMEWHERE ALONG THE FAULT LINE, AND THIS IS WHY SCIENTISTS ARE WATCHING AND PONDERING ITS EVERY WHIM.

Debris produced by the earthquake litters Mission Street while the fire rages

In fact, the San Andreas fault comprises a system of branching faults stretching almost the length of California. The system marks the boundary where the Pacific Plate on the west has been sliding past the North American Plate on the east for about 30 million years and has caused a horizontal displacement totalling 300km (186½ miles – the distance from London to Manchester). The faults are often locked together until the pressures force the rocks apart again. The earthquake that results may displace the rocks by a few metres in seconds.

There has been a number of serious earthquakes in California in recent years, including those at Loma Prieta in 1989 and Northridge in 1994, but the scale and location of the 1906 San Francisco earthquake meant that it became the foundation of present-day seismology. It also illustrates the devastating effects of the fires caused by earthquakes.

On the morning of 18 April 1906 the northernmost 430km (267 miles) of the San Andreas fault system ruptured, from near San Juan Bautista in the south, to Cape Mendocino in the north; no other recorded Californian earthquake has sprung from such a long dislocation. The magnitude has been estimated at 8.3 although some believe it may have been as low as 6.9. The lateral displacements were visible in the north where they exceeded 6m (19½ft) around the epicentre at Olema, north-west of San Francisco.

In terms of the damage caused by

San Francisco ablaze. The elegant mansions built on the solid rocks of Nob Hill survived the earthquake but were destroyed by the fire

the earthquake, there was a distinct correlation between the intensity of the damage, and the nature of the buildings' foundations. Well-constructed buildings on solid rock stood reasonably firm, whilst houses built on sands and silts vibrated much more, and destruction was therefore greater. In a valley at the seaward end of the main thoroughfare, Market Street, small wooden houses and brick blocks of flats inhabited largely by the poor, and many wharves near the ferry station, were flung down into the cracked streets. Land reclaimed from mudflats, especially alongside the Bay, suffered the most. Buildings on the unstable infilled land vibrated so wildly that they collapsed completely. The water pipes and the gas mains broke all over the city.

On the other hand poor construction methods were to blame for the destruction of the expensive and newly finished City Hall: all that remained was the grand dome surrounded by rubble and twisted girders. Nearby, however, well-built steel-caged 'skyscrapers' were left practically unscathed. Throughout the city the tramlines and railway lines were twisted in all directions and the roads were cracked and subsided. Three-quarters of the headstones and monuments in the cemeteries were broken, twisted and displaced.

No sooner had the shocks of the main earthquake stopped than the fires started. The shocks threw furniture and beams into open hearths, flames spread from cracked chimneys and shattered stoves, gas hissed from broken pipes and was set alight. By noon on 18 April the badly-

The aftermath. The ruins stretch as far as the eye can see in this picture taken after the fires were finally extinguished

destroyed wooden houses of the poor south of Market Street were an inferno. The earthquake had severed the water pipes and there was no water to combat the flames. The fire spread northwards. It engulfed the commercial area and gutted many skyscrapers that had withstood the shocks. It went on spreading northward to Chinatown and the homes of the wealthy on the hills nearby. Then it turned westward. To stop its advance, they had to blow up buildings alongside Van Ness Avenue, one of the main arteries of the city. The fire burnt more than 28,000 buildings and made 350,000 people homeless. The officials admitted a death toll of about 700 but there must have been at least four times as many – notably among the unregistered immigrants in the areas near Market Street and Chinatown.

Largely spared by the earthquake, the steel-caged skyscrapers in the financial district were also badly damaged by fire. Here the fire is still burning; it was many days before the flames were finally brought under control

the Loma Prieta
earthquake
17 October 1989

ON 17 OCTOBER 1989 ABOUT 40KM (25 MILES) OF THE SAN ANDREAS FAULT MOVED BETWEEN LOS GATOS AND SAN JUAN BAUTISTA. THE FOCUS WAS 17KM (10½ MILES) DEEP. IT CAUSED A MAGNITUDE 7.1 EARTHQUAKE WITH AN EPICENTRE NEAR LOMA PRIETA PEAK IN THE SANTA CRUZ MOUNTAINS, ABOUT 100KM (62 MILES) SOUTH-EAST OF SAN FRANCISCO.

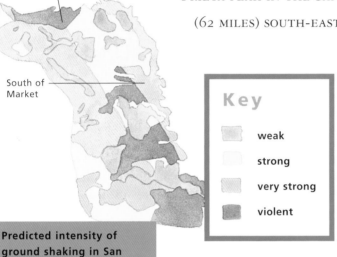

Marina district

South of Market

Key

weak

strong

very strong

violent

Predicted intensity of ground shaking in San Francisco during major earthquakes

In 1988, the US Geological Survey had forecast that this particular zone of the San Andreas Fault had a 30 per cent chance of suffering an earthquake above magnitude 6.5 in the next 30 years, but they could not predict exactly when it would happen. It happened, most inconveniently, at 17.04, just before an important baseball game was due to start in San Francisco. The earthquake shook the stadium and its 60,000 fans and was probably the first ever to be shown live on network television. The game, on the other hand, was cancelled, and some of the fans soon discovered that there were no roads fit to drive over, and no homes to go to. It was the third largest earthquake (in terms of magnitude) to hit the United States since 1906. It was also the most costly because it caused about US$6 billion damage to property, destroyed 414 houses and 97 businesses, damaged 18,306 homes and 97 businesses, made 18,892 people homeless, injured 3,757 and killed 62 people. Although the city of Santa Cruz was damaged, the Santa Cruz mountains, near the epicentre, are sparsely populated.

An aerial view of a collapsed section of the Cypress Viaduct in Oakland, California. The earthquake struck at 17.04 when the roads were busy; many people were trapped by falling concrete blocks

A right-hand displacement occurred, and the Pacific Plate slipped about 1.9m (6¼ft) north-west. The fault did not reach the surface, but the earthquake caused millions of surface cracks. But, very unusually for the San Andreas system, there was a distinct movement of about 1.3m (4¼ft) upwards over the North American Plate, causing, for instance, 25cm (10in) of crustal compression in the town of Los Gatos.

The earthquake caused damage reaching VIII on the modified Mercalli Scale in the area around the epicentre between Los Gatos, Santa Cruz and Watsonville, where wooden and non-reinforced buildings were damaged. But

Fires and gas explosions in the Marina district of San Francisco added to the dangers faced by the inhabitants

intensities of IX occurred away on Interstate roads 880 in Oakland and 280 in San Francisco and also in the marine area of north San Francisco. There were thousands of landslides and rockfalls, especially in the Santa Cruz Mountains.

The most intense damage occurred where land infill liquefied along the shores of San Francisco Bay about 80km (50 miles) from the epicentre. On the eastern shores of the Bay, the sandy fill liquefied and

An apartment block slumped on its foundations; huge quantities of debris were created by falling buildings

sand boils spurted out on the runways at Oakland airport. But the worst liquefaction, and the worst damage, occurred in the Marina area on the northern shore of San Francisco, opposite old Alcatraz. Much of this area had been an old lagoon, and had been filled with sand and rubble from the buildings damaged in 1906 to make the site of the International Panama-Pacific Exposition in 1915. By 1989 it had been built over. The earthquake liquefied the ground and heavily damaged many buildings. Sand boils even brought up pieces of charred wood from the earthquake in 1906.

The most spectacular damage occurred to motorways on stilts: the pillars sheared and sections of their upper decks dropped onto passing traffic on the lower decks. The most dramatic collapse took place on the Cypress Viaduct on the Nimitz Freeway in Oakland where inadequate design was compounded by ground liquefaction. The shock rolled on like a wave causing section after section of the upper deck to collapse onto the deck below. Three viaducts in San Francisco itself were also very badly damaged along with hundreds of bridges throughout the area.

The Marina area also experienced a terrible fire, but it was brought under control within 12 hours, thanks to the help of many volunteer fire-fighters. As all the district's water pipes were broken and useless they compensated by pumping water straight from the Bay.

INTERVIEW

LOMA PRIETA, 1989

An aerial view of earthquake and fire damage in the Marina district of San Francisco

Sherra Cox

Sherra Cox had a busy afternoon planned for October 17 1989:

 'I had left my office a little early that day in order to get home and perhaps unpack some boxes – I just moved into the apartment – and to watch the World Series. When I got there, however, I decided I was too lazy and took a little nap and just as I got up at 5 o'clock, I turned on the TV and the building started to shake ... it very quickly turned into a big wave-type motion. The building seemed to tilt to one side so you couldn't stand ... so I just automatically went to a door to hold on to be able to stand up but ... the building fell down on itself. It was a four storey building and it fell to the street and it tilted from the front towards the back'.

During the earthquake Sherra was conscious of a deep roar; before the building collapsed she was conscious of the structural changes that were going on around her:

 'The first thing I saw was the ceiling dropping and the walls just like an accordion ... I sort of turned back towards the entrance door in the hallway and that's when the door popped out ... the ceiling dropping caused the door to buckle and come out.'

Sherra's heavy front door knocked her down, pinning her to the floor. At that moment she heard a voice.

 'I heard someone say "Is anyone in there?" ... and I shouted "Yes, I'm here" ... Whoever it was did not hear me ... I reached back and ... there was a pipe ... and I could bang on the door with it and make a definite sound ...'

Sherra's quick thinking meant that she was found relatively quickly. After being alerted by passers-by a fireman crawled into the debris to see whether there was indeed a survivor trapped in the rubble.

 'I heard them say "Is anybody there?" again. I was shouting as loud as I could because they couldn't hear my voice, but they said "We hear a tapping. Tap louder, as loud

as you can if you can hear our voice." So I tapped as loud as I could. They said "We hear you ... we're coming to get you ... just keep shouting."'

It took about an hour for the fireman to locate Sherra but finally he got close enough for them to talk.

'He told me his name was Gerry [Shannon, San Francisco Fire Department]. I said "I'm very glad to know you Gerry".'

Eventually he reached her but soon realized that any further progress was blocked by huge beams that had fallen in the bedroom.

'... he told me that he had to go out and get some chain saws ... but it was getting dark and he put his hand under this one beam and I could see his fingers ... I saw him and I grabbed hold of him and I begged him not to leave me, and he said he had to go but he would be back.'

Inadequately built garage walls meant that this apartment block was in danger of collapsing following the earthquake

Meanwhile the situation outside in the street was getting worse: broken gas pipes meant there was a high risk of explosions. Sherra could hear people warning Gerry not to go back into the building but she was unaware that sparks from the chain saw could possibly trigger a gas explosion.

'When he started back in he said he ... was going to start a chain saw and it would be very loud and just to be calm ... he started it and nothing happened and he was able to cut through quite a few beams ... then he had to get another chain saw ... when he went out the second time he said there was just no way he could not come back even though ... they were really shouting even more so not to come back in.'

Finally all that lay between Gerry and Sherra was the door. It took several men to lift it, and even then they were only able to shift it slightly. By this time the building was already on fire. Salt water was being used to control the flames but in the final stages of the rescue these had to be turned off to stop the building collapsing further under the weight of the water. At last the men began to pull Sherra clear of the rubble. A large crowd of photographers and camera crews began to applaud as she finally emerged.

'I wanted to know where Gerry was because ... there was no way I was going to let this fireman get away without knowing who he was. There was an ambulance they put me in right away, and some of the other people followed and asked for Gerry, and he came over to the stretcher and I just put my arms around him and kissed him on the cheek.'

the Alaskan earthquake

27 March 1964

ALASKA IS 'BIG COUNTRY' AND EXPERIENCES BIG EARTHQUAKES TO MATCH. EIGHT EARTHQUAKES EXCEEDING MAGNITUDE 8.0, AND ABOUT 70 OVER MAGNITUDE 7.0, HAVE STRUCK SOUTHERN ALASKA AND THE ALEUTIAN ISLANDS DURING THIS CENTURY ALONE. ONE OF THE LARGEST EARTHQUAKES EVER RECORDED IN NORTH AMERICA STRUCK SOUTHERN ALASKA AT 17.36 ON GOOD FRIDAY, 27 MARCH 1964. ITS EPICENTRE WAS NEAR THE NORTHERN SHORE OF PRINCE WILLIAM SOUND, 130KM (81 MILES) EAST OF ANCHORAGE, AND ITS FOCUS WAS 20KM (12½ MILES) DEEP.

Epicentre of main shock
Anchorage • *Valdez* •
Seward •
Region of aftershock epicentres
Prince William Sound
Gulf of Alaska

It measured magnitude 8.4 on the Richter scale, caused damage over an area of 80,000km² (31,000 square miles), was felt over an area of more than 800,000km² (310,000 square miles) and caused water levels to fluctuate in wells as far away as Florida by as much as 5m (16½ft). The level of the land and sea-floor changed over 160,000km² (62,000 square miles). A long trough, running north-east to south-west and including most of the Kenai Peninsula subsided by as much as 2m (6½ft). Parallel to it, a long hump like an upturned boat rose by as much as 15m (49ft), especially near Montague Island.

Anchorage, the largest town in Alaska, had 100,000 inhabitants, half the population of the largely empty, wilderness state. The earthquake tossed the buildings in the city about like ships in a storm for nearly four minutes. It was just the same in the smaller towns in the district, including Seward, Kenai and Valdez. These primary effects were then followed by secondary effects.

Anchorage is built on sands and clays left behind when the glaciers melted. The vibrations

One span of the 'Million-dollar' truss bridge was dropped into the Copper River by the earthquake; the other truss spans were shifted on their piers

liquefied these water-laden terrains – and sand sometimes spouted from the ground. Shops and bars in central Anchorage subsided, landslide after landslide began to slip downslope, taking their crown of buildings with them. A fashionable suburb slid 600m (1,970ft), leaving behind a chaos of homes and gardens as if they had suddenly frozen on a stormy sea. A school split in two, fissures formed in the playground and supplied another landslide that swamped the railway yard. A radio-announcer broadcast and recorded his own vivid 'Anchorage Experience' as it was happening. It is a striking contrast to the written accounts of other earthquakes (see panel p.72).

A similar pattern was repeated throughout the district. The communications system suffered badly. Embankments, bridges, roads, railways and harbours cracked, subsided and

These rails were buckled by lateral ground movement

sometimes even rose up. It was to cost US$22 million to repair the damage to the Alaska Railroad and its harbour alone. Cracks and subsidence made many roads impassable. Harbours were lifted out of the water: the quayside at Cordova rose 3m (9¾ft), but other areas were flooded.

Submarine subsidence and landslides then produced a number of tsunamis. They washed ships up onto land at Kodiak and Seward and dumped them amidst the tangle of wrecked harbour installations. The tsunamis swept down the Canadian and American coasts as far as northern California.

A whole range of shocks and secondary effects struck the port of Valdez. The earthquake damaged the buildings, cracked the oil-storage tanks, and liquefied the sands of the old delta where the town was built. The resulting landslide swept the quayside – and 30 people

Alaska's communication system was badly damaged by the earthquake. Cracks and subsidence made many roads impassable and many bridges collapsed into the water. In this picture the road bridge over the River Kenai Pen has been broken in several places

Testimony of R Pate, KHAR Radio announcer,
Anchorage, Alaska

'Hey, boy – Oh-wee, that's a good one! Hey –
boy oh boy oh boy! Man, that's an
earthquake! Hey, that's an earthquake for
sure! ... Man – everything's moving – you
know, all that stuff in all the cabinets have
come up loose ... I've never lived through
anything like this before in my life! And it
hasn't even shown signs of stopping yet,
either ... the whole place is shaking ... Hold
it, I'd better put the television on the floor.
Just a minute – Boy! Let me tell you that sure
scared the hell out of me, and it's still
shaking. I'm telling you! I wonder if I should
get outside? Oh boy! Man, I'm telling you
that's the worst thing I've ever lived
through! I wonder if that's the last one of
'em? Oh man! Oh – Oh boy, I'm telling you
that's something I hope I don't go through
very often. Maa-uhn! ... I'm telling you, the
whole place just moved like somebody had
taken it by the nape of the neck and was
shaking it ... I wonder if the KHAR radio
tower is still standing up. Man! You sure
can't hear it, but I wonder what they have to
say on the air about it? ... Man, that could
very easily have knocked the tower down – I
don't get anything on the air – from any of
the stations – I can't even think! I wonder
what it did to the tower. We may have lost
the tower, I'll see if any of the stations come
on – No, none of them do. I assume the radio
is okay – Boy! The place is still moving! You
couldn't even stand up when that thing was
going like that I was falling all over the place
here. I turned this thing on and started
talking just after the thing started, and man!
I'm telling you, this house was shaking like a
leaf! The picture frames – all the doors were
opened – the dishes were falling out of the
cabinets – and it's still swaying back and
forth – I've got to go through and make a
check to make sure that none of the water
lines are ruptured or anything. Man, I hope I
don't live through one of those things again.'

waiting for a boat – into the sea. Then tsunamis
wrecked the waterfront, fire broke out in the
broken oil-storage tanks and spread through the
remains of the harbour area. Valdez was so badly
damaged that the town had to be moved to a
new site altogether at a cost of US$37.5 million.

How could anyone have survived such an
onslaught in southern Alaska? Many taller
buildings of heavy materials suffered badly, but
well-made wooden framed buildings often
survived, if not exactly on an even keel, or in
their original positions. The tsunamis wrecked

The business area of Anchorage was
very badly damaged. The cracks in the
foreground were caused by lateral ground
spreading

the coasts as much as the earthquake shocks. But
even for such a sparsely-populated area, the
number of deaths was remarkably small. Many
more people would have died had the earthquake
not taken place on a holiday evening when
schools and businesses were empty. The
earthquake claimed 131 lives, 122 of which
resulted from tsunamis in Alaska, British
Columbia, Oregon and California.

ABOVE Tsunamis washed ships up onto the waterfront at Seward and dumped them among wrecked harbour installations

BELOW This truck was bent around a tree by the surge waves generated by underwater landslides along the Seaward waterfront

the Kobe earthquake

17 January 1995

IN 1978, THE JAPANESE EARTHQUAKE PREDICTION PROGRAMME CHOSE TEN AREAS FOR SPECIAL MONITORING. KOBE WAS ON THE EDGE OF ONE OF THESE SELECTED AREAS THAT STRETCHED ACROSS HYOGO PROVINCE, AND EASTWARDS THROUGH OSAKA TO NAGOYA. THIS IS A HEAVILY-INDUSTRIALIZED, HIGHLY-POPULATED REGION, AND IT WAS CLEAR THAT AN EARTHQUAKE WOULD CAUSE A HIGH DEGREE OF COSTLY DAMAGE. AT THE TIME, HOWEVER, THE TOKYO AREA IN KANTO PROVINCE, AND THE NEARBY PROVINCE OF TOKAI, WERE JUDGED TO BE AT GREATER RISK. SEVENTEEN YEARS LATER KOBE WAS STRUCK BY A HIGH-MAGNITUDE EARTHQUAKE WHICH PROVIDED A GRAPHIC ILLUSTRATION OF WHAT COULD HAPPEN IN TOKYO IN THE FUTURE.

The magnitude 7.2 earthquake caused the Kobe intersection of the Hanshin Motorway to topple sideways

Therefore, the experts thought that there could be an earthquake in the Kobe area, but had no real reason to expect one. The shocks came as a surprise and also occurred along a fault that had previously been obscured by a blanket of coastal alluvium. It is a fairly short fault, one of many branching from a much longer, well-known fault called the Median Tectonic Line. This fault line has developed because the Philippine plate is squeezing up against southern Japan. The pressure has produced a crack that is forcing some of the blocks of crust to slide horizontally out of the way with a right-handed horizontal movement. Gradually, the block to the north of the fault is carrying Kobe and Osaka towards the east, whilst the block to the south of the line is moving intermittently westwards. This kind of movement has built up energy which has been released periodically, not only on the main fault, but also on the many parallel faults that these forces have created.

At 05.46 on 17 January 1995 one of these smaller faults was producing a right-lateral movement, ie. when the observer faces the fault-line, the block on the other side moves to the right. In all, between 40km (25 miles) and 60km (37 miles) of the fault moved. The focus of the magnitude 7.2 earthquake was 19km (12 miles) below the Akashi Straits. The epicentre lay in the channel between Kobe and Awaji Island. In seconds, Kobe moved 1.7m (5½ft) further away from Awaji Island, as the fault jerked to the right and also thrust a maximum of 1.3m (4¼ft) upwards.

The Hanshin trains were thrown off the collapsed railway viaduct; buildings in the surrounding area were crushed

The fault gave out two warning foreshocks about 12 hours before the main earthquake and it produced 6,000 aftershocks. These ranged from a magnitude 4.9 earthquake, two hours after the main shock, to hundreds of little tremors during the following month. There had also been some ground deformation beforehand and on Awaji Island some strange animal behaviour had been noted. In spite of these warnings, the people of Kobe were totally unprepared for what was to happen next.

The earthquake cut a swathe of devastation across Kobe. It stretched 25km (15½ miles) north-westwards from Awaji Island in a band 500m (1,640ft) wide. In this corridor, the intensity of damage reached the maximum of 7 on the Japanese intensity scale – the equivalent of XI on the modified Mercalli Scale. Elsewhere, the damage was less severe.

There were many small, and a few moderate, landslides of up to 100m (328ft) in length, and all occurred within 4km (2½ miles) of the fault. Where the soil liquefied, the results were altogether more disastrous. It naturally affected the coastal sediment and the vast areas of reclaimed land used for additional harbour space and, unfortunately, for housing. Within minutes, the port of Kobe was useless, hundreds of houses collapsed and sand spurted out onto

The fires that followed the earthquake caused huge amounts of damage. Some smoke is still visible in this picture taken on 18 January 1995

the surface. On Port Island, the weathered, granitic infilling liquefied and not only subsided about 50cm (19¾in), but also pushed the concrete walls of the container quays about 2m (6½ft) into the sea.

Meanwhile, amplified by the alluvial ground, the earthquake shocks powered through central Kobe, Ashiya and on to Nishinomiya. More than 100,000 houses collapsed. Within two hours, 234 fires had broken out. Eventually, about 1km² (⅓ square mile) of closely spaced, compact, largely wooden buildings burnt down in the Kobe metropolitan area – the equivalent of a century of accidental fires.

Ten per cent of the infrastructure of the area was lost (roads, railways, electricity, gas, sewerage), 10 per cent of educational facilities, 5 per cent of housing, 12 per cent of the raw materials industrial sector and 14 per cent of the wholesale-retail trade sector. The disaster cost 0.2 per cent of GNP. In contrast, damage caused by the Tokyo earthquake of 1923 cost 7 per cent of GNP.

Around 5,500 people were killed, about 36,500 were injured and 188,000 houses badly damaged or completely destroyed in the Kobe metropolitan area. 52,000 people were left homeless, and there were 350,000 refugees at the height of the crisis. 316,000 out of 3,021,091 people living in the Kobe area were evacuated to refugee camps in the days after the calamity.

The earthquake destroyed several bridges and the Hanshin Expressway viaduct collapsed for a distance of 600m (1,968ft). All the lifeline services were shut down over 150km² (58 square miles). The electricity supply was cut when half the substations in the zone of severe damage were destroyed: 2,000,000 homes were left without power. Underground cables were more vulnerable than aerial cables. Many gas pipes failed at the screw joints but the polyethylene pipes resisted. Many water pipes cracked at the joints – especially the smaller service pipes inside buildings. Repairs were handicapped when the Water Works office collapsed and buried the maps of pipeline networks! Over 1 million homes had no water for ten days. Telecommunications were badly damaged too and were not fully restored until the end of January – except where buildings had collapsed. The earthquake severely damaged the railways, but happened before the 'bullet' train began its daily service. Although there were no railway injuries, many railway viaducts and bridges collapsed and several stations were damaged. The bullet train was fully restored to service after 81 days on 8 April, but many commuter lines were closed until June. The roads, of course, also lost many bridges.

The ports suffered most of all: 30 per cent of Japan's container trade operated from Kobe and the disaster badly damaged 234 out of the 240 container berths.

The earthquake caused Daikai Street to cave in; the Daikai station of the Kobe Express Underground lies beneath the central subsided section of this road

ABOVE At night fires raged, devastating the densely populated areas of Hyogo and Nagata

BELOW The main street of North Sannomiya. The buildings seen here show varying degrees of earthquake damage

INTERVIEW

KOBE, 1995

Mrs Komazawa and Mrs Iio

Hokkaido

Sapporo

Pacific Ocean

Sea of Japan

Tokyo

Kobe • *Kyoto* • *Yokohama*

• *Osaka*

Shikoku

Kyushu

Mrs Komazawa was working in an office in Yokohama when the earthquake of 1923 struck the Kanto province of Tokyo.

'During the earthquake I was hiding under the desk ... Then I was trapped among fallen objects and could not move at all. A man ... tried to save me by pulling ... with all his might, then at last all my body could move and I was taken out of the building and carried outside.'

She lay under a tree in Yokohama Park for a day and a night, before a kindly passer-by sent word to her family of her plight, and her aunt came to find her. It was some time before Mrs Komazawa recovered from her injuries. Shortly afterwards, her husband was transferred by his company from Yokohama to Kobe, 440km (273 miles) away. Although sad to leave her home, Mrs Komazawa was relieved to have moved from the earthquake danger zone around Tokyo.

A detail showing damage to Daikai Street. Huge cracks appeared all along the road as it simply caved in when the ground started to shake

'I never thought I would have such an earthquake in Kobe.'

Sixty years later, on 16 January 1995, Mrs Komazawa and her friend Mrs Iio were preparing for the New Year Tea Ceremony. Mrs Iio did not go to bed until 03.00 on the morning of 17 January. She remembers,

 '... I saw the moon shining extraordinarily bright in the sky ...'

She woke again at around 05.40, it was pitch black. Then at 05.46 the earthquake struck.

 '... at the moment of the jerk, the shelf of the home shrine fell off ... and then the home shrine fell nearly squashing me but narrowly missing my head ... I was caught under the shrine at my back ... and I was lying there helplessly.'

Mrs Komazawa was not trapped, and began to crawl towards Mrs Iio, who reached out to hold her friend's hand. For the first time she noticed the scene around her.

 'I looked around the room ... paintings, scrolls on the wall were hanging off the wall or fallen on the debris ... I told Mrs Komazawa "Don't panic! Someone is looking for us from the fallen roof." ... they were calling "Are you all right?" ... The people saved us by pulling off the room slate, and broke into the ceiling and pulled us out.'

The rescuers had to work carefully when they pulled out Mrs Komazawa so as not to cause further damage that would crush Mrs Iio.

 'They managed to lift and hand down Mrs Komazawa on the ground and I crawled down the roof with bare feet and took rest at the house across the road ... We stayed there until 4pm or so, then we moved to the temporary shelter placed on the parking lot.'

The scene that greeted them was terrible,

 'It was the end of the world ... The road in front of our house was covered up by the collapsed houses ... the only thing left to us was our own lives.'

Mrs Komazawa is fatalistic. Although she is 90 years old and has survived two earthquakes, she knows that another could strike at any moment, and that this time she may not be so lucky.

Large areas of the city were devastated by the earthquake and later by fire. This aerial view gives an idea of the extent of the damage

the Northridge earthquake

17 January 1994

On 17 January 1994 a magnitude 6.7 earthquake shook the San Fernando valley 30km (18½ miles) north of Los Angeles in California. Its focus was 19km (12 miles) deep, the fault slipped an average of 2m (6½ft), and its epicentre was at Northridge. Fifty-seven people died, a further 9,000 were injured, and damage was estimated at over US$13 billion.

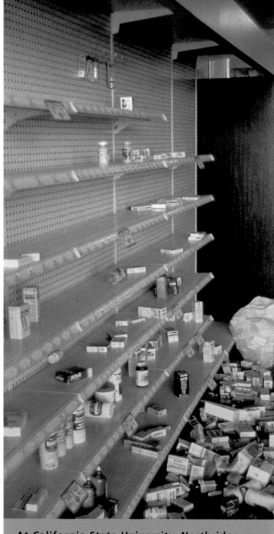

At California State University, Northridge, shaking knocked the contents of the shelves in the pharmacy to the floor

Some railway crew members saw the earthquake rush towards them in their engine headlights. The rails twisted from the ground, 'exploded' into the air, and the train was then thrown off the tracks. In this densely-populated area, 1,600 buildings were declared unsafe and 7,300 others were damaged; freeway bridges collapsed, and broken gas pipes caused explosions and fires. Fortunately, the 10–20 seconds of violent shaking took place at 04.30 in the morning, when many roads and bridges were empty. If the earthquake had happened during the day then lists of casualties would have been far longer. Improved building techniques since the nearby San Fernando earthquake of 1971 also limited damage and loss of life, but nevertheless, the intricate network of Los Angeles freeways collapsed in seven places.

In southern California the San Andreas Fault system and its associated faults bend round so that they trend east to west around Los Angeles. The Pacific Plate is moving towards the north-west, and tends to push against this bend rather than slide past the North American Plate, as it does along the rest of the San Andreas system. The area around Los Angeles and San Diego is continually being forced up against this bend, and the rocks of the crust are squeezed, folded or broken into slices, and pushed upwards along reverse or thrust faults. This is also what happened in the earthquakes at San Fernando in

These sections of Interstate 5 at Gavin Canyon were sheared apart during the earthquake

1971 and at Whittier Narrows in 1987.

The Northridge earthquake took place on a fault in the bedrock that was completely hidden by sediments. It was a 'blind' or 'masked' fault. No-one knew that it even existed. Such events demonstrate just how difficult it is to predict earthquakes in extremely mobile zones of the Earth's crust – the very places where prediction is needed most. The Northridge fault remains hidden because the displacement along the fault took place 19km (12 miles) underground and did not break through to the landsurface. It did, however, cause the greatest earthquake damage in the United States since San Francisco was devastated in 1906.

During the Northridge earthquake there was a great deal of ground movement. Damage recorded on the modified Mercalli Intensity Scale reached between VIII and IX in the San Fernando valley. Nevertheless, many houses survived mainly because they had been built after earthquake-resistant design and building codes had been enforced. What happened inside the houses, however, was a different matter: pictures were thrown from walls, refrigerators and cupboards were emptied onto the floor, furniture was moved, pipes were broken, some fires were started, and there were many landslides out in the country. Bricks and masonry fell from buildings and damaged parked cars, and some wooden homes were shaken from their foundations, and flopped over onto the crawl-space between the foundations and their ground floors. More than 50km (31 miles) from the epicentre, damage was only slight, although the scoreboard did fall down at Anaheim Stadium, 75km (46½ miles) away.

West central Los Angeles suffered some of the worst damage, because it lay within 20km (12½ miles) of the epicentre, and because its buildings were constructed

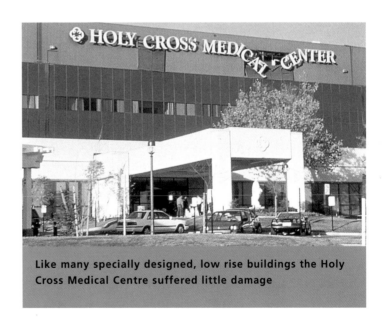
Like many specially designed, low rise buildings the Holy Cross Medical Centre suffered little damage

before earthquake-resistant provisions were incorporated into the building codes. Raised sections of freeways produced the most spectacular failures. On the Santa Monica freeway (Interstate Highway 10) at Venice Boulevard in Los Angeles, the circular steel 'ties' or belts wrapped around the columns were meant to reinforce them and hold them together. But they were too thin and the spaces between them too great. The earthquake broke them apart, and the weight of the concrete freeway crushed the columns and whole sections collapsed. The columns, however, which had been properly strengthened after the San Fernando earthquake in 1971, remained intact. Similarly, most buildings that were designed and built to resist known earthquake forces survived with little or no damage. The Olive View Hospital at Sylmar, 16km (10 miles) from the epicentre, survived intact except that its fire-sprinkler system was damaged. It had been designed to resist earthquake forces, with a steel-framed structure with concrete and steel load-bearing walls, and proved to be a successful replacement for its predecessor that had collapsed during the San Fernando earthquake of 1971.

Buildings with a 'soft' ground floor (called the first floor in the United States) were damaged more than those around them. 'Soft' ground floors are those with large open areas such as garages and shops, which have little lateral strength and, therefore, cannot withstand strong vibrations. At Reseda in Northridge, 14 people were killed when a block of flats dropped onto the ground floor garage, crushing all the cars. The car-park of California State University at Northridge – full of soft storeys – collapsed inwards in a tangled wreckage. As expected, many steel-frame buildings withstood the earthquake well, but many of them developed cracks after six months that would weaken them in any future earthquake.

Tall buildings are particularly vulnerable during earthquakes because shaking is usually several times greater on upper floors than at ground level – hence tall buildings are more likely to collapse. In some cases the problem can be overcome by placing base-isolators (huge rubber pads) between the building and its foundations. One seven-storey building with base-isolators on the UCLA campus in central Los Angeles, 37km (23 miles) from the epicentre, survived the earthquake relatively unscathed.

Most structural damage occurred to the following types of construction: older buildings that had not been built to post-1971 seismic provisions; recent garages with weakly-

Reseda was one of the areas in Northridge that was badly affected by the earthquake

ABOVE Damage to the 'soft' lower storeys of the car park at California State University, Northridge
BELOW This five-storey building partially collapsed

connected, load-bearing columns; buildings with a 'soft' ground floor storey; and tall buildings. Buildings of 18 or more storeys with a natural swaying motion of 2 secs or more were particularly vulnerable. The natural period of such buildings matches the seismic surface waves that are propagated in areas of highly-populated sedimentary basins in southern California.

On the plus side, by far the majority of buildings in the area resisted the earthquake extremely well. About 90,000 buildings were inspected in Los Angeles following the earthquake: only two per cent were deemed unsafe to enter; ten per cent could be entered only to a limited extent; and 88 per cent were judged to be safe enough for unlimited access and use. The survival of so many buildings in the area illustrates the immense value of well-conceived building codes and modern, earthquake-resistant design and construction practices.

Although reinforced, the frame of this 15-storey building cracked

The third and fourth storeys of this unreinforced masonry building were damaged while the floors below were left relatively unscathed

the Messina-Calabria earthquake

28 December 1908

THE AREA AROUND THE MEDITERRANEAN HAS BEEN SHAPED BY THE COLLISION BETWEEN THE EUROPEAN PLATE IN THE NORTH AND THE AFRICAN PLATE IN THE SOUTH. ONE OF THE MAIN RESULTS OF THIS COLLISION IS THAT GREECE AND ITALY SUFFER THE MOST FREQUENT EARTHQUAKES IN THE WHOLE OF EUROPE. EARTHQUAKES CAUSED BY PLATE COLLISION ARE OFTEN THE MOST VIOLENT OF ALL.

The relatively small area in eastern Sicily and nearby Calabria, the toe of Italy, experiences some of the most destructive earthquakes on Earth. The whole area is riddled with major active faults, different sections of which have moved at various times in recent years. These displacements have been happening ever since Africa and Europe began to collide about 40 million years ago. The result is that the crust of Calabria has been broken into blocks that have risen up to form the Sila and Aspromonte uplands. The Peloritani mountains form a similarly upraised block in northern Sicily. The area between them, however, has collapsed and has been flooded to form the Straits of Messina. It is in this area that the most savage earthquakes are concentrated.

The search for survivors in the aftermath of the earthquake

Particularly destructive earthquakes seem to occur in this area about once every 90–125 years. In 1908 the epicentre lay in the Straits of Messina itself, between Messina in Sicily (population then 150,000) and Reggio in Calabria (population then 45,000), two of the most populous cities in the region. If this pattern persists there could be another earthquake in the area within the next 30 years.

The Messina earthquake has thus far been the most deadly natural disaster to occur in Europe in the 20th Century. It happened at 05.21 on the morning of 28 December 1908, the Feast of the Massacre of the Innocents. The focus of the earthquake was relatively shallow, perhaps only 10km (6¼ miles) deep, and its magnitude was 7.5. For an earthquake of such magnitude the shocks were felt over a relatively small area – 1,000km (621 miles) – as far away as Palermo, Naples, Tunis, and Joanina in Greece.

Soldiers had to police the ruined buildings the protect them from looters

There was just a single foreshock, a light tremor lasting for 20 secs that increased in intensity and then declined. This was followed by a 7.5 magnitude earthquake that rocked the ground for over 30 secs. The Feast of the Massacre of the Innocents claimed 160,000 lives.

The most serious damage was concentrated along the shores of the Straits of Messina where the buildings had been constructed on alluvium soil. Here the seismic waves were greatly magnified and liquefaction also occurred. These areas included the centres of Messina, Reggio, Villa San Giovanni, and most of the towns along the neighbouring coast. The fish market in Messina sank below sea-level, the railway station foundered and the façade of the cathedral crashed into the Piazza del Duomo and the roof fell into the nave. In Reggio, the city centre, the harbour and the cathedral met the same fate. In a 40km (25 mile) zone along the Straits scarcely a single building remained undamaged. In the 30km (18½ mile) wide band around the coastal area the

destruction was less severe, but damage did occur throughout most of southern Calabria and north-east Sicily. Tsunamis 3–6m (9¾–19¾ft) in height caused additional devastation.

The stricken area was isolated. News of the disaster filtered out only slowly. The trains from Palermo and Catania, for example, were unable to reach Messina because landslides had blocked the tracks. Roads were destroyed and telegraph cables were severed. The sea appeared to be the only point of access. Several Italian naval vessels had survived in the harbour at Messina. The Captain of the *Serpente* set sail to find a place where the telegraph cables were intact: he had to sail a distance of 70km (43½ miles) up the Calabrian coast to the town of Marina di Nicótera. That evening Roman newspapers released the first reports of the earthquake.

In Messina and Reggio the survivors and the first Red Cross workers to reach the area began to pull the bodies from the wreckage and line them up on the shores. On 30 December King Vittorio Emmanuele III visited the scene of the disaster. He was horrified by what he saw and immediately sent a personal telegram to Rome 'There is complete havoc here: fire, blood and death; send ships, ships, ships and more ships'. Even when the rescue operation was complete, it was many years before the villages were rebuilt.

This makeshift hospital was set up amongst the wreckage to treat those wounded by the earthquake

the Mexico earthquake

19 September 1985

MEXICO CITY IS ONE OF THE LARGEST AND OLDEST SETTLEMENTS IN THE AMERICAS. ORIGINALLY THE SITE OF THE GREAT AZTEC CAPITAL OF TÉNOCHTITLAN, WHEN HERNÁN CORTÉS LED THE SPANISH CONQUISTADORS INTO TÉNOCHTITLAN IN 1519, HE DECLARED THAT HE HAD NEVER SET EYES ON ANYTHING SO SPLENDID.

The Aztecs had built their capital on islands in the midst of Lake Texcoco which were joined to the shore by impressive causeways. Within five years, the Spaniards had overthrown the Aztec Empire, reduced all its 'pagan' public buildings to rubble, and started to build Mexico City, their own Christian capital, upon the ruins. It quickly became a flourishing city but soon the islands began to restrict expansion. In the demand for building space, the waters that surrounded the island were filled with rubble, rocks and soil. Lake Texcoco was drained and buildings were constructed on the weak sands and clays of its floor. Mexico City was then free to grow and soon attracted a huge, densely-packed population.

This brief summary of the city's history helps to explain why the 1985 earthquake caused much more damage in Mexico City than at its epicentre, 380km (236 miles) away in the province of

Key

- former shore of Lake Texcoco
- city centre boundary
- zones of maximum earthquake damage
- main N–S avenues

Michoacán. The rocks of Michoacán were volcanic and solid and withstood the ground movement well. The weak infilling and lake-floor sediments

Many buildings in Mexico City were reduced to rubble by the earthquake that reached 8.1 on the Richter scale. Few people survived in buildings that were as badly damaged as this one

In the aftermath of the earthquake debris littered the streets

beneath Mexico City increased the effects of the seismic waves: foundations shook far more violently. Liquefaction was common.

At 07.18 on 19 September 1985, the Cocos Plate on the floor of the Pacific Ocean pushed further into its subduction zone under Mexico, unleashing an earthquake of magnitude 8.1. The seismic waves reverberated throughout the world and reached Mexico City within 1 min. Many people were getting up, or were already on their way to work, and there were no warning foreshocks. The earthquake waves threw down buildings, burying and killing thousands under the masonry. Many old, 1–2 storey buildings managed to remain upright. Larger, more modern buildings collapsed like packs of cards. This was especially common in some of the more recently-constructed public buildings such as blocks of flats, hotels and hospitals. The fashionable Zona Rosa area, in the centre of town, was particularly badly affected.

The combination of poor construction and an unconsolidated substratum once again proved lethal. It was calculated that 412 major buildings had collapsed and that a further 3,124 were very badly damaged. Controversy has raged over the number of people killed in the disaster. Official figures suggest that at least 9,500 people died, but according to unconfirmed reports, the death-toll could have been as high as 35,000. About 30,000 people were injured and over 100,000 were left homeless. Damage occurred over an area of nearly 1 million km² (386 square miles), and the earthquake was felt by 20 million people.

Still standing, but badly damaged, this apartment block was one of many left unfit for habitation by the earthquake

INTERVIEW

MEXICO, 1985

Elizabeth, Cielo and Roberto Marquez

On 19 September 1985 Cielo Marquez was on her way to work. At 07.19 she felt the earthquake that shook the city but it was only later that she became aware of its strength.

'I could hear the radio in the bus station and it said that buildings were destroyed in the Zona Rosa and Colonia Roma areas. The most affected area was the Juarez complex where we used to live, so I immediately went back but it took me four hours to reach the place. They were cordoning off the area to stop people going back into the danger zones, but when I saw the collapsed buildings I thought the worst, that my family was already dead.'

Cielo was soon joined by other members of her family, her brother and sister, and they looked on appalled at the tangle of metal and glass that confronted them.

'The building where we used to live twisted and leaned to the side and the upper floors were sandwiched together ... But the rest of the buildings collapsed into dust, all of them were totally destroyed, you could smell gas, hear screams ...'

Cielo's parents and her children were all inside the apartment. The earthquake caught her daughter, Elizabeth, completely by surprise.

'Suddenly I felt the ground moving ... We ... tried to open the door and it slammed shut by itself and it opened again and at that moment we felt the building shake and the structure sank ... my sister and I jumped under the table and the walls fell down. The building remained standing but inside the apartment the walls and ceiling fell down and the floor cracked. The building split and suddenly there was this noise like an explosion. The windows blew out and at that moment the building came away from the pavement.'

Like the building above, the General Hospital was badly affected by the earthquake.

The members of the Marquez family were injured by the flying debris, their eyes were irritated by the dust, there was a terrible smell of gas, and they were all in shock.

'We were afraid of not being rescued and that another earthquake would happen ... There were 14 floors and we were on the ground floor and with all that weight on us we believed ... we would be crushed and would die here.'

Elizabeth's brother Roberto was also in the apartment.

 'I was sleeping when the earthquake happened. My sister ... pulled me by the hair and she said "There is an earthquake, wake up", and she pulled me under the bed because the ceiling started to fall down ... The structure of the building shook and sank ... Thankfully the building didn't collapse and

Miraculously, live babies were still being rescued from the wreckage several days later

there were some holes which protected us from the collapsed upper floors.'

Already a large number of people had arrived at the scene to begin pulling people from the rubble. The priority for the Marquez family was now to make themselves heard.

Unstable debris and weakened buildings made rescues particularly dangerous

 'There was very little oxygen because of the gas and we didn't have much space inside. My sisters couldn't shout really loud, [our] parrot was the one who started screaming really loud, asking for help, "Mama, mama, take me out of here. Help, help". It was thanks to the parrot that we were rescued and those were words the parrot had never said before.'

Elizabeth says that the parrot must have been mimicking their cries for help. She adds:

 'There was even a moment when the parrot's screams hurt our ears so we told him to shut up but at the same time we wanted him to continue screaming because we couldn't do it ... When [the rescuers] got close to the parrot, they discovered that we were there as well.'

It was about eight hours before the Marquez family were finally rescued. Although physically they escaped relatively unscathed, the psychological wounds inflicted by their ordeal have taken longer to heal.

 'Every time there's an earthquake we get really ill, we get really nervous, we feel despair and believe the building will collapse at any minute. But we have got through it. Thanks to our effort and some other help we have got over this.'

volcanic earthquakes

EARTHQUAKES THAT OCCUR ON OR AROUND VOLCANOES CAN ACT AS WARNING SIGNS OF IMPENDING ERUPTIONS. THEY CAN ALSO HAVE DEVASTATING CONSEQUENCES, OR MAY EVEN BE FALSE ALARMS. HERE ARE FOUR VERY DIFFERENT STORIES.

Iceland

Time: Sunday morning, 7 April 1727. Place: Sandfell Church, at the foot of Öraefajökull volcano in south-east Iceland. Rev. Jón Thorláksson has just started his sermon. Suddenly, the building begins to rock and the congregation stops listening. An old man rushes out of the church, throws himself to the ground, and starts to listen. People laugh nervously at his peculiar behaviour. The old man hurries back to the minister, shouting 'Be on your guard, sir. The Earth is on fire!' Then a second earthquake threatens to cause the church to collapse on top of them. Rev. Thorláksson abandons the service and they all hurry home. The earthquakes are already making the shimmering ice-cap heave up and down on the crest of Öraefajökull. That afternoon, the shocks become more violent, overturning furniture and throwing loose utensils and ornaments to the ground in every house in every hamlet at the foot of the volcano. The ground begins to rumble. At 09.00 on Monday 8 August, Öraefajökull erupts for the first time since 1362, showering the district with ash, blacking out the daylight for three days, and flooding the villages with water melted from the ice-cap. The earthquakes had acted as a warning system but unfortunately people were not aware of the signs.

Volcanic earthquakes shook Pompeii during the eruption of Vesuvius

Such warnings are common. The magma has a consistency something like molten glass. It rises into the volcano, invading the chimney and neighbouring cracks in the rock. As it moves upwards, each surge causes displacements of the solid rock, thereby generating earthquakes. These are shallow, usually less than magnitude 5.0; their effects are usually limited to within 25km (15½ miles) of the volcano. Only rarely do they reach destructive intensities.

Vesuvius

Volcanic earthquakes also continue during violent eruptions, not just because of rising magma, but also because gases explode from it and cause the ground to shake. During the climax of the eruption of Vesuvius in AD 79, Pliny the Younger described the effects of the earthquakes at home in Misenum, 32km (20 miles) from the volcano. 'The buildings around were already tottering and we would have been in danger in our confined space if our house had collapsed.'

He and his mother climbed to the safety of the hill above Misenum. The earthquakes continued. 'The carriages we had ordered began to lurch to and fro although the ground was flat, and we could not keep them still, even when we wedged their wheels with stones.' Both Pliny and his mother survived.

Mount St Helens

There are times, too, when volcanic earthquakes can have even more disastrous consequences. Rising magma caused Mount St Helens to tremble for a week before its first eruption on 27 March 1980. Then there were far more earthquakes than eruptions during the following 52 days. Meanwhile the rising magma had caused the north flank of the cone to swell out by over 150m (492ft), so that it became unstable.

The magnitude 5.1 earthquake that took place at 08.32 on 18 May 1980 was unusually large. It shook loose the top of the north flank of Mount St Helens. Half the summit swept down the side of the volcano in a huge landslide. The magma was then exposed and, in a matter of seconds, it exploded outwards and upwards in one of the largest recorded eruptions in North America.

This great eruption was inevitable, but the earthquake had brought it forward by several days and had perhaps increased its violence by wrecking the summit of the volcano. Thus Mount St Helens showed that earthquakes and eruptions are not only related, they can also be inter-related: earthquakes could warn of eruptions and – sometimes at least – provoke them.

The Old Roman Market, Pozzuoli. Originally thought to be a temple dedicated to the Egyptian goddess Serapis, because of an inscription found there, it is often incorrectly called the 'Temple of Serapis'

Pozzuoli

Unfortunately, the pattern is not invariably simple and direct, otherwise predicting eruptions would be much easier. There are false alarms, and sometimes no alarms at all. One example is the entrance to the Underworld of the Ancient Romans, the area around Pozzuoli, west of Naples, in the Phlegraean, or 'Burning' Fields. It is pock-marked with old volcanoes but only La Solfatara is still fuming sulphurous smoke and steam. However, the ancient Roman gods Pluto and Vulcan have not been entirely idle, because upsurging magma has shaken the ground, and made the land swell up, and then subside again, four times in the past 3,000 years. Only once has the magma erupted onto the landsurface – for a single week in 1538. The first changes in ground level were registered on the columns of the Old Roman Market, incorrectly called the 'Temple of Serapis' (see caption above). No sooner had it been built in about 100 BC than the land started to sink, sea-water soon flooded in, and a new pavement had to be built 2m (6½ft) higher than the previous one. After the Roman Empire fell, the market was abandoned, but the land continued to subside.

Stone-boring molluscs began to eat into the columns and the holes they made show that the building had sunk at least 5.8m (19ft) by about AD 1000.

Then, sometime before 1500, the land began to jerk upwards again in a series of earthquakes that were caused by rising magma. The land probably rose by as much as 8m (26ft) at Pozzuoli in the 50 years before 1538. The ruined 'Temple of Serapis' was on dry land again. But all the houses in the district were being shaken to their very foundations. The earthquakes reached a climax in the area on 27 and 28 September 1538. At 18.00 on 28 September the land at Pozzuoli suddenly rose by about 5m (16½ft) and exposed a band of sea-floor, 350m (1,150ft) wide, that was covered with stranded fish. The accompanying shocks had ruined practically every building in Pozzuoli. At 20.00 on Sunday 29 September, the ground cracked open at the village of Tripergole, 4.5km (2¾ miles) west of Pozzuoli and molten rock exploded out. The terrified citizens fled to Naples. When the eruption ended a week later, on Sunday 6 October 1538, one eyewitness, Francesco Marchesino, claimed that 'there were

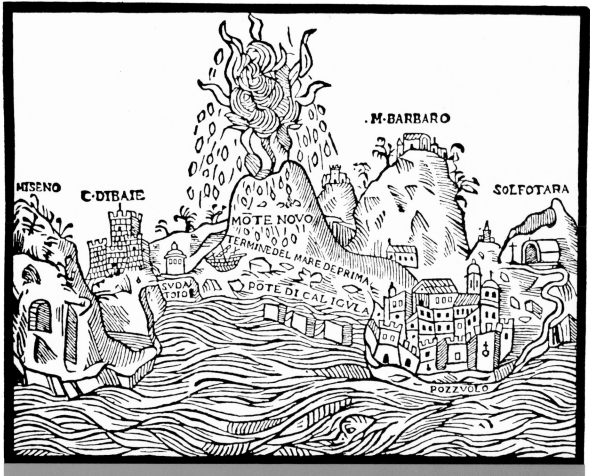

Labels on image: MISENO · C·DIBAIE · M·BARBARO · SOLFOTARA · MOTE NOVO · TERMINE DEL MARE DE PRIMA · SVDA TOIO · POTE DI CALIGVLA · POZZVOLO

Monte Nuovo as seen from the Bay of Naples. Misenum is to the left while Pozzuoli and La Solfatara are to the right

not ten houses still intact, most were crushed or ruined... hardly one stone remained standing above another ... and half the Cathedral had collapsed.' The earthquakes had done most of this damage. The eruption had merely coated the empty ruins of Pozzuoli in ash. It had also completely buried Tripergole beneath a cone 130m (426ft) high that they christened Monte Nuovo.

Southern Italy was in Spanish hands at the time. Luckily the Viceroy, Pedro de Toledo, was a passionate builder and he soon restored Pozzuoli. In the following centuries the land subsided again, but generally without intensely damaging earthquakes. Monte Nuovo fell silent.

Then, in 1969, the earthquakes started again at Pozzuoli, cracking masonry and terrifying its citizens. Little by little the city jerked upwards by about 1.7m (5¹/₂ft) as magma rose towards the surface. But, just as suddenly, the earthquakes stopped and the land began to subside again. There was no eruption.

But the crisis was not over for long. In August 1982, the earthquakes began again and the land started to rise. The centre of the swelling was at the harbour in the very heart of Pozzuoli. The people were even more terrified and the buildings even more damaged than before. The shocks continued for more than two years and over 500 were recorded on 1 April 1984. At that time 40,000 people had been evacuated from the city centre and panic was widespread. Then, once again, the earthquakes stopped, as if the magma had halted. There was no eruption. But the harbour quaysides had been carried too high to be used by the local boats and another set of quays had to be built in front of them and 2m (6¹/₂ft) lower.

chapter**3**

VOLCANOES

volcanic eruptions

VOLCANIC ERUPTIONS CAN BE SPECTACULAR AS THE PHOTOGRAPHS IN THIS BOOK ILLUSRATE ONLY TOO CLEARLY. CONSEQUENTLY MOST PEOPLE HAVE HEARD OF VESUVIUS, ETNA AND MOUNT ST HELENS. EARTHQUAKES, ON THE OTHER HAND, ARE FRIGHTENINGLY ANONYMOUS, SUDDEN, DESTRUCTIVE AND DEADLY, AND HAVE NONE OF THE SAVAGE BEAUTY OF THEIR EXPLOSIVE COUNTERPARTS.

It is easy to assume that all volcanoes erupt only sporadically, producing huge lava flows, and billowing clouds of ash. However, volcanic eruptions are far more varied than earthquakes, and volcanoes throw out much more than just molten lava and ash. Eruptions last far longer than earthquakes and often tend to build up to a climax over a period of several months of activity. Volcanoes can, therefore, be watched and studied in detail, and familiarity with their behaviour has produced a worldwide network of devotees.

major volcanic eruptions

Date	Volcano and location	Deaths	Date	Volcano and location	Deaths
1500 BC	Santorini, Greece	unknown	1892	Awu, Indonesia	1,532
AD 79	Vesuvius, Italy	c. 5,000	1902	Soufrière, St Vincent	1,565
1006	Merapi, Indonesia	unknown	1902	Montagne Pelée, Martinique	29,000
1362	Öraefajökull, Iceland	c. 200	1902	Santa María, Guatemala	7,000
1586	Kelut, Indonesia	10,000	1906	Vesuvius, Italy	200
1631	Vesuvius, Italy	4,000	1911	Taal, Philippines	1,335
1638	Raung, Indonesia	1,000	1919	Kelut, Indonesia	5,110
1669	Etna, Sicily	0	1929	Santiaguito (Santa María) Guatemala	5,000
1672	Merapi, Indonesia	3,000			
1711	Awu, Indonesia	3,000	1930	Merapi, Indonesia	1,369
1727	Öraefajökull, Iceland	2	1937	Rabaul, Papua New Guinea	505
1730–6	Lanzarote, Canary Islands	0	1943	Parícutin, Mexico	3
1760	Makian, Indonesia	2,000	1951	Mount Lamington, Papua New Guinea	2,942
1772	Papandajan,Indonesia	2,957			
1783	Laki, Iceland	9,350	1951	Hibok-Hibok, Philippines	500
1783	Asama, Japan	1,377	1953	Ruapehu, New Zealand	151
1792	Unzen, Japan	14,524	1963	Agung, Indonesia	983
1794	Vesuvius, Italy	18	1966	Kelut, Indonesia	212
1812	Awu, Indonesia	963	1968	Arenal, Costa Rica	78
1814	Mayon, Philippines	1,200	1979	Etna, Sicily	9
1815	Tambora, Indonesia	60,000+	1980	Mount St Helens, USA	57
1822	Galunggung, Indonesia	4,011	1981	Semeru, Indonesia	265
1835	Cosegüina, Nicaragua	7	1982	El Chichón, Mexico	2,000+
1843	Etna, Sicily	59	1985	Nevado del Ruiz, Colombia	23,000
1845	Nevado del Ruiz, Colombia	1,000	1986	Lake Nyos, Cameroon	1,742
1856	Awu, Indonesia	2,806	1990	Kelut, Indonesia	35
1877	Cotopaxi, Ecuador	400	1991	Unzen, Japan	43
1883	Krakatau, Indonesia	36,417	1991	Pinatubo, Philippines	1,202
1886	Tarawera, New Zealand	153	1993	Mayon, Phillipines	75
1888	Bandai San, Japan	461	1994	Merapi, Indonesia	61

eruption styles

Here we provide a summary of they way in which volcanic eruptions have been categorized in this book.

A. MILD ERUPTIONS
Hotsprings and pools: usually no lava
Geyser: small extent
Mudpot: short-lived
Fumaroles: fragile
Solfataras: not threatening

B. MODERATE ERUPTIONS
Strombolian eruptions: cinders, ash, lava-flows, cinder cones
Icelandic eruptions: lava-flows and cinder cones on fissures
Deepwater eruptions: pillow lavas
Subglacial eruptions: glacier bursts
Hawaiian eruptions: cinders, ash, lava-flows, huge shields
Basaltic floods: massive lava-flows

C. VIGOROUS ERUPTIONS
Vulcanian eruptions: ash, cinders, blocks, noise, ash cones

Surtseyan eruptions: tuffs, noise, tuff-cones
Steam-blast eruptions: fine fragments, blocks, maars
Volcanic gas eruptions: gas only

D. VIOLENT ERUPTIONS
Ash and pumice floods: ash and pumice, ash-plains
Blasts and debris avalanches: landslides, shattered rock, hummocky land
Peléan eruptions: nuées ardentes, ash, domes
Plinian eruptions: ash, nuées ardentes, pumice, strato-volcanoes
Caldera collapse: ash, pumice, calderas
Stratospheric aerosols: atmospheric cooling, jet problems, sunsets

E. MAJOR SIDE-EFFECTS OF ERUPTIONS
Volcanic mudflows: mud, mud plains
Volcanic tsunamis: large devastating on-shore sea-waves

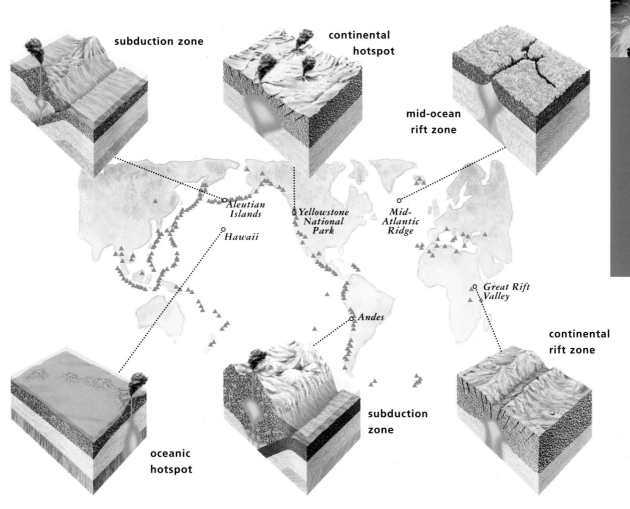

subduction zone

continental hotspot

mid-ocean rift zone

Aleutian Islands

Yellowstone National Park

Mid-Atlantic Ridge

Hawaii

Great Rift Valley

Andes

continental rift zone

oceanic hotspot

subduction zone

what is an eruption?

In basic terms a volcano is a hole in the Earth's crust, on land or on the sea floor, from which materials are expelled naturally from below. These materials may include hot lava, commonly in the form of flows, cinders, blocks, ash or pumice, cold rock fragments of all sizes, gases, aerosols, steam and water. Some materials cool and pile up around the hole, or chimney, and often form a cone-shaped hill. Other fine materials can be blasted into the stratosphere, carried around the world within about 15 days, and then remain as aerosols that veil the sun for several years.

Volcanoes, therefore, can eject a variety of different materials, and can erupt in a number of ways. A few of the main reasons for this variation are discussed here.

1. TYPE OF MAGMA

The material that rises to the surface inside the volcano is called magma (see pp.24–25). When the volcano erupts, the magma usually breaks up into lava and gases. The lava either runs across the surface as flows, piles up as domes, or, underwater, oozes out to form pillow-like lumps. Depending on the strength of the explosion, the gases that are released can break the lava into fragments that can be as small as dust. The dust aerosols described above can be responsible for producing cooler weather than normal for a period of several years, and can also produce spectacular, coloured sunsets. The chemical composition of the magma is a fundamental factor in the variability of volcanic eruptions, because it influences the fluidity of the lava, the way in which gases escape from it, and also the degree of shattering of both the magma itself, and the surrounding rock.

The top layer of this slow-moving Hawaiian lava-flow has started to solidify, but the red-heat of the lava is visible around the edges, where it is setting fire to vegetation as it

Basic magma

Basic magma, with less than about 55 per cent silica, is hot – about 1200°C – and fluid enough to flow easily. Gases can usually escape without causing huge explosions. The molten lava flows out, often in great fountains, and then forms long flows before it solidifies. Greater concentrations of gas tear the molten lava into clots and droplets that solidify into smaller particles. These volcanic fragments pile up in layers around the volcanic chimney and build a cone about 100–200m (328–656ft) high.

Silicic magma

Silicic magma behaves differently. It contains between 55 per cent and 70 per cent silica, its temperature is commonly between 700 and 900°C, and it

moves along the ground. Solidified flows can be seen towards the back of the photograph

is viscous. As the magma approaches the surface, gases can only escape from their bubbles by causing vast explosions. Hence the lava may be shattered into dust or fine ash that can mix with escaping sulphur dioxide, for example, to form aerosols that can travel around the world. Other lavas can be changed into froth like a meringue,

which solidifies as pumice that can float across oceans. Coarser ash and pumice, and the occasional lava-flow, accumulate in large cones such as Vesuvius or Mount St Helens. As the eruption ends, the remaining viscous lava often oozes out of the volcanic chimney and piles up in a dome above it. This dome then becomes the first victim of the violent explosions of the next eruption. These violent eruptions of silicic magma are concentrated in the subduction zones (see pp.22–25), and the calmer, more effusive eruptions of basic magma are characteristic of other plate edges and many hotspots such as the Hawaiian chain of volcanic islands (see pp.114–115).

2. WATER

A second agent of variability in volcanic eruptions is their relation to the depth and quantity of water surrounding them. The pressure of deep water stifles explosions, but shallow water greatly intensifies the vigour of an eruption. Each upsurge of red-hot magma suddenly changes the cold water into steam and explosions shatter the magma into fine ash. These are called Surtseyan eruptions. On land, stream waters or ice meltwater can filter down to meet a rising hot magma. This meeting in a confined space produces a few vigorous explosions before the water supply is exhausted. These eruptions are called steam-blast, or 'phreatic' from the Greek word *phreatos* meaning 'well', and are amongst the shortest-lived of all eruptions. Longer-lasting eruptions occur when the downward-percolating water reaches rocks heated by red-hot magma below. This generates convectional water circulation below ground and causes geysers and mud-volcanoes to erupt at regular intervals.

Mauna Loa, Hawaii

Krakatau, Indonesia

Etna, Sicily

Vesuvius, Italy

3. SUPPLY OF MAGMA

Another general factor is the supply of the magma. At the mid-ocean ridges it is practically continuous and so are the eruptions. Almost everywhere else on Earth, the magma only surges upwards from time to time, and, even then, much of it solidifies in the crust before it can erupt onto the surface. Stromboli has probably erupted at least a dozen times nearly every day for the past 2,500 years. Some volcanoes, like Sakurajima in Japan, Izalco in El Salvador and the north-east crater of Etna, have erupted frequently for several decades this century. They, too, are exceptional. Most volcanoes only erupt for brief and irregular periods, separated by long interludes of silence, and may be dormant for most of their active lives. Many smaller volcanoes are active only briefly, with magma rising intermittently for less than a decade before it stops, or finds a better path to the surface elsewhere. Thus, many of the cones in the Chain of Puys in central France were probably active for only a few years before they fell silent. However, it is never safe to assume that any volcano is dormant or extinct; several apparently extinct volcanoes, including Bezymianny in Kamchatka, Pinatubo in the Philippines, and El Chichón in Mexico, have erupted with some force since 1956 alone.

4. SIDE EFFECTS

A final feature that makes volcanic eruptions so variable is their side effects which can sometimes be more life-threatening than the eruptions themselves. Eruptions near the sea sometimes unleash great tsunamis. These were the major cause of death following the eruption of Krakatau in 1883. Eruptions can also cause ice to melt on the crests of volcanoes and generate mudflows, such as the one from Armero, Colombia, in 1985, that killed 23,000 people. In Iceland, meltwater produced by sub-glacial eruptions can match the discharge of the River Amazon. Luckily, floods such as this occur in sparsely-populated areas. Lakes on the summits of volcanoes can also cause mudflows. The lake in the crater of Kelut, Indonesia, produced three devastating mudflows since 1586 before efforts were made to drain it. Many volcanoes also develop secondary mudflows. Pinatubo provides the best recent example. The 1991 eruption blanketed the slopes of Mt Pinatubo in the Philippines with fine ash, and killed the tropical vegetation that bound the soil together. Now, every year, the rainy season storms generate mudflows on its flanks that have so far killed almost as many people as the main eruption itself. Famine is another major secondary effect of eruptions. Volcanic ash and gas kill crops and animals, and aid may not arrive in time to prevent famine. After Tambora erupted in 1815, 60,000 or more people are said to have died in the resulting famine.

volcanic materials

Type	% Silica content by weight	Typical temperature on emission	Typical forms	Comments
Basalt	50	1200°C	Ocean floors, flows, cinder cones	Fluid. By far the most common volcanic rock
Andesite	60	1000°C	Flows, cinder cones, domes	Fairly fluid; subduction zones (e.g. Andes)
Dacite	60-65	800°C–900°C	Ash, pumice, domes	Viscous; subduction zones
Rhyolite	70+	700°C–800°C	Ash, pumice, domes	Very viscous; volcanic glass (Obsidian) is often rhyolitic Rare
Trachyte	65	1000°C	Flows, domes, ash, pumice	Viscous; rich in sodium and potassium
Phonolite	55–60	1000°C	Pumice, flows, domes, ash	Viscous; rich in sodium and potassium

volcanic flows

	Origin	Danger level	Av. speed + temperature
Lava-flows	Basaltic and Andesitic effusions	Not lethal	Soon slow to 500m (1,640ft) a day or less
Mud flows	Secondary features: ice meltwater or lake water + loose surface soil and rock	Lethal	30–50km/h (18½–31mph); usually cold
Glacier burst	Ice and ice meltwater + loose glacial materials first accumulating under ice-cap	Lethal	50km/h (31mph); vast discharge. Cold
Nuée ardente	Ash, pumice, gas, lava fragments in ground hugging mass and aerosols	Extremely lethal	500km/h (311mph); hot: 500°C

airborne volcanic fragments

Type	Size	Comments
Dust	0.5mm	Impalpable, often like flour
Ash	0.5–2mm	Sand-like, often called sand in older descriptions
Lapilli	2–64mm (½–2½in)	Rough, rounded nut-sized (from the Italian meaning 'little stones')
Cinders	6.4–30cm (2½–12in)	Very rough chunks, like clinker
Blocks	0.5–1m+ (20–40in+)	Angular, like masonry. Often old material blown from a volcano
Bomb	0.5–1m+ (20–40in+)	Twirled and rounded often almond-shaped.
Pumice	1–10cm+ (½–4in+)	Solidified 'foam' of silicic magma. Floats on water
Tuff	2–64mm (½–2½in)	Yellowish fragments shattered by magma-water interaction. Thin beds

eruption styles

VOLCANOES ERUPT IN SO MANY DIFFERENT WAYS, AND EJECT SUCH A VARIETY OF MATERIALS, THAT IT SEEMS IMPOSSIBLE TO GROUP THEIR ACTIVITY INTO PARTICULAR STYLES. IT IS, HOWEVER, AN EXERCISE THAT EARTH SCIENTISTS HAVE PRACTISED FOR A LONG TIME. AT THE TURN OF THE CENTURY, FOR INSTANCE, THE GREAT FRENCH VOLCANOLOGIST, LACROIX, DESCRIBED FOUR MAIN ERUPTION STYLES: HAWAIIAN, STROMBOLIAN, VULCANIAN AND PELÉAN, AFTER THE BEST-KNOWN VOLCANOES TYPICAL OF EACH GROUP.

Scientists soon realized that there were types of eruption that did not easily fit into these groups, and many more were subsequently described. At present, more than 12 different styles are commonly distinguished, and even these groups are not exclusive. Here we will place eruption styles into four broad groups: mild, moderate, vigorous and violent. Each group contains smaller sub-groups, depending, for example, on what is expelled from the volcano, or whether the eruption takes place on land or underwater.

Mild eruptions

On land, mild eruptions are limited to emissions of gas, steam, hot water, sulphurous fumes and bubbling mud from geysers, hissing holes and fissures. They are the glory of Yellowstone Park in Wyoming, United States, central Iceland and the North Island of New Zealand. They are also common on dormant or dying volcanoes that have had a much more violent past, such as Lassen Peak in California and Teide in Tenerife.

Such activity is termed hydrothermal, and heated water is one of its basic components. The water comes from the rain and melting snows and percolates down into the crust. In many volcanic areas, magma still lies in relatively shallow masses long after violent eruptions have ceased. The rocks above it remain hot and they heat the water that filters into them to temperatures of over 200°C without boiling. In the simplest case, this now less dense water returns to the surface and forms hot-water pools.

Probably more often, steam bubbles and hisses continuously from the rising water and forms more typical hot springs such as those at Furnas in São Miguel in the

ABOVE Organ terraces at Mammoth Hot Springs, Yellowstone National Park, formed when hot waters stream downslope.
BELOW Mud-pots at Yellowstone

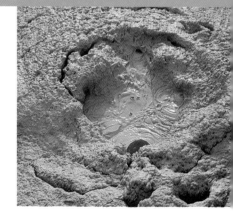

Azores, or in Bumpas Hell on Lassen Peak, California. Towns in several countries have tapped these hot waters for heating and power, including Larderello in Italy, Chaudes-Aigues in France and Reykjavík and Hveragerdi in Iceland.

In some cases steam from the percolated water mixes with sulphurous fumes produced by the magma. These fumes are called solfataras and fumaroles, names derived from the Italian. The Ancient Romans believed their Underworld lay below the volcano known as La Solfatara, near Pozzuoli. The poet Virgil compared these wispy fumes to ghosts; 'bodiless, airy, flitting behind an empty figment of a form'. Steam and fume emissions are common on many dormant or declining volcanoes, where holes hissing with escaping hydrogen sulphide or sulphur dioxide are surrounded by halos of yellow sulphur crystals.

If the hot water cannot circulate freely underground, or rise to the surface easily, then two things may happen: the water only gushes out intermittently and/or it becomes contaminated and muddy. The restricted circulation means that, as the water becomes hotter, the steam is placed under great pressure and forces the water to spurt out onto the surface in a geyser. These fountains can reach as much as 20m (65½ft) high and last for over 5 mins. The interval between eruptions varies from geyser to geyser. Old Faithful in Yellowstone Park now erupts about once every 67 mins, and its timetable is posted daily for visitors, but Beehive nearby only erupts about once a year.

The hot waters often dissolve various chemicals as they circulate through the rocks. They then precipitate them again on the surface, where they can form cowls or cones around the fissure. Where the hot waters stream downslope they form magnificent organ-pipe terraces such as Mammoth Springs in Yellowstone Park.

Where the water lingers longer underground and the rocks are easily weathered or dissolved, boiling, bubbling mud erupts at the surface in mud-pots that sometimes reach 20m (65½ft) across. A mud-pot on Vulcano in the Aeolian Islands is reputed to cure rheumatism.

Many of these mild eruptions are products of fragile systems that can be disrupted by earth-tremors, changes in rainfall patterns or human intervention, for example. As a result their activity is often short-lived. The Great Geyser in Iceland has been active for 8,000 years. Now, however, it has to be stimulated into action using soap-powder.

ABOVE Steam from La Solfatara (named after the Italian word for sulphur), near Pozzuoli, Italy
BELOW Yellowstone's world-famous geyser, Old Faithful

volcanoes

During Icelandic eruptions, lava erupts along fissures or cracks in the Earth's crust, producing red-hot fountains that can reach 100m (328ft) in height

Moderate eruptions

Moderate eruptions expel lava and some gases. The lava is nearly always of the basic, basaltic kind that emerges in a hot, fluid form from the chimney, and streams away in lava-flows. At the same time, moderate gas explosions can also shatter some of the basalts into clots and droplets that solidify into cinders and ash that pile up in cones around the crater hole. Columns of gas and ash might also rise about 2km (1¼ miles) above the crater. The eruptions often happen on fissures that can be anything from 5–50km (3–31 miles) long. Away from the chimney, however, they are rarely dangerous because flowing lava predominates over the explosions. Nevertheless, 'moderate' does not necessarily mean small, because such eruptions are by far the most common form of volcanic activity, and have piled up some of the largest lava accumulations on the planet. Strombolian eruptions are the most common in the moderate group. The two main variants are Icelandic eruptions which extend along fissures, and Hawaiian activity which is concentrated on a central hub. Basaltic flood eruptions are an extreme case brought about when vast volumes of lava are expelled. Eruptions in deep water and under ice-caps are other special cases.

Etna in Sicily erupts its lavas, on average, at rates of 25m³ (883ft³) per second, forming flows reaching 7.5km (4½ miles) long and 12m (39½ft) thick

Hawaiian eruptions are characterized by slow-moving, wide-spreading lava-flows. These lava-flows build up into huge, shield-like volcanoes

Stromboli

STROMBOLI BEGAN LIFE ABOUT 1 MILLION YEARS AGO, 2,000M (6,560FT) DOWN ON THE SEABED NORTH OF SICILY IN THE MEDITERRANEAN. CONSTANT MODERATE ACTIVITY HAS PRODUCED A VOLCANIC ISLAND THAT NOW RISES 926M (3038FT) ABOVE SEA-LEVEL. THREE, AND SOMETIMES AS MANY AS SIX, CRATERS ERUPT APPROXIMATELY EVERY 20 MINS, AS THEY HAVE USUALLY DONE FOR THE PAST 2,500 YEARS.

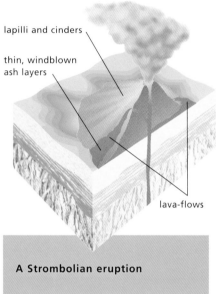

lapilli and cinders

thin, windblown ash layers

lava-flows

A Strombolian eruption

The first warning of an impending eruption is a low, shuddering rumble. A red glow then brightens in the necks of the craters. The chimneys begin to hiss like old steam engines, rumble like thunder, or explode like shells. Soon the gases explode and shatter the molten lava into red and orange clots and droplets that curl about 200m (656ft) into the air. Gas and steam swirl around them. The fragments then fall back and cool on the cones they are forming around the craters. Meanwhile, the wind scatters fine ash and sulphurous steam. These explosions continue for perhaps 5 mins until the craters can manage no more than a dull groan. The red-hot molten fragments settle on the cones and the colour gradually fades as the embers cool. Then there is silence until the whole process begins again.

Occasionally the molten lava pours out in continuous streams on the Sciara del Fuoco (the 'Scar of Fire') on the northern flank of the volcano below the craters. But the steep slope causes the lavas to cascade and shatter as they career down the Sciara and head straight into the sea.

Sometimes Stromboli remains quiet for a day or two. On most volcanoes such periods of repose represent a good time to visit the crater. But not on Stromboli. The rest period only means that the volcano is preparing a more vigorous eruption which is usually unleashed without warning.

Strombolian eruptions

Strombolian eruptions epitomise moderate activity and Stromboli, appropriately enough, is the best place to see them. However, although the eruptions on Stromboli are typical of the style, they have not produced a typical Strombolian volcano. Stromboli has grown far too big for that, because it has been erupting for at least 2,500 years. In fact, elsewhere, most Strombolian eruptions only last for a year or two at most before they become extinct. Usually, there is never time for them to build up cinder cones more than 250m (820ft) high, or send out lava-flows over 10km (6¼ miles) long. The cones have a shallow, bowl-shaped crater directly above the chimney,

key features

Strombolian eruptions are characterized by:

◆ constant, but usually short lived, moderate activity
◆ cinder cones with a shallow, bowl-shaped crater
◆ dust and ash
◆ lava-flows; Initially fast-moving, soon slow down

Strombolian eruptions are usually short-lived. The prolonged activity exhibited by Stromboli itself is exceptional and has produced a strato-volcano that rises 3,000m (9,840ft) from the sea floor

which stays open during the eruption, but is plugged with solidified lava when it stops. Sometimes lava gushes out from one side of the chimney so fast that it carries away all the fragments that have fallen on it. In this case, the cinders never pile up in that sector and the cone is 'breached' and forms a crescent in plan rather than a perfect circle. The main problem caused by the fragments is that the wind sends the dust and ash swirling for as much as 5km (3 miles) from the volcano. The lava-flows are more dangerous at first, because the molten basalt at temperatures between 1000 and 1200°C can travel at up to 50km/h (31mph). Fortunately this does not continue for long as edges of the flow soon solidify until it resembles a red-hot molten river that moves forward between solid lava walls. In some cases, the surface solidifies too, but the molten lava continues to press forward within a tube of lava that also feeds the advancing snout of the flow. In either case the flows travel forward fastest immediately after they are erupted and soon slow down to walking pace. As a result, lava-flows often reach three-quarters of their ultimate length after only a quarter of the eruption period has elapsed.

Thus, Strombolian eruptions are only potentially dangerous for those within about 1km (⅔ mile) of the chimney. In fact, they rarely kill anybody except by odd quirks of fate. In 1843, the people of Bronte, Sicily, were watching a flow approaching their town from a Strombolian eruption on the western flank of Etna. The hot lava tongue encroached upon a marshy field and the heat suddenly converted the water to steam that exploded from the confined space under the flow. Molten clots of lava showered onto the startled spectators, killing 59 people. Three people were killed whilst Parícutin was erupting in Mexico between 1943 and 1952. They were struck by lightning generated in the column of ash and gas rising above the volcano.

Strombolian cones and lava-flows are the most common volcanic forms on land in the world. There are, for instance, over 75 in the Chain of Puys in central France; over 200 decorate the flanks of Etna; and over 1,000 Strombolian cones are scattered around Parícutin in Mexico.

the eruption of Etna

11 March 1669

THE FAMOUS ERUPTION ON THE SOUTHERN FLANKS OF ETNA IN 1669 SHOWS THE LIMITS OF WHAT STROMBOLIAN ERUPTIONS CAN ACHIEVE. IT BEGAN AT NICOLOSI, 2,000M (6,560FT) AND 14KM (8¾ MILES) BELOW THE SUMMIT OF ETNA. IN EARLY MARCH 1669, THE EARTH BEGAN TO QUAKE WITH INCREASING VIOLENCE. ON 11 MARCH A FISSURE 12KM (7½ MILES) LONG RIPPED OPEN ON THE FLANKS OF ETNA AND REVEALED A WOUND LIVID WITH MOLTEN LAVA. THE VILLAGERS LEFT EVERYTHING AND FLED.

That evening exploding gas began to throw ash and cinders into the air 'with a most terrible and vigorous din' (this was the birth of the Monti Rossi cone). Almost at once, a bright orange stream of lava surged out nearby. Within three days it had buried most of Monpilieri, La Guardia, Malpasso, Mascalucia, San Pietro and Camporotondo, whose people had only time to pack up their valuables before they left. By this time, however, the flow was slowing down markedly so that the snout was advancing at no more than 100m (328ft) an hour, but the tongue was already 6km (3¾ miles) long by 16 March. By the end of March the flow stretched 10km (6¼ miles) from Nicolosi and was strong enough to shift aside fields of both wheat and vines. In early April, the snout of the flow was poised outside the walls of Catania and 13km (8 miles) from its source. On 14 April, the lavas wrapped around the western city wall and turned south-eastwards towards the Ursino Castle. The following day the lava pushed down a sector of the western wall – and halted for Easter week. On 23 April, the Tuesday after Easter, the lava

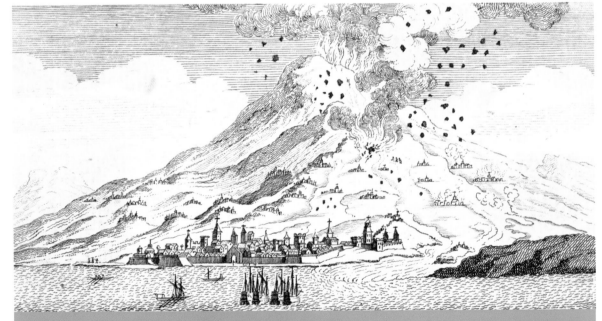

The origin of Etna's activity is something of a mystery: it lies neither on a subduction zone nor on a large crustal fissure. Instead it seems to be located on an intersection of secondary fractures produced by the collision of the African and Eurasian Plates

This painting, depicting the lava-flows invading the west side of Catania in 1669, hangs in the Cathedral at Catania. It was painted shortly after the eruption

uninhabitable. It was so thick that trees and crops had burnt, animals were starving, and there was 'great store of a strong sulfureous smoak, wherewith some of our company were at first almost stifled through inadvertency.' The wind was blowing the finest ash to Catania, and 100km (62 miles) away to Calabria; it even reached Zante (Zakynthos) across the Ionian Sea.

Most terrifying of all was the current of molten lava issuing from the foot of Monti Rossi. At night the glow from the lavas was so bright in Catania that 'books and writings printed in the smallest characters could be read with ease.' At times, the lavas surged forward without warning and then stopped again equally quickly. On 8 June lava swamped the ground floor of Ursino Castle, and built a terrace, 1km (⅔ mile) wide, between the fortress and the sea. The final burst came on 26 June when a brilliant red torrent rushed southwards, straight into the sea, for a period of four hours. The Catanians were amazed and mesmerized by the spectacle and thanked their lucky stars, Saint Agatha or any other protector they could invoke, that this lava had not chosen to travel over Catania.

Then, on 11 July 1669 the eruption near Nicolosi stopped. By then, the Monti Rossi formed a cone 250m (820ft) high and the area 3km (1¼ miles) around was blanketed in thick ash a century later. The lava flow formed a great rugged black scar all the way down to Catania. Nearly 1,000m³ (35,300ft³) of lava had erupted and now covered 37.5km² (14½ square miles). About 27,000 people had been made homeless and only 3,000 out of 20,000 citizens were still in Catania. Over a dozen villages were destroyed or badly damaged. Nobody had been killed.

also entered the sea south of the city, causing 'a superb and terrifying spectacle' full of hissing, crashing, black and red-hot rocks.

The lava-flows were now advancing much more slowly than a month before but this time a large city was in the way. On 30 April, the lavas started to spill once again over the western walls. The panic-stricken Catanians turned to their protecting patron, Saint Agatha, whose veil had stopped many lava-flows in the past. This time the veil was presented to the advancing snout in vain, and soon the lavas piled up against the Church of San Nicolo, but were making only slow progress. The citizens had time to remove all their property from their homes. As some English merchants of Messina commented, the citizens 'not only, at good leisure, removed their goods, but the very tiles, and beams, and what else was moveable.' They also took the brass cannons from Ursino Castle and church bells from their steeples; and they barricaded the streets with the masonry from already ruined houses to arrest the flow.

Meanwhile, the explosions of gas cinders and ash were continuing at the Monti Rossi. The swirling ash made Nicolosi completely

Icelandic eruptions

ICELANDIC ERUPTIONS OCCUR WHERE FISSURES IN THE EARTH'S CRUST DOMINATE VOLCANIC ACTIVITY. THE BEST PLACE TO SEE THEM IS ICELAND, WHOSE ERUPTIONS HAVE BUILT UP A SECTION OF THE MID-ATLANTIC RIDGE ABOVE SEA-LEVEL. THE BASALTIC PLATEAUX OF WESTERN ICELAND BELONG TO THE NORTH AMERICAN PLATE AND ARE MOVING TO THE WEST; EASTERN ICELAND BELONGS TO THE EURASIAN PLATE AND IS MOVING TO THE EAST.

Modern activity is centred on the ridge crest, a broad band, 70km (43½ miles) wide and 400km (249 miles) long, that curves diagonally across the country from north-east to south-west. Thousands of fissures spring from the volcanoes dotted along this band, that run at right angles to the direction of plate divergence. They form when the crust cracks in response to the stretching caused by the strains of the separation of the plates. Basaltic magma moves up towards the surface, but most of it fails to reach the open air, and solidifies below ground. The basalt that does reach the surface, erupts along the fissure in fountains reaching 100m (328ft) into the air. After a few days, the eruptions are concentrated in many individual chimneys where they build up cinder cones as the lavas spread outwards. These eruptions are strongest during their early weeks, and become

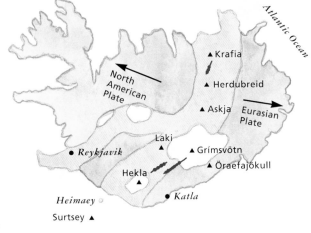

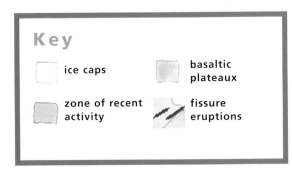

Key

- ice caps
- zone of recent activity
- basaltic plateaux
- fissure eruptions

key features

Icelandic eruptions are characterized by:

- ◆ lava fountains
- ◆ cinder cones on fissures
- ◆ vast lava-flows
- ◆ fine ash
- ◆ sulphur dioxide emissions

less powerful over time. They leave behind rows of 50–100 cinder cones, commonly less than 100m (328ft) high, and vast lava-flows. The magma that solidifies below ground welds the walls of the fissure strongly together. As crustal stretching continues, the basalt-choked fissure resists the pressure and cracks, and eruptions thus occur alongside it. The result is that Icelandic fissures only erupt for one episode and then become extinct. In this way they differ from fissures that produce Strombolian eruptions, which can be active at different points, and at different intervals.

The Laki eruption in Iceland

At 09.00 on Whit Sunday, 8 June 1783, the south-east side of Laki mountain split open. From 8 June until 25 July 1783, the fissure became increasingly wide on the south-western flanks of Laki. Fluid basalt, as hot as 1250°C, spurted 1km (⅔ mile) into the air in swishing fountains, and surged into the River Skaftà gorge. Gas explosions built cone after cone of ash and cinders and hurled ash and dust 12km (7½ miles) into the air. The basalts gushed out at about 5,000m³ (177,000ft³) per second – double the discharge of the Rhine. In a few days they had filled the River Skaftà gorge to the brim and spread out onto the coastal plain. On 11 July, woodcutters working in the gorge had to run for their lives when the molten lava charged down the gorge. The next day, the farmers on the plain had just enough time to drive off their stock, load their valuables onto their carts and flee.

Then, from 25 July until 30 October, the north-eastern flank of Laki burst open. This time lavas gushed into the River Hverfisfljót gorge, filled it, and spread out over the coastal plain.

By the end of October 1783, 90 per cent of the lava had erupted, and activity slowed down and stopped altogether on 7 February 1784. In all, the fissures were then 27km (16¾ miles) long, they had erupted 140 cones and 14.7km³ (3½ cubic miles) of lavas that covered an area of 599km² (231 square miles). Perhaps as many as 21 farming hamlets were swamped.

Although no-one was killed directly as a result of the advancing lava-flows this was to be the worst human disaster in Iceland since it was first settled in AD 875. The fine ash stunted the growth of the summer grazing lands, sulphur dioxide contaminated the rain producing sulphuric acid, and fluorine poisoned the animals. Half the Icelandic stock of cattle, three-quarters of the horses and three-quarters of the sheep, all perished. Fish catches were vastly reduced. The famine spread quickly and caused at least 9,300 of the 10,521 deaths registered in Iceland before the end of 1785: nearly a quarter of the population.

It was called the 'Haze Famine' because it was associated with a mysterious, dry blue fog that spread over Europe and beyond during the summer of 1783. The haze irritated the eyes, reeked of sulphur and persisted through storms and changes of winds. It killed trees and crops in Iceland, and scorched leaves and new growth throughout much of Europe. It also produced huge variations in weather conditions: in July 1883 the weather was cold in Iceland, there was snow in Poland and Russia, but there were high temperatures and mighty thunderstorms in western Europe. In Japan, frost and high rainfall ruined the rice harvest in 1783 causing a terrible famine.

The acid and dust aerosol lingered in the lower stratosphere and reduced the amount of the Sun's heat reaching the Earth's surface for 1–2 years. The winters of 1784, 1785 and 1786 were amongst the coldest of the latter half of the century. Annual temperatures from 1783–86 were probably 1–3°C below average. The winter of 1783–84 ranks as the coldest in Europe and North America during the last 250 years.

A typical Icelandic rift and fissure swarm showing both cones and fissures on the surface

crater row and new flows

new flows from fissure

developing fissure

divergent movement

open fissure

sealed fissure

lava channel to surface

dykes filled with lava failing to reach the surface

divergent movement

deepwater and sub-glacial eruptions

NOT ALL VOLCANIC ERUPTIONS ARE CHARACTERIZED BY FOUNTAINS OF RED-HOT LAVA. DEEPWATER AND SUB-GLACIAL ERUPTIONS ARE TWO CASES WHERE MAGMA DOES NOT REACH THE LANDSURFACE. THE HEAT THAT IS GENERATED PRODUCES SOME DRAMATIC EFFECTS.

Deepwater eruptions

Deepwater eruptions take place in the sea where the water pressure prevents any explosions. They occur especially along the crests of all mid-ocean ridges and from ocean floors where they are often linked to volcanic seamounts related to hotspots. When the eruptions are more than 100m (328ft) deep, the lavas ooze out, and solidify in piles of pillow-shaped lumps. Gases such as hydrogen sulphide and carbon dioxide bubble up in 'black smokers'. All these eruptions were virtually unknown until the 1960s, but they are the most voluminous in the world, and generate new oceanic crust. Their remote location and the cushion of the water means that we are protected from the power of these eruptions. If they were to take place on land, mid-ocean ridge eruptions would probably adopt the Icelandic style. If they were to occur on emerged seamounts, they would probably follow the Hawaiian style.

Sub-glacial eruptions

Eruptions that occur underneath glaciers also can be almost stifled by thick ice-caps. In Iceland, when Grímsvötn erupts beneath the Vatnajökull ice-cap, the hot basalt melts some of the ice, and the water accumulates until it suddenly bursts from beneath the ice-cap. This is called a 'jökulhlaup' or glacier burst. Sub-glacial eruptions may also form table mountains (see right).

Glacier-burst from Vatnajökull

Vatnajökull, 'the water glacier', the largest ice-cap in Iceland, is aptly named because the eruptions that occur beneath it have generated a succession of brief, but formidable, floods. Grímsvötn is the largest of the volcanic fissure systems in Iceland. At its summit is a huge, ice-filled hollow, probably a volcanic caldera. This is where meltwater accumulates whenever eruptions melt some of the ice, thus forming a lake which eventually lifts up the 500m (1,640ft) of covering ice and makes it float. Within a few days water breaks through the now buoyant ice-barrier. It drains southwards under the ice and cascades out from its edge in an enormous flood of meltwater, ice-blocks, mud, sand and boulders: the glacier bursts.

volcanoes

Water pressure prevents explosions during deepwater eruptions; lava oozes out in pillow-shaped lumps

The latest volcanic eruption beneath Vatnajökull occurred in 1996. At 10.48 on Sunday 29 September, a magnitude 5.0 earthquake shook Vatnajökull. Almost 30 hours of volcanic tremors followed. By the morning of 1 October, lava was erupting from a fissure under the ice. It soon began to melt the ice until several lakes formed across the surface of Vatnajökull. At first the explosions were stifled, but increased lava emissions soon built up a ridge above the fissure, bringing the volcanic chimneys closer to the surface. Explosions were then able to blast fine fragments into the atmosphere. At 05.18 on 2 October, Surtseyan explosions began, firing out block plumes of ash 500m (1,640ft) into the air, while a white column of steam rose into the sky.

About 10km (6¼ miles) to the south, meltwater was pouring into the Grímsvötn hollow. On 4 October, 2km³ (½ cubic mile) of water had accumulated and reached levels 20m (66ft) higher than ever previously recorded. All the authorities could do was dig trenches and raise dykes on the coastal plains to try to concentrate the flow into channels.

On 13 October, the eruption stopped. It had built up a long ridge of tuff and ash, and a Surtseyan cone rising 40m (131ft) above the open-air lake where the main activity had been. The heat from the rocks, however, continued to melt the ice, and meltwater kept accumulating under the ice on the summit of Grímsvötn. On 2 November the water level reached 1,509m (4,950ft) – 60m (197ft) above the level when glacier-bursts were usually unleashed.

Eventually, at about 08.30 on Tuesday 5 November, the River Skeidar clouded with mud and began to smell of sulphur. Suddenly it flooded, its discharge increasing by 100 times in less than two hours. It swept across the coastal plain with a frontal wave, 4m (13ft) high. Ice, rocks, water and mud ripped away 10km (6¼ miles) of the Icelandic coastal ring-road, damaged bridges and tore down electricity and telephone cables. No-one was killed. But the long-delayed onset and unusually quick climax are still a puzzle.

Formation of table mountains by sub-glacial eruptions

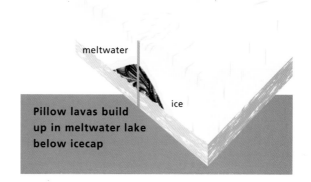

Pillow lavas build up in meltwater lake below icecap

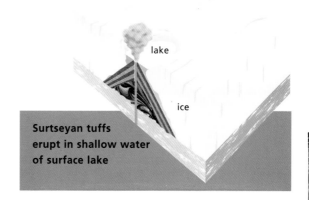

Surtseyan tuffs erupt in shallow water of surface lake

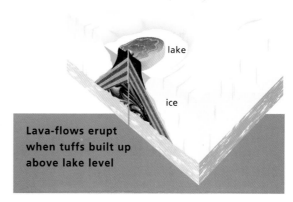

Lava-flows erupt when tuffs built up above lake level

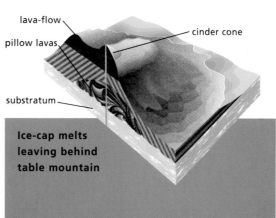

Ice-cap melts leaving behind table mountain

Hawaiian eruptions

According to Hawaiian mythology the spectacular volcanic activity seen in Hawaii is caused by the fire goddess Pelé, who was chased from her home in Tahiti, and settled in the crater of Kilauea. The scientific explanation may be less poetic but it is certainly no less dramatic.

The volcanic islands of Hawaii are situated over a hotspot in the Pacific Ocean where the Pacific Plate is sliding north-west at a rate of 10cm (4in) per year. The diagram (right) shows how they were formed. Magma rises in a central vent from which thin flows of basalt emerge and spread over a wide area. As the layers accumulate and the volcano grows larger, lava flows may also emerge from vents on either side of the summit, in flank eruptions. The characteristic, broad-based shape of this type of volcano has given them the name 'shield volcanoes'.

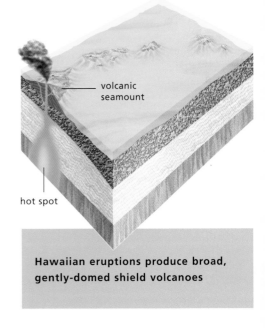

Hawaiian eruptions produce broad, gently-domed shield volcanoes

Five shields join to make the islands of Hawaii, three of which are still active: Kilauea, Mauna Loa and Hualalai. Mauna Loa is probably the largest active volcano in the world, rising 9km (5½ miles) from the floor of the Pacific Ocean, with a diameter of 100km (62 miles). Another example is Réunion Island in the Indian Ocean, which is composed of two huge shields.

The weathered lava-flows that surround shield volcanoes are extremely fertile and often become highly populated. In Hawaii, although eruptions are frequent – Kilauea has erupted every three years on average since 1830 – they are generally non-explosive, and relatively slow-moving, flows of basalt.

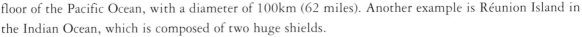

Therefore, although damage to crops and property can be immense, the number of human lives claimed by eruptions is relatively low; even when fluid lava flows into narrow valleys, people usually have time to pack their bags and leave.

The Piton de la Fournaise in Réunion is also extremely active, erupting once every ten months on average. But in contrast to Hawaii, most of the active craters lie on the barren, sparsely populated, eastern part of the island.

Volcanic activity in this part of the world is continuing with a new Hawaiian island, Loihi, lurking beneath the surface. It will be many centuries, however, before the crest rises above the Pacific: at present eruptions are still taking place 1,000m (3,280ft) below sea-level.

key features

Hawaiian eruptions are characterized by:

♦ frequency
♦ hot, fluid, wide-spreading emissions of basalt
♦ relatively non-explosive nature
♦ destructive but slow-moving lava-flows
♦ shield volcano

The islands of Hawaii are part of a long chain of volcanic islands, known as seamounts, stretching from Siberia. New volcanic islands are now being formed to the south of Hawaii, and in thousands of years, Kilauea (above) will become extinct

INTERVIEW

KALAPANA, HAWAII

Todd and Mary Dressler

Todd and Mary Dressler were living in Kalapana, a small town in the shadow of Kilauea, when a new fissure on the volcano's side began erupting in 1983. On that day they received a phone call from Todd's mother:

'... it was dark, maybe 3 o'clock in the morning ... she asked me to look out of the window ... there was this huge glow in the mountain, like a nuclear glow. And then I realized that there was a major eruption, so all of us got in the car ... we drove all the way around to realize that the eruption was happening really close to us, because we couldn't see it better than in our own back yard.'

The eruption began along a crack in the side of the volcano 6.5km (4 miles) in length, in an area of forest, east of the summit caldera. The Dresslers went to have a closer look at the area.

'We flew up in an airplane with a friend of ours ... and took a look at it and realized where the crack was and it really didn't look that scary ... but as the months went on ... and the mountain then really started erupting, when there were 1,500ft [457m] fountains ... then it started really coming to us, that something serious was going to happen.'

The eruptive phases consisted of lava fountains lasting up to a few days, followed by a period of inactivity, that averaged about a month. Fifty phases were recorded between 1983 and 1986.

' ... the mountain would expand and then it would erupt for like ten days. And they would have these incredible fountains on the mountain that ... were so alluring ... and then the mountain would ... stop. And the lava flow would stop. And it would just come down through the forest and burn lots of forest and maybe catch a few houses, and then it would go away ... And then the mountain would inflate again and then it would do the same thing again, over and over for years.'

The eruptions continued without respite until, ominously, the mountain and the type of lava flow began to change.

The lava-flows at Kalapana spread out over the land and began to run off into the sea.

'... this went on for seven years ... it was many phases of eruption, many different flows came down the mountain, and when Kupaianaha was born ... that is when it finally took everything out, because the volcano had changed into a shield, which meant that there was much volume every day, 500,000 cubic yards [382,300m^3] a day coming into the area ...'

On 1 April 1990 the Dresslers finally began to move out of the house they had lived in for 15 years:

 'And from that moment until April 22, when our house was actually taken down, ... those were the most threatening days of my life. It would come close to the house and then it would subside and stop. But April Fool's Day was the last day my girls were able to be at their home, they went to school never to return.'

In the last few days before their house was engulfed Todd and Mary watched the approach of the lava.

The slow-moving lava-flows produced by Kilauea destroyed everything in their path

Here we can see steam produced as the red-hot lava is cooled by the water

 '... it is really interesting because you look down ... and you see all the ants leaving, all the roaches leaving, all the insects leaving and one day the birds aren't there. And ... the explosions [caused by methane gas released by the lava] get closer and closer ... one night I watched my wife get blown 5ft [1.5m] off the ground ... from a methane explosion. Some think we were crazy for hanging out as long as we did but ... you become one with the area for so long you just want to be there till the end.'

Todd made a video of the final moments.

 '... it was devastating, ... each little sparkle and each little crackling, ... watching the house getting gutted took about 35–45 minutes, ... what really kept me sane through that 45 minutes was knowing that ... we can rebuild again and ... that my children were safe and we were safe ... but it was very emotional ... we thought this was where we would always be.'

INTERVIEW

VOLCANO CHASERS

Steve and Donna O'Meara

Steve and Donna O'Meara are passionate about volcanoes. They live in Hawaii, a group of islands created entirely by volcanic activity, in a village called Volcano. Their second date was on a volcano; they got married on a volcano and they spend their holidays chasing volcanoes.

 '... we travel all over the world photographing volcanoes and mainly having fantastic adventures ... the first time I saw an erupting volcano ... it just gives you a sense of awe ... what we do is embrace the fact that we know our lives are short and make the most of every moment ... I'd rather have ten minutes of something wonderful than a lifetime of nothing special'.

Steve had been Donna's astronomy teacher and for their second date it seems that he was determined to make an impression:

 '... it was the day before Christmas Eve and Steve called me at my office ... and he said "how would you like to see an erupting volcano?" and I said "sure" ... 18 hours later we were hovering in a helicopter over Kupaianaha which is a Hawaiian lava lake that was about 700ft [213m] wide and it was churning and bubbling and I was screaming ... I guess that was it, I was hooked, and it was the most incredible experience I ever had in my life.'

 '... I never forget my first eruption, it was a large fire fountain ... 1km [²⁄₃ mile] long, and these fire fountains going up 100 sometimes 200ft [30–60m] high ... it went from sounding like a waterfall – its liquid lava sounded just like a waterfall – but then more gas started coming out than lava and it was breathing, it was choking ... it was inhaling ... and then it could cough and all this molten phlegm would fly out, spat all over the ground, and you're in awe and the sounds echoing off the cold air, all the phlegm would fall back in the throat, the stuff would go flying out, and it would fall back into the throat. Ultimately the volcano made its last gasp and that was it ... it just died ...'

For two people with such a fascination with volcanoes, as well as nature and science in general, it is no surprise that they have settled in

The characteristic shield-shaped profile of Mauna Loa, Hawaii

Lava fountains produced by Stromboli in the Mediterranean are among the most spectacular, and the most regular, on Earth

Hawaii. Hawaiian volcanoes have both a characteristic form and style of eruption.

 '... it is called a shield volcano, so it looks like an overturned saucer. The eruptions are very gentle ... the molten rock is fed almost directly from the centre of the Earth ... [the Pacific Ocean floor is on] a moving plate under which is there is a hotspot [like] a blow-torch, and it blows right through and makes a hole in the plate ... now the plate is moving, it moves off the hotspot and a new blow-torch hole comes up and that's another island ... this continues and you get [a] chain of islands.'

In keeping with their courtship, when Steve and Donna decided to get married, they were both keen for the ceremony to take place on a volcano. After gaining permission from the Hawaii National Park, they flew out to a vent on Kilauea, made an offering of lilies to Pelé, the goddess of the volcano, and exchanged vows.

 'We were married on a lava flow that was about three hours old ...'

 'And then it was covered over so no-one will ever step on it again.'

In spite of their love-affair with volcanoes the O'Mearas are very aware of their dangers.

 'There is always a dark side to volcanoes ... so we always respect them. When we visit volcanoes we go to the experts ... we just go up with the geologists, they know the land best ... it is when you do not respect the volcano ... if you have no fear ... that's when you'll die.'

 'But even then, every year photographers, journalists, vulcanologists, geologists ... who know these volcanoes very well, die, ... their sheer unpredictability is always a factor ...'

basalt floods

BASALT FLOODS ARE THE MOST SPECTACULAR AND POSSIBLY THE MOST DEADLY OF ALL LAVA ERUPTIONS. MODERATE ONLY IN TERMS OF THEIR LOW LEVEL OF EXPLOSIVITY, VAST QUANTITIES OF HOT, FLUID BASALTS GUSH OUT FROM LONG FISSURES, FORMING SHEETS THAT MOVE SO FAST THEY CAN TRAVEL 150KM (93 MILES) BEFORE THEY STOP AND SOLIDIFY. THE COLUMBIA VOLCANIC PLATEAU OF OREGON AND WASHINGTON HAVE INDIVIDUAL FLOWS COVERING 1,000KM² (386 SQUARE MILES) AND THEY FLOODED A TOTAL AREA OF 130,000KM² (50,000 SQUARE MILES) ABOUT 12 MILLION YEARS AGO. THE ROZA ERUPTION IN OREGON WAS ONE OF THE MIGHTIEST, DISCHARGING BASALT AT OVER 1 MILLION M³ (35.3 MILLION FT³) PER SECOND.

lava-flows

earlier flows

fissures

A fissure eruption of highly fluid basalt. Lava forms layers rather than building volcanic cones

Even the outpourings of the Columbia Plateau (see right) were dwarfed by the eruptions that formed the Deccan Plateau in India, about 65 million years ago. These lava-flows cover 500,000km² (193,000 square miles). Many scientists believe that these eruptions shut out the sunlight and produced poisonous gases that between them killed off the dinosaurs. There are similar vast basaltic plateaux in the Karoo of South Africa, central Siberia and southern Brazil. There are also smaller basaltic plateaux in Northern Ireland and in the Isle of Skye in western Scotland. Luckily, there have been no remotely comparable basaltic floods since the evolution of man. It is not clear what exactly caused these

outpourings in the geological past, so predicting the next one is indeed hazardous. It would, however, be extremely difficult to run away from liquid basalts gushing out at a rate of 5km³ (1¼ cubic miles) an hour, especially if they were also producing huge quantities of noxious gases. This is the only type of basaltic eruption that is really to be feared on a world scale. It is just as well that so far there are no signs of another.

Death of the dinosaurs

About 65 million years ago, a cataclysmic event killed off many different species, both on land and at sea. It was so widespread and significant that it is recognized as marking the end of the

Secondary and the beginning of the Tertiary Era. Although scientists have resisted attributing this to a single, abrupt event, evidence suggests that, by geological standards, it took place within a relatively short period of time.

Some scientists believe that a huge meteorite hit the Earth, its impact scattering rock fragments over such a wide area that a freezing darkness persisted until many species starved or died of cold. The geological beds laid down at this time apparently support this theory as they are rich in particles of the metal iridium, common in meteorites, but usually very rare on Earth. A possible culprit could be the large meteorite that formed the huge Chicxulub crater on the edge of the Yucatán Peninsula in Mexico. This meteorite was perhaps 10km (6¼ miles) across. Its impact made a crater 200km (124 miles) in diameter and released energy equivalent to a million eruptions of Mount St Helens in 1980. In addition, tests have also shown that this particular meteorite did hit the Earth 65 million years ago.

Other scientists have proposed that eruptions of the flood basalts forming the Deccan Plateau in India caused the demise of the dinosaurs and their companions. Like all volcanic rocks the Deccan basalts were magnetized at the time they were created (see pp.18–19). At this time the Earth was experiencing magnetic reversals once or twice every million years. The vast volume of the Deccan basalts only registers two changes of magnetic polarity, so, they must have all erupted within less than a million years. It is possible that the eruptions were not continuous throughout that period but it is a fact that between 10–100km³ (2½–24 cubic miles) of basalt gushed onto the continental mass of India each year. The lavas have also been dated and results show that they are also 65 million years old. The cause of this volcanic outburst seems to have been the sudden development of a hotspot under part of the Indian plate.

The noxious quality of these basalt flows lies in their gas content. The lavas were abnormally rich in sulphur dioxide and carbon dioxide, which together would form sulphuric acid,

thereby killing the vegetation upon which the dinosaurs depended. The carbon dioxide would have spread far enough to kill animals in nearby valleys but could also have had a profound effect on the cycle that delivers carbon dioxide to marine sediments. Hence many marine species would have suffered just as much as those on land. Scientists have also discovered that hotspot volcanoes such as Réunion in the Indian Ocean, also give off iridium, and that it is not just present in meteorites.

Therefore, although there is evidence to support either theory, no direct link has yet been demonstrated between the death of the dinosaurs and the impact of the Chicxulub meteorite or the Deccan eruption.

Basalt flood lavas at Columbia Volcanic Plateau, Picture Gorge, Oregon, United States

vigorous eruptions

VIGOROUS ERUPTIONS ARE MORE EXPLOSIVE THAN MODERATE ERUPTIONS AS THEY OFTEN CONTAIN A STRONG ELEMENT OF GAS OR STEAM, PRODUCED WHEN MAGMA COMES INTO CONTACT WITH WATER, EITHER ON THE SURFACE OR UNDERGROUND. THE AMOUNT OF WATER AND THE SITE OF THE EXPLOSIONS DETERMINE THE ERUPTION STYLE. MOST TYPES OF MAGMA INVOLVED ARE BASALTIC, AND THE CONFLICT WITH WATER GIVES THEM FAR MORE VIGOUR THAN THEY WOULD OTHERWISE ACHIEVE. WITHOUT WATER THEY WOULD PRODUCE MODERATE, USUALLY STROMBOLIAN, ACTIVITY. VULCANIAN ERUPTIONS BELONG TO THIS VIGOROUS GROUP, BUT THEIR EXPLOSIONS MAINLY OCCUR WHEN GASES ESCAPE FROM RISING MAGMAS THAT ARE VISCOUS AND SILICIC.

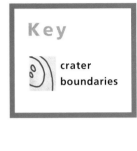

Key

crater boundaries

Vulcanello

Porto di Levante

Forgia Vecchia

Fossa

Pietre Cotte

Gran Cratere

Caldera del Piano

South Vulcano

volcanoes

ocean

tuffs

A Surtseyan eruption. Fragments known as tuffs are expelled by repeated explosions caused when magma rises into water less than 100m (328ft) deep

All vigorous eruptions produce cones and blankets of finely-shattered fragments. Lava-flows are small and usually rare; if they occur at all, it is towards the end of the vigorous activity. The main threat from vigorous eruptions comes from falling ash and larger fragments. Vigorous eruptions can be alarming, as the explosions they produce are loud and abrupt, but they pose little danger to those more than 2km (1¼ miles) away.

Vulcanian eruptions

Vulcanian eruptions are named after the activity of Fossa cone at Vulcano in the Aeolian Islands off Sicily. The Ancient Romans believed that Vulcano was the site of the forges of Vulcan, armourer to the Gods. The eruptions start suddenly: quick successions of explosions shatter new magma and old fragments of the volcano and shoot them from the chimney as if they had been fired from a gun. The noise is deafening. A black cloud of ash and steam rises 5km (3 miles) into the air. Volcanic fragments rain down on and around the cone. Several days of these explosions can be followed by several days of total calm until the eruptive spasm is over. Vulcano last erupted between 2 August 1888 and 22 March 1890 and Arenal, in Costa Rica, produced a Vulcanian eruption in 1968. Sakurajima in Japan has produced over 5,000 Vulcanian eruptions since 1955.

Vulcanian eruptions tend to produce bigger cones than their Strombolian counterparts, often 500m (1,640ft) high and about 2km (1¼ miles) across. Craters are large and deep. If they produce lava-flows they are often remarkably viscous.

Surtseyan eruptions

Surtseyan eruptions are named after Surtsey, the island that formed in the sea off the coast of Iceland between 1963 and 1967. They occur when basaltic magmas rise into areas of shallow water less than 100m (328ft) deep, and are thus quite common in coasts surrounding volcanic areas, such as Iceland, the Azores and Hawaii. Hot basalt at 1200°C that meets water at less than 20°C, suddenly produces steam that expands rapidly, shatters the magma into fine fragments, and fires them out in pointed jets of black fragments. The explosions are repeated every minute or so for several months at least. Each explosion expels a thin layer of fine fragments called tuffs, that accumulate in a tuff-cone, that can reach 500m (1,640ft) in height. Billowing clouds of ash and steam also rise in a column 5km (3 miles) above the crater. Sometimes this column collapses and surges out from the volcano like the collar around the base of a nuclear explosion. Like Vulcanian eruptions, Surtseyan activity is less dangerous than it first appears, and presents no threat (except from wind-blown ash) at distances of over 2km (1¼ miles). But the eruptions are disconcerting: the water appears to explode and looks as if it is 'on fire'.

The tuff-cones are fragile and a few days of Atlantic storms, for instance, can sweep them away. This is what happened to Sabrina tuff-cone that formed off São Miguel, in the Azores, in 1811. When the tuffs accumulate in such quantity that water can no longer reach the magma in the chimney, the eruptions change to the Strombolian style. The Strombolian lava-flows that emerge form an armour-plate around the cone, and often create an apron that protects the cone from attack by waves. This change is what saved Surtsey from destruction on 4 April 1964.

The crater of Vulcano looking towards two of the other Aeolian islands, Lipari and Salina

A fumerole on Vulcano. Yellow sulphur produced by the volcano can be seen in the foreground

the eruption of Surtsey

ERUPTIONS REPEATED OVER MILLIONS OF YEARS PRODUCED THE MID-ATLANTIC RIDGE AND FORMED ICELAND. THE RIDGE CONTINUES SOUTH-WEST OF ICELAND, AS A SHALLOW VOLCANIC PLATFORM, WHERE WEAKER ACTIVITY HAS CREATED THE SMALL AND SCATTERED VESTMANN ISLANDS JUST ABOVE SEA-LEVEL. THEY HAD BEEN QUIET FOR AT LEAST A THOUSAND YEARS WHEN, SUDDENLY, OUT OF A GREY NOVEMBER DAWN, AN ERUPTION STARTED TO CREATE AN ENTIRELY NEW ISLAND. IT MADE A FASCINATING NEW WORLD FOR THE EXPERTS TO STUDY AND A WONDERFUL SPECTACLE FOR EVERYBODY TO ADMIRE. THEY CALLED IT SURTSEY, AFTER THE NORSE GIANT SURTUR, WHO HAD FOUGHT FREYR, THE GOD OF FERTILITY AND PROSPERITY, IN THE BATTLE BEFORE THE END OF THE WORLD.

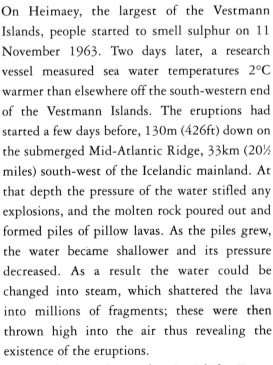

Reykjavik •

▲ Hekla

Atlantic Ocean

Myrdalsjökull

Heimaey • Vestmannaeyjar

Surtsey

On Heimaey, the largest of the Vestmann Islands, people started to smell sulphur on 11 November 1963. Two days later, a research vessel measured sea water temperatures 2°C warmer than elsewhere off the south-western end of the Vestmann Islands. The eruptions had started a few days before, 130m (426ft) down on the submerged Mid-Atlantic Ridge, 33km (20½ miles) south-west of the Icelandic mainland. At that depth the pressure of the water stifled any explosions, and the molten rock poured out and formed piles of pillow lavas. As the piles grew, the water became shallower and its pressure decreased. As a result the water could be changed into steam, which shattered the lava into millions of fragments; these were then thrown high into the air thus revealing the existence of the eruptions.

On 14 November 1963, the *Isleifur II* was fishing south-west of the Vestmann Islands. Ólafur Vestmann, the cook, was on watch. At 07.15, he felt the ship swirl and roll, and, peering into the dawn half-light, he saw dark smoke rising out of the sea about 1,500m (4,900ft) away. He awoke Captain Tómasson. Both thought another vessel was on fire, but radio enquiries revealed that there had been no S.O.S. signals. Captain Tómasson grabbed his binoculars and saw black columns erupting from the sea. He called the radio post on Heimaey to report that an eruption seemed to have started. For the next few hours, the captain sailed the *Isleifur II* around the growing eruption. At 08.00 the columns of ash and steam were 70m (230ft) high and, by 10.30, explosions every 30 secs sent columns 400m (1,312ft) skywards. The temperature of the sea nearby rose to 12°C — about 5°C above normal.

Soon explosions every few seconds were firing out shattered lava fragments in curved black plumes like a cockerel's tail. By the next morning they had piled up into an island 10m (33ft) high, which quickly increased in size. At first the eruptions came from a fissure, 500m (1,640ft) long, but then they concentrated on one spot and formed the crater and cone called

'The eruption was most vigorously active, the eruption column rushing continuously upwards.' Icelandic geologist, Sigurdur Thorarinsson, on the eruption of Surtsey in 1964

Once the eruption began the island grew quickly: within 24 hours the lava fragments contained within the plumes of smoke and ash had piled up to a height of 10m (33ft)

Surtur I. Even the experienced Icelandic geologist, Sigurdur Thorarinsson, was enthralled by the sight: 'The volcano was most vigorously active, the eruption column rushing ... upwards, and, when darkness fell, it was a pillar of fire and the entire cone was aglow with bombs which rolled down the slopes into the white surf around the island. Flashes of lightning lit up the eruption cloud and peals of thunder cracked above our heads. The din from the thunderbolts, the rumble from the eruption cloud, and the bangs resulting from bombs crashing into the sea produced a most impressive symphony ...'

Eruptions went on with the same vigour for some weeks. On 6 December, three Frenchmen made the first landing on Surtsey, to take photographs for *Paris Match*, but the volcano drove them back after 15 mins. Some Vestmann islanders landed on 13 December in an attempt to name the island Vesturey (West Island). Sigurdur Thorarinsson and another scientist landed on 16 December and collected lava samples that proved to be basalts just like those of Katla on the mainland nearby.

The new island needed the protection of solid lava-flows if it were to survive the attacking waves. These flows could only erupt, however, if the fragments piled up so thickly that the sea could no longer flood into the chimney. The Surtseyan eruption would thereby lose its character and become a Strombolian eruption. But the sea was fighting back all the time, eroding a cliff all around the accumulating cone of tuff fragments, and spreading them in a beach, 150m (490ft) wide at its base. On 29 December 1963, Surtsey started also erupting from a subsidiary chimney, 2km (1¼ miles) to the north-east. Activity went on until 6 January 1964, but never succeeded in building an island.

Then the eruptions on Surtsey abandoned their original chimney and broke out from another, just to the north-west, on 1 February 1964. Surtur Junior, as it was called, quickly built up another cone, alongside the first, that was 180m (590ft) high by the end of March. The waves found it harder and harder to penetrate into the new chimney. On 4 April, a lava lake welled up in the crater of Surtur Junior, lava fountains spurted 50m (164ft) into the air, and lava flows ran along the beach. These Strombolian eruptions gave Surtsey just the armour-plating that it needed to survive the onslaught of the Atlantic waves. Thereafter, activity continued on and off, until July 1967.

Meanwhile on 5 June 1965, another chimney began to erupt in the sea, 500m (1,640ft) north-west of Surtsey, forming an island called Syrtlingur. Throughout the summer, Surtseyan

Strombolian lava flows prevented Surtsey from being washed away by the powerful Atlantic seas

eruptions piled up fragments, and the Atlantic waves washed them away again. Syrtlingur reached its maximum height of 65m (213ft) on 15 September. It was last seen on 17 October 1965 before a week of bad weather. When it finally calmed on 24 October, the eruption had stopped, and Syrtlingur had vanished.

Another subsidiary chimney also started erupting on 28 December 1965, 500m (1,640ft) south-west of Surtsey, forming an islet called Jolnir. Jolnir lasted a little longer than Syrtlingur, and disappeared on 20 September 1966. Neither Jolnir nor Syrtlingur produced enough fragments to stop the sea entering the chimney, and therefore could erupt no lava-flows to defend them against the waves. Rapid creation and subsequent sea erosion characterizes most islands formed by Surtseyan eruptions. Surtsey itself only survived because it adopted a different style of eruption.

steam-blast and volcanic gas eruptions

THE TWO FINAL CATEGORIES OF VIGOROUS ERUPTIONS ARE VERY DIFFERENT IN TERMS OF THE THREATS THAT THEY POSE. STEAM-BLAST ERUPTIONS PRODUCE SCARS IN THE LANDSCAPE BUT ARE SHORT-LIVED AND POSE RELATIVELY LITTLE DANGER IN THEMSELVES. VOLCANIC GAS, ON THE OTHER HAND, CAN BE DEADLY AND CAN ESCAPE PRACTICALLY UNNOTICED.

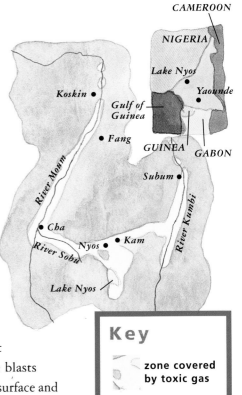

Steam-blast eruptions

Steam-blast or phreatic eruptions on land are broadly similar to Surtseyan eruptions, but much less water is available, and the explosive contact with the hot magma takes place in a confined space about 250m (820ft) underground. Water usually infiltrates the rocks from surface streams or melting ice and snow. Several big blasts will quickly exhaust such a water supply, and so steam-blast eruptions may last just a day, or even less than an hour. The blasts can, however, be vicious enough to blow huge holes in the landsurface and shoot fragments of rock for a distance of 5km (3 miles). Two such holes, Big Hole and Hole-in-the-Ground, in Oregon, United States, are still dry, but they soon fill with water in humid areas and form distinctive circular lakes. The most famous are the *maars* (*meers*) of the Eifel area in western Germany, and there are many more in central France.

Similar eruptions occur when magma is rising into large explosive volcanoes, where they often offer preliminary warnings of more violent activity. One of their major distinguishing characteristics is that the fragments expelled are cold because they are shattered from old rock, not from new magma. Such eruptions went on for almost a year before new magma reached the surface at Nevado del Ruiz on 13 November 1985, and they continued for two months at Mount St Helens from 27 March to 18 May 1980. Individual eruptions in this style produce limited threats because they are confined to a short time and a small space.

Volcanic gas eruptions

Volcanic gas escapes from most eruptions and plays an essential role in explosions. But it is nearly always accompanied by lava-flows or fragments or both. Thus the sulphur dioxide and fluorine expelled from Laki in 1783–84 were almost a by-product of the great lava-flows, although they indirectly caused huge losses of human and animal life.

Eruptions of volcanic gas alone are very rare; in fact, many scientists do not believe that they are produced directly by eruptions. They happen absolutely without warning and release lethal volumes of

Key

zone covered by toxic gas

Lake Nyos where gas killed 1,700 people in 1986

invisible carbon dioxide. Since it was first identified in 1979 this type of eruption has caused more deaths than all other forms of vigorous eruption combined.

On 20 February 1979 on the Diëng Plateau in central Java, a sudden explosion of carbon dioxide from a dry crater killed 142 people. In Cameroon on 15 August 1984 carbon dioxide exploded from Lake Monoun causing 37 deaths. Neither eruption created much scientific interest. A third case, at Lake Nyos, Cameroon, in 1986, produced great controversy about the origin of the gas. Some scientists thought that the gas had gradually accumulated on the floor of the lake where it had remained trapped by dense layers of water until a landslide, earthquake or heavy rainfall had disturbed the layers, releasing the gas. Others believed that the gas was produced by a volcanic eruption.

The gas eruption from Lake Nyos, Cameroon

Lake Nyos is one of many lakes in the North-west Province of Cameroon that have been formed by steam-blast explosions. On 19 August 1986, a local healer became suspicious when herb leaves turned red near the lake, perhaps because some gas had escaped. At 16.00 on 21 August, some herdsmen heard the lake gurgling, and some strange bangs were audible between 21.30 and 22.00. About 20.30 Mr Malanjaï saw water begin to shoot upwards making sounds like gunshots. A cloud of water droplets and carbon dioxide covered his house, 120m (394ft) above the lake, at about 22.00. It gave him a headache and his children fell down as they tried to leave the house. Kalus Keituh in Upper Nyos village saw the water quickly spurt up and change colour from red to white. The cloud covered the house of his neighbour Mr Pakalé, about 100m (328ft) above the lake, killing one of his children and all his cows. Next morning it became clear that about 600 of the 606 inhabitants of Nyos village had been gassed.

About 1km³ (¼ cubic mile) of concentrated, almost pure carbon dioxide spread northwards from Lake Nyos about 23.30 on 21 August 1986. As the gas is denser than air, it moved along the ground in a long cloud about 40m (131ft) thick, travelling at 20–50km/h (12½–31mph). Human beings are asphyxiated if they breathe air containing more than 20–30 per cent carbon dioxide for more than 10 mins. The gas did not mix readily with the air and the cloud kept its lethal concentrations until it had spread 23km (14 miles) from the lake. Many people in villages in this area were also killed.

Many people in Nyos village died in their beds. Others tried to escape before they were overcome by fumes. The small number of survivors said that they had smelt something similar to rotten eggs (hydrogen sulphide) or gunpowder (sulphur dioxide). Both gases would only have come from a volcanic eruption.

Steam-blast or phreatic eruptions produced by the south-eastern crater of Etna, Sicily, during 1971

violent eruptions

VIOLENT ERUPTIONS ARE USUALLY PRODUCED BY LARGE, ACTIVE VOLCANOES. ALMOST ALL OF THESE VOLCANOES ARE MORE THAN 10,000 YEARS OLD AND MANY ARE OVER 1 MILLION YEARS OLD. THE MAJORITY HAVE GROWN UP OVER SUBDUCTION ZONES, WHICH IS WHY SO MANY OF THEM FORM THE IMPRESSIVE 'RING OF FIRE' THAT SURROUNDS THE PACIFIC OCEAN. THESE ERUPTIONS ARE FAR FROM CONTINUOUS, AND MANY OF THESE VOLCANOES ARE DORMANT FOR MOST OF THEIR ACTIVE LIVES, UNTIL SPORADICALLY, AND DRAMATICALLY, THEY BURST INTO ACTION.

Violent volcanic activity is generally short-lived but is always highly destructive. Among the weapons at its disposal are ash clouds, nuées ardentes, mudflows, landslides, tsunamis and climatic changes. Due to the difficulties of studying such eruptions at close range their behaviour tends to be categorized according to the types of deposits that are left behind. The repetition of huge and violent eruptions over thousands of years creates large structures called strato-volcanoes, so-called because they are composed of many layers of material.

Ash and pumice floods

Ash and pumice floods are vast and rare, and lie on the boundary between vigorous and violent eruptions. Nobody has seen them happening, which is fortunate because they are wide-spreading and very fast-moving. They are composed mainly of rhyolite, and apparently emerge as fine, frothy, ashy, pumice, like milk boiling over from a pan at 700km/h (435 mph). At Yellowstone Park, USA and Taupo in New Zealand, they have volumes of 3,000km³ (720 cubic miles) and have blanketed nearly 20,000km² (7,700 square miles). Ash and pumice floods spread so quickly that they

occasionally trap masses of fossils: the 20 million year-old flood in Oregon, called the John Day Formation, has proved to be a paleontologist's treasure trove.

Only one ash and pumice flood has been recorded in recent times. It happened unobserved at the foot of Katmaï volcano in an unpopulated area of Alaska on 6 June 1912. Although it was relatively small, it was nevertheless one of the biggest eruptions of the

key features

**Blasts and debris avalanches
are characterized by:**

◆ **highly powerful blasts**
◆ **ash clouds**
◆ **landslides**
◆ **shattered rock**
◆ **hummocky land**
◆ **huge volcanic craters left by
   landslides**

20th Century. About 35km³ (8½ cubic miles) of pumice, 200m (656ft) thick, covered the Ukak valley within 60 hours. Those who first saw it many months later called it 'The Valley of 10,000 Smokes', because the entire surface of the flood emitted wispy columns of gas and steam.

Blasts and debris avalanches

Blasts and debris avalanches have only just been fully recognized. In June 1956, a blast blew off the top of Bezymianny, and deposited an apron, covering 100km², (39 square miles) at its base. Although there had been months of preliminary eruptions, the blast occurred in the remote, inhospitable and inaccessible Kamchatka Peninsula off eastern Siberia. The volcano was hardly known (in fact its name means 'no name') and no-one was killed by the blast.

Then, on 18 May 1980, the same thing – but on a smaller scale – happened at Mount St Helens. Specialists had closely followed the volcano's two months of preliminary activity when journalists and television crews had often joined thousands of visitors. The climactic moment was actually photographed, but sadly 57 people were killed, including the geologist monitoring events that day. The blast blew off the crest and north flank of Mount St Helens and spread 3km³ (¾ cubic mile) of the volcano in a debris avalanche that covered 60km² (23 square miles) at its feet. Mount St Helens became world-famous, and has been studied every day since the eruption. Specialists have now found evidence of previously unsuspected blasts and debris avalanches on more than 150 other strato-volcanoes.

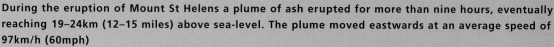

During the eruption of Mount St Helens a plume of ash erupted for more than nine hours, eventually reaching 19–24km (12–15 miles) above sea-level. The plume moved eastwards at an average speed of 97km/h (60mph)

the eruption of Mount St Helens

IN WASHINGTON STATE, NATIVE AMERICAN LEGEND TELLS
OF AN UGLY OLD WOMAN CALLED TAH-ONE-LAT-CLAH ('FIRE
MOUNTAIN') WHO LIVED IN THE CASCADE RANGE. ONE DAY
THE SPIRIT GOD TURNED HER INTO A BEAUTIFUL VIRGIN, AND
TWO GREAT WARRIORS, WYEAST AND PAHTO, SOON BEGAN TO
COMPETE FOR HER AFFECTIONS. SHE WAS UNABLE TO CHOOSE
BETWEEN THEM, AND THE WARRIORS BEGAN A DUEL, HURLING FIRE,
LIGHTNING, AND BURNING ROCKS AT EACH OTHER SO FIERCELY THAT
THE EARTH SHOOK, THE SUN WAS BLACKED OUT, AND THE PEOPLE WERE
TERRIFIED. THE SPIRIT GOD WAS SO DISGUSTED BY SUCH BEHAVIOUR THAT HE
TURNED ALL THREE INTO MOUNTAINS NEAR
THE RIVER COLUMBIA VALLEY: WYEAST
BECAME MOUNT HOOD, PAHTO BECAME
MOUNT ADAMS AND TAH-ONE-LAT-CLAH
BECAME MOUNT ST HELENS.

Geologists have discovered that Mount St
Helens is younger and more violent than any
large volcano in the Cascade Range. It is only
30,000 years old, and it erupts violently about
once every 3,000–4,000 years. In 1975, the
geologists D.R. Crandell and D.R. Mullineaux
declared that Mount St Helens could well erupt
before the end of the present century. The
beautiful virgin was turned back into an old
woman on 18 May 1980.

Mount St Helens issued warnings for two
months. Small earthquakes centred just under
the volcano began at 15.37 on 20 March 1980.
On 25 March the volcano was closed to climbers.

Mount St Helens is the smallest of five major vol[c]
peaks in the Cascade Range. It measured 2,950m
(9,678ft) before the eruption in 1980

On 26 March an emergency co-ordination centre was set up at Vancouver, Washington. At 12.36 on 27
March the first gas-blast, phreatic eruption exploded cold black ash 3km (1¾ miles) into the air.
Residents and forestry loggers were evacuated from the mountain area and roadblocks were placed
around a restricted zone. It was also on 27 March that the northern sector of the cone began to bulge
outwards. Geologists began to monitor the mountain.

By the beginning of April, and especially at weekends, the whole area swarmed with visitors. The
eruptions continued, with spectators buying bags full of ash. Then the eruptions stopped between 22

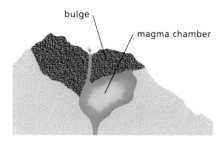

bulge / magma chamber

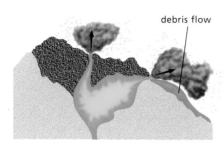

debris flow

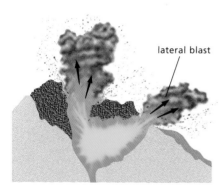

lateral blast

The eruption of Mount St Helens. 1. Bulge on north side of mountain, 90m (295ft). 2. Magnitude 5.0 earthquake dislodges weakened rocks of north face causing huge landslide. 3. Pressure of carbon dioxide and water that has been building up over a period of months is finally released producing a lateral blast which blows out the north face of the mountain

As well as the main blast that took place on 18 May other eruptions followed. This one happened on 22 July, sending pumice and ash 10–18km (6¼–11 miles) into the air, and was visible 160km (100 miles) away in Seattle

April and 7 May, but the earthquakes went on, and the north flank continued to swell alarmingly at a rate of 1.5m (5ft) a day. On 30 April, Governor Dixy Lee Ray of Washington State established a Red Zone, ranging from 5–13km (3–8 miles) around the volcano that was prohibited to all except appropriate scientists and officials. The Geological Survey moved its chief observation post to a new site, Coldwater II, 9km (5½ miles) from the volcano.

Meanwhile Harry Truman, 83, owner of 16 cats, refused to leave his Mount St Helens Lodge on Spirit Lake, north of the volcano. 'This damn mountain won't ever do me any harm. In any case, if it explodes, well then, I'll go up with it'. One local geologist thought that the Coldwater II observation post was badly placed, facing onto the bulging flank. 'It was like looking down the barrel of a loaded gun.'

Mount St Helens started erupting again on 7 May and the earthquakes and bulging continued. Then, on 14 May, the eruptions stopped again; earthquakes fell to their lowest levels for a month; and the rate of bulging stopped increasing.

Events over the next few days happened as follows:

15 May: bulging rate constant; fewer earthquakes; no eruptions.
16 May: bulging rate constant; fewer earthquakes; no eruptions. Scout leaders allowed to remove equipment from camps in restricted zone. Evacuated home-owners also granted permission to retrieve belongings after a protest.
17 May: bulging rate constant; fewer earthquakes; no eruptions. 30 car-loads of home-owners go in a police-escorted convoy to salvage belongings from their houses. Geologist David Johnston is on duty at Coldwater II observation point.
18 May: beautiful, cloudless morning; bulging rate constant; few earthquakes; no eruptions ... until 08.32.

At 08.32 on 18 May 1980, a magnitude 5.0 earthquake destabilized the bulging north flank of the volcano, and 3km³ (¾ cubic mile) of it shuddered and collapsed in a debris avalanche landslide that hurtled northwards at 250km/h (155mph). In an instant it buried Harry Truman, his lodge and his cats. Within a second the exposed magma exploded. The blast shot outwards and downwards at speeds approaching 500km/h (311mph) and burnt and devastated 600km² (232 square miles) within two minutes. David Johnston at Coldwater II just had time to radio his base at Vancouver: 'This is it! This is it!' Those were the last words he uttered. The blast knocked down the conifers on the nearby hills as if they were matchsticks. The explosions

Sunset over the eruption of 22 July 1980, three months after the main blast

This car was caught in the mudflow 16km (10 miles) north of the volcano

More than 200 homes and over 300km (186 miles) of roads were destroyed by mudflows during 1980

The mudflows engulfed everything in their path. These mailboxes were situated near the Cowlitz River

Clearing-up operations began soon after the eruption. This photograph was taken about 16km (10 miles) north of Mount St Helens

pulverized the magma into dust, hot ash, steam, gas and pumice that soared skywards in a roaring, billowing column that reached a height of 25km (15½ miles) within 15 mins. At Bear Meadow, 17km (10½ miles) from the volcano, Gary Rosenquist and Keith Ronnholm took some of the most dramatic pictures ever filmed and then drove off to safety as fast as they dared.

Meanwhile, the column went roaring into the stratosphere. The upper winds began to transport the fine ash and dust earthwards, darkening the sky, clogging car engines, spoiling the Lilac Festival 430km (267 miles) away at Spokane, making breathing difficult and causing cars to skid. Three days later, the ash had spread over New York, and had completed its first world tour before the end of May 1980.

About noon, a series of incandescent clouds, or nuées ardentes, comprising hot ash, steam and gas, spurted northwards from the gaping crater that had been left by the debris avalanche. On the fringes of the scorched and devastated area, waters from rivers and several lakes, and melted snow and ice combined with the debris avalanche, the incandescent clouds, and forest trees to form mudflows that charged down the River Toutle valley that afternoon. The bridge taking the Interstate 5, the main west-coast road across the River Toutle, only just held out as the mudflow threw lorries, twisted bridge segments and shattered wooden houses against its supports.

When the eruption calmed down at about 17.30 on 18 May, Mount St Helens had lost 400m (1,312ft) from its crest and in its place was a fuming horse-shoe-shaped hole 3.2km (2 miles) long, 1.6km (1 mile) across and 700m (2,297 ft) deep. Mount St Helens had released energy equal to 27,000 nuclear bombs of the type dropped on Hiroshima in 1945. About 57 people died, 250 homes, seven bridges and 300km (186 miles) of roads were destroyed completely. Some of the local wildlife had a miraculous escape. Snow protected the lee-sides of the more distant ridges, and the snow melted, seedlings and sapling trees, frogs, mice and beavers emerged as if nothing had happened!

INTERVIEW

MOUNT ST HELENS, 1980

Sue Ruff-Nelson

On the morning of 18 May 1980 Sue Ruff-Nelson was camping with some friends about 19km (12 miles) from the volcano. She and her boyfriend Bruce were making coffee, their friend Terry was fishing while his girlfriend Karen was still in bed.

 'Terry ... lost the fish and came up to replace his line ... he looked up and saw a small black cloud on the horizon and said there must be a forest fire ... and then

A detail of the ash cloud produced by the eruption of Mount St Helens on 18 May 1980

within 30 seconds it was huge and filled the whole horizon, and then it just kept getting bigger and bigger, and coming at us faster and faster, and it was dark and black ...'

The sound of the eruption was not audible to those in the immediate vicinity of the volcano, although it was heard 322km (200 miles) away in Canada. The cloud of ash was the first indication to Sue and her friends that something had happened.

 'It wasn't like a smoke cloud, it was like a boiling, moving, solid thing that had ... stuff shooting out of it ... it was alive and it was massive and dense ... and it was very black ... and there was no noise, it was the strangest thing, it was totally silent really, until it got down onto the canyon where we were and then there was a huge roaring ... you could hear the limbs on the trees creaking and the trees themselves moving back and forth ... I remember looking at the fire and the wind just blew the flames out low along the ground, and watching the handle of my coffee pot just kind of melt in the flames and then this cloud, ... it was like a wall ... solid, roaring, grinding, crashing and ... it just engulfed us.'

Sue started to run back towards Bruce and the tent but then the cloud hit them,

 '... it was a like a thump or an explosion of sound and I fell over backwards and I was covered with dirt and it was cold.'

Together Bruce and Sue fell to the ground. Bruce reached out in the darkness to touch Sue and asked if she was okay. They got up and realized

Mount St Helens and Spirit Lake were popular with tourists before the eruption, attracted by the tranquil surroundings and the natural beauty of the area

its own weather and there were streaks of lightning going horizontally across the sky instead of down to earth and the lightning was blue and pink and it was really quite pretty.'

Sue still remembers vividly what it felt like to walk through a cloud of volcanic ash:

 ... it was nearly a foot [30cm] deep in places and it was so hot underneath ... you could only stay in it for a short period of time and then we would have to get up on a stump and ... take our shoes off and dump [the ash] out and unroll our pants and ... within a few minutes it would be filled up ... like slogging through a huge field of talcum powder and it just smelled terrible ... it was the smell of rotten eggs.'

that there were trees all around them: they had fallen down into a hole left by the roots of a tree which was then covered over by other falling trees. Bruce started to climb out of the hole but was driven back by the heat. They waited until the air had cooled slightly and then tried again. Sue was met by a scene of total devastation.

 'It was completely destroyed. There were maybe a few trees standing, but halfway up they'd been snapped off and most of the trees were down ... it was silent ... it happened so fast ... it was too hard for us to even comprehend what had happened.'

Another ash cloud full of debris engulfed them. They tried to climb out of the valley because they were afraid that the ash contained poisonous gas from the eruption.

Bruce and Sue both survived but Terry and Karen were not so lucky. Just as the first cloud hit, Terry dived into the tent that he and Karen shared. Seconds later a tree fell on top of the tent killing them both. After a few days Bruce returned to the scene to find out what had happened to his friends.

 '... about a week later, Bruce went back in and they found them ... together, with their arms around each other, and they were dead'.

 '... it was so dark and so heavy with ash coming down that I felt we were going to asphyxiate ... so we took our shirts off and wrapped them around our head and so we couldn't see anyway, it was dark so it was like blindly climbing up and over and falling off the trees ... we started getting hit by bigger pieces and decided we'd better wait that part out and we climbed underneath a log and I remember ... the ash cloud made

After the eruption Mount St Helens was only 2,550m (8,364ft) high, with a crater 1.5km (1 mile) wide

Peléan eruptions

PELÉAN ERUPTIONS WERE ONLY FULLY APPRECIATED AFTER MONTAGNE PELÉE DESTROYED ST PIERRE, MARTINIQUE, ON 8 MAY 1902. THEY ARE A LETHAL AND DEVASTATING COMBINATION OF HOT SIDEWAYS BLASTS, NUÉES ARDENTES OR GLOWING AVALANCHES, AND LARGE LAVA DOMES. THE DORMANT VOLCANOES SHOW VIRTUALLY NO ACTIVITY FOR DECADES OR CENTURIES, THEN, FOR A FEW WARNING WEEKS, STEAM-BLAST ERUPTIONS SHATTER THE WALLS OF THE CHIMNEY, CRATER THE SUMMIT, AND SCATTER FRAGMENTS 10KM (6¼ MILES) OR MORE FROM THE VOLCANO.

nuées ardentes

lava dome

beds of lava and ash

A Peléan eruption showing the creation of a large crater by repeated steam-blast eruptions

At the same time, the viscous, silicic magma rises towards the top of the chimney where pressures upon it are much reduced. The gases in the magma quickly separate out into bubbles that push the whole mass faster upwards. Near the top of the chimney, the gases explode and blow the magma into smithereens, forming a turmoil of fragments ranging from dust and gas to blocks of the old volcanic crest. The whole mass can be as hot as 700°C when it bursts out from the chimney. Sometimes a blast of hot air, gas and fine ash shoots out directly for 10km (6¼ miles) or more. At other times, the gases and fine ash mix with much larger fragments which surge downslope under gravity at speeds of 500km/h (311mph), smashing and picking up trees, buildings, bridges, and people on the way. These are nuées ardentes – incandescent clouds or glowing avalanches – that hug the ground as they move. There is no means of diverting or avoiding them and this is why they are the most lethal of volcanic eruptions. Blasts and nuées ardentes only last for two or three minutes, but this is enough time to devastate 50km² (19 square miles), and burn everything in their path.

Almost at the same time, magma surges up the chimney forming a lava dome. Spines of glowing lava can often rise up 100m (328ft) before they weather and crumble as they solidify. The solidified dome can withstand most of the weaker gas explosions that happen as the eruption wanes. In some cases, such as Merapi in Java, the dome remains at the summit throughout most eruptions, but one sector is not

An artist's impression of the aftermath of the eruption as viewed from the French Naval vessel *Suchet*, one of the first ships to reach the stricken area

supported by the crater wall. This collapses about every two years, releasing small blasts and nuées ardentes that career down the slopes.

The eruption of Montagne Pelée

In almost 300 years since the French first settled in St Pierre, Martinique in 1635, the volcano that dominated the area, Montagne Pelée, had only had two small eruptions, in 1792 and 1851. By the beginning of the 20th Century, St Pierre had become known as the 'pearl of the West Indies', and was the commercial and intellectual centre of the island. Its buildings were made

St Pierre with the dome of Montagne Pelée visible in the background. Le Prêcheur is around the bay to the north

of stone, it had a busy port, electricity, a piped water supply, many mechanized distilleries, fine squares, a Grand Hotel, a college, a chamber of commerce, a cathedral and an elegant theatre. It was the hub of the island's wealth, earned from the production of sugar and rum, that was controlled by the French colonial administrators and plantation owners.

Early in 1902, a sickly smell of hydrogen sulphide began to spread into Le Prêcheur and to St Pierre, 7km (4½ miles) from the volcano. A minor steam-blast eruption on 24 April expelled a small amount of ash – the first real indication of renewed activity. On 27 April the mountain was calm enough for groups to climb to the summit. The crater of the Étang Sec was no longer dry, but contained a lake that looked 'like quicksilver', and a new cinder cone was producing boiling water and the fumes tarnished the visitors' silver buttons. This was also the day of the French Parliamentary elections. None of the candidates won an overall majority and so a second ballot, between the two leading candidates, was set for 11 May.

Montagne Pelée burst into action on 1 May. The next day at 23.00, terrifying explosions wakened the inhabitants of St Pierre. The first ash fell on the city since 1851, and was soon 3cm (1¼in) deep. On 3 May, Governor Mouttet arrived to visit St Pierre and Le Prêcheur. The Governor promised that the people of Le Prêcheur could shelter in the barracks in St Pierre, if conditions got worse, and many people from the slopes of Montagne Pelée had already crowded into St Pierre. One of the election candidates, Fernand Clerc, called for the evacuation of St Pierre. The mayor Raymond Fouché, however, issued a counter-call for calm, closed the schools, and ordered the firemen to hose away the ash.

Two days of relative calm followed and attention turned to the strange behaviour of the Rivière Blanche that drained from the crater rim to the coast between St Pierre and Le Prêcheur. For a week it had been flooding and drying up. On 5 May it was in full spate. At 12.45, the crater rim gave way, and the waters that had accumulated in the crater swirled into the Rivière Blanche and formed a mudflow 10m (33ft) high that rushed down the valley, threw the Guérin rum factory into the sea, and killed 23 people. The mudflow sent a small tsunami across the bay that crashed onto the Place Bertin 15 minutes later. Governor Mouttet made a second visit to St Pierre, and the day ended when ash clogged the generators, and cut off the electricity supply.

Montagne Pelée ▲

● Le Prêcheur

Morne Jacob ▲

● St Pierre

Caribbean Sea

Fort de France ●

The inhabitants of St Pierre and Le Prêcheur were becoming more and more frantic. On 6 May food supplies were provided by the Governor himself but no evacuation order was given. The same day, the mayor of St Pierre issued a poster to try and diffuse the tension, affirming that 'lava will not reach the city'. That evening, a glow from the crater lit up the eruption. Nobody realized that this showed that the molten rock had finally reached the surface. Throughout 7 May Montagne Pelée spewed ash over all north-western Martinique; in Le Prêcheur roofs began to collapse under its weight.

Finally on 7 May, the mayor of St Pierre asked the Governor to send troops to help distribute food to refugees, and patrol the city streets. Governor Mouttet arranged for them to go the following morning. He and his wife, and several senior administrators, went to spend the night in St Pierre to demonstrate his confidence in their future and calm the citizens. The Governor's Scientific Commission (apart from one member) met in St Pierre and concluded that the town was in no danger from earthquakes, landslides, or mudflows. The area's wildlife appeared not to share this opinion: reports claimed that the rats, cats, snakes and birds – even a boa constrictor from the town's Botanical Gardens – escaped and headed south.

There was a terrible thunderstorm during the night, and the rain washed the ash from St Pierre. 8 May, Ascension Day, dawned bright and sunny and, at 07.00, holiday-makers from Fort-de-France disembarked from the steamer Diamant. At 07.15 a skiff carrying Governor Mouttet and three members of the Scientific Commission left for Le Prêcheur. They were never seen again. From time to time dark clouds shot from Montagne Pelée right over St Pierre. The climax came at 08.02. It was not the most powerful eruption of the 20th Century, but it was the most deadly, killing 28,000 people.

At 08.00 the telegraph clerk at St Pierre signalled 'Go ahead' to his colleagues in Fort-de-France to start the day's work. At 08.01 (the times were calibrated on the international network) his colleague asked for the morning's news, and then at 08.02 he heard a 'short trill on the line. Then nothing more'. At the same time, a businessman was phoning a friend in St Pierre. 'He had just finished his sentence, when I heard a dreadful scream, then another much weaker groan, like a stifled death rattle. Then silence'.

A blinding flash, a tremendous blast and a violet-red nuée ardente blasted straight down to St Pierre at 500km/h (311mph). The swirling mixture of gas, steam, scalding mud, scorching ash, glowing stones and boulders, and drops of

The ruins of St Pierre. Repeated blasts and nuées ardentes flattened most of the buildings in the town

molten rock, picked up and smashed buildings, trees and huts. In St Pierre a few walls parallel to the blast stayed upright, but nearly everything else was cut down: the theatre, hotel, chamber of commerce, the college, the bank and hundreds of shops and houses. The rum distilleries blasted apart, the rum casks ignited, and soon St Pierre had become a raging inferno. The cathedral collapsed upon the Ascension Day worshippers and its dome came to rest in the sea.

It is usually said that there were only two survivors in St Pierre: a cobbler and a prisoner. This story is untrue; there were, in fact, about 70 survivors in the city, on the edges of the nuée ardente, and on boats out to sea. The cobbler,

The cover of this issue of *Petit Parisien* featured an artist's impression of a family running from an approaching nuée ardente

A prisoner named Sylbaris (or Cyparis) was being held in this cell on the morning of 8 May. He was one of only 70 survivors

Léon Compère-Léandre, found himself covered in burns and was then plunged into darkness. When daylight returned he saw the mass destruction around him and fled. The prisoner, Louis-Auguste Sylbaris (or Cyparis), had been jailed for disorderly conduct the previous day. He had been put in a stone cell, built like a bomb-shelter, in a hollow in the prison courtyard. Its only window faced away from the nuée ardente. 'All of a sudden, there was a terrifying noise', he said. 'Everybody was screaming "Help! Help! I'm burning! I'm dying!" Five minutes later nobody was crying out any more – except me'. He was rescued a few days later, badly burnt and extremely thirsty. Offshore, the nuée ardente destroyed or overturned all but one of a dozen large vessels, and smashed all the smaller craft. At sea, the survival rate was low, but better than on land, as there was slightly more warning and some people were able to rush to shelter below deck.

As far as the rest of the island and mainland France were concerned, after 08.02 St Pierre had fallen silent. A steamer set out from Fort-de-France and managed to reach St Pierre at 11.00. The city was blazing and it was impossible for the ship to land. That afternoon the steamer and a Naval vessel the *Suchet* were able to rescue the small number of burnt, incoherent survivors. At 21.55 on 8 May the captain of the *Suchet* telegraphed to the Navy Ministry in Paris. 'Back from St Pierre, city completely destroyed by mass of fire about 8 this morning. Suppose all population annihilated. Have brought back the few survivors, about thirty. All ships in roads burnt and lost. Eruption volcano continues. I am leaving for Guadeloupe to get supplies.'

During the next few days rescue operations concentrated on Le Prêcheur and the coastal villages to the north. At Le Prêcheur, a mudflow earlier that morning had already killed 400 villagers, so soon after dawn, about 400 others had climbed up to a hill south of the village to find refuge. Sadly they were then killed by the nuée ardente which missed the village by 500m (1,640ft).

For the rest of the month nuées ardentes were produced almost daily. Finally the explosive eruptions stopped and a huge dome arose in the old crater. A single spine of lava lasted for several months but it quickly weathered away when the eruption stopped in 1904.

Plinian eruptions

PLINIAN ERUPTIONS ARE NAMED AFTER PLINY THE ELDER, THE MOST FAMOUS VICTIM OF THE ERUPTION OF VESUVIUS IN AD 79, AND HIS NEPHEW PLINY THE YOUNGER, WHO DESCRIBED THE EVENT IN TWO LETTERS TO THE ROMAN HISTORIAN, TACITUS. THE MOST POWERFUL OF ALL VOLCANIC ERUPTIONS, THEY RELEASE HUGE AMOUNTS OF ENERGY, MUCH OF WHICH IS USED TO EXPEL A BILLOWING, ROARING COLUMN OF GAS, STEAM, ASH AND PUMICE FROM THE CHIMNEY INTO THE STRATOSPHERE.

This enormous, rising column is sustained by convection and incessant gas explosions for many hours. In its upper reaches, 25km (15½ miles) or more above the crater, the power wanes and the column branches out into a characteristic umbrella-pine shape. Vast areas are plunged into darkness as dust, ash and pumice rain down upon an area of as much as 500km^2 (193 square miles), choking streams, blocking roads, suffocating people and animals, destroying crops, defoliating forests and causing rooftops to collapse. Although the ash and pumice falls are dangerous, they build up gradually over several hours, and can allow time for evacuation. The most hazardous feature of a Plinian eruption is nuées ardentes.

The eruptive column may soar upwards for several hours or for as long as two or three days. From time to time its rising impetus may be checked by a decrease in the intensity of the gas explosions, or a sudden widening of the chimney. If this occurs, the column collapses and crumbles in a dark, fiery mass, and rushes down the volcano as nuées ardentes at a speed of 500km/h (311mph).

It is these nuées ardentes that often cause the greatest devastation and death-tolls in Plinian eruptions because it is impossible to escape from them. In AD 79, the column erupting from Vesuvius collapsed and generated nuées ardentes at least six times, and caused most of the deaths in Herculaneum and Pompeii. Similar nuées ardentes seared the slopes around El Chichón in Mexico on 3 April 1982 and killed over 2,000 villagers. As they are rarely observed first-hand

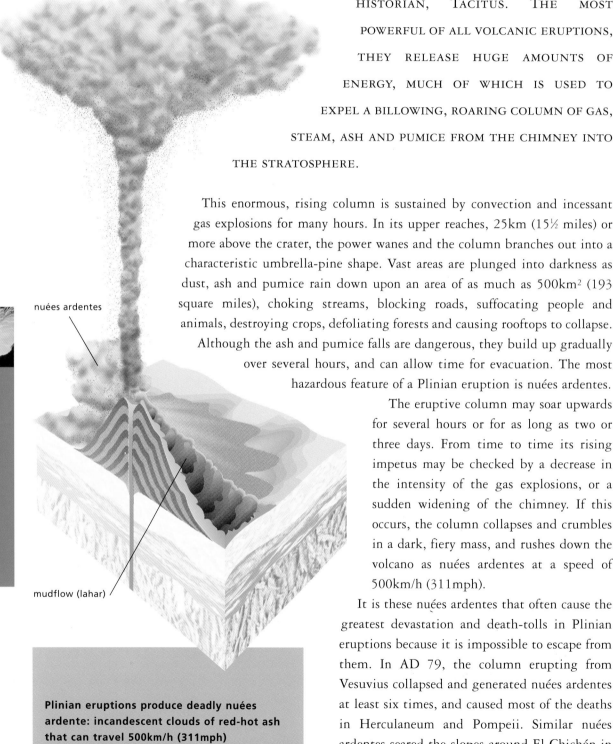

nuées ardentes

mudflow (lahar)

Plinian eruptions produce deadly nuées ardente: incandescent clouds of red-hot ash that can travel 500km/h (311mph)

'Lancaster Sands' by J.M.W. Turner, c.1816. During a tour of the north of England in 1816 Turner and his party were caught in a rain storm. Note the spectacular colours in the sky

the existence of nuées ardentes was frequently overlooked until scientists recently began to study more closely the deposits that were left behind by Plinian eruptions.

The tremendous release of energy in a Plinian eruption shakes and cracks the summit of the volcano, and the removal of huge quantities of magma from the reservoir destabilizes the whole structure. The summit can then collapse, with an enormous additional explosion, down into the spaces left behind when the magma departed. Within a few minutes, a vast fuming hole, or caldera, sinks into the old crest of the volcano which can be anything from 2–10km (1¼–6¼ miles) across. The volcano is decapitated and may lose perhaps 400m (1,312 ft) in height. Subsequently, small eruptions begin to fill the caldera with domes, cinder cones and lava-flows.

Many, but not all, Plinian eruptions expel enormous quantities of sulphur dioxide which combines with water condensed from rising steam to form sulphuric acid. The acid droplets and the finest dust particles make aerosols that

the high altitude winds blow around the world in about two weeks. They remain in the stratosphere for 2–3 years, reducing the amount of heat reaching the Earth from the sun, and causing cooler weather. Some sulphurous Plinian eruptions have reduced world temperatures by 1°C or more for about three years.

The most remarkable example of climatic effects followed the largest recorded Plinian eruption at Tambora, in Indonesia, on 10 and 11 April 1815. The eruptive column rose at least 40km (25 miles) high and about 125km³ (30 cubic miles) of fragments were expelled. The top 1,000m (3,280ft) of the volcano was blown to smithereens, and the crest was replaced with a caldera, 700m (2,296ft) deep and 6km (3¾ miles) across. The dust and acid aerosols circled the Earth for several years and reduced temperatures in 1816 so that it became known as 'the year without a summer', particularly in Europe and North America. The aerosols also produced brilliant sunsets that inspired many paintings by British artist J.M.W. Turner.

the Plinian eruption
of Vesuvius in AD 79

THE EVENT THAT GAVE PLINIAN ERUPTIONS THEIR NAME, AND VESUVIUS ITS REPUTATION, LASTED FROM 24–26 AUGUST IN AD 79. IT LAID WASTE TO MUCH OF CAMPANIA, ONE OF THE MOST DAZZLING PROVINCES IN THE ROMAN EMPIRE. NAPLES WAS ITS CHIEF CENTRE, WITH A POPULATION OF ABOUT 50,000; POMPEII WAS A BUSY COUNTRY TOWN WITH 20,000 INHABITANTS, AND HERCULANEUM, OPLONTIS, STABIAE AND PUTEOLI (POZZUOLI) WERE ALL PROSPEROUS SEA-SIDE TOWNS, EACH WITH ABOUT 5,000 INHABITANTS.

A view of the Bay of Naples with Vesuvius dominating the skyline

The most famous victim of Vesuvius was Pliny the Elder, author of a vast *Natural History*, and commander of the Imperial Roman Fleet. He was 56. His nephew, Pliny the Younger, aged 17, was staying at Cape Misenum on the north shore of the Bay of Naples with his mother when Vesuvius erupted. A number of years later, the historian, Tacitus, invited Pliny the Younger to describe his uncle's death, and his own experiences at Misenum. The two letters he wrote are the oldest surviving detailed descriptions of a volcanic eruption – and recent geological research has also shown how remarkably accurate and perceptive they were. The only regret is that they do not describe events in the cities that were destroyed.

In his first letter Pliny describes the death of his uncle:

'At that time, my uncle was at Misenum in command of the fleet. On 24 August, about one in the afternoon, my mother pointed out a cloud of an odd size and appearance that had formed [over Vesuvius] ... The cloud could best be described as more like an umbrella pine than any other tree, because it rose up high in a kind of trunk and then divided

Soldier, scholar and naturalist, Pliny the Elder, who died during the eruption in AD 79

into branches ... Sometimes it looked light-coloured, sometimes it looked mottled and dirty with the earth and ash it had carried up. Like a true scholar, my uncle saw at once that it deserved closer study and ordered a boat to be prepared.'

'[He was about to leave when he got a message from his friend Rectina, begging him to rescue her.] He changed plan and ... ordered the large galleys {quadriremes} to be launched ... He steered bravely straight for the danger zone that everyone else was leaving in fear and haste, but still kept on noting his observations.'

'The ash already falling became hotter and thicker as the ships approached the coast, and it was soon superseded by pumice and blackened burnt stones shattered by the fire. Suddenly the sea shallowed where the shore was obstructed and choked by debris from the mountain. [Instead of turning back, as the Captain advised,

he decided to push on to Stabiae, across the bay where his friend Pomponianus lived.] Pomponianus had already put his belongings into a boat to escape as soon as the contrary, onshore wind changed ... My uncle calmed and encouraged his terrified friend'.

'Meanwhile, tall, broad flames blazed from several places on Vesuvius and glared out in the darkness of the night. My uncle ... went to bed and apparently fell asleep ... but, eventually, the courtyard outside began to fill with so much ash and pumice that, if he had stayed in his room, he would never have been able to get out. He was awakened, and joined Pomponianus and his servants who had stayed up all night. They wondered whether to stay indoors or go out into the open, because the buildings were now swaying back and forth and shaking with more violent tremors ... After weighing up the risks, they chose the open country, and tied pillows with cloths over their heads for protection.'

An artist's impression of the despair of the inhabitants of Herculaneum as the ash cloud from the volcano approaches

A view of Vesuvius from the excavated ruins of the Forum at Pompeii. Much of Pompeii and the surrounding towns buried during the eruption have yet to be excavated

'It was daylight everywhere else by this time, but they were still enveloped in a darkness that was blacker and denser than any night ... My uncle went down to the shore to see if there was any chance of escape by sea, but the waves were still running far too high. He lay down to rest on a sheet, and called for drinks of cold water. Then, suddenly, flames and a strong smell of sulphur giving warning of yet more flames to come, forced the others to flee. He himself stood up, with the support of two slaves, and then suddenly collapsed and died, because, I imagine, he was suffocated when the dense fumes choked him. When daylight returned the following day, his body was found intact and uninjured, still fully clothed and looking more like a man asleep than dead.'

The eruption was one of the greatest natural catastrophes ever to inflict Imperial Rome. As well the events at Cape Misenum, thousands more died in other settlements in the area, particularly Pompeii and Herculaneum. The ash and pumice buried the cities which are now among the best-known archaeological sites in the world. Their aggressor, Vesuvius, became the most famous volcano on Earth.

When Vesuvius exploded on 24 August, it hurled a huge column of ash and pumice more than 25km (15½ miles) into the air. The northwesterly winds carried the fragments directly over Pompeii, where they soon began piling up thickly in the streets. A suffocating, pitch-black darkness engulfed the area. Many people panicked and fled, including the baker Modestus who left 81 loaves in his oven, where they remained for 1,800 years. By late evening the fates of Pompeii and nearby Oplontis appeared to be sealed, but up to that point only a sprinkling of ash had fallen on Herculaneum, upwind to the west. Its inhabitants were, however, anxious to be evacuated. Many took to their boats and others waited on the shore for help.

In fact Herculaneum was the first town to be completely destroyed. At 01.00 on 25 August, a nuée ardente raced down the western slopes of the volcano at over 100km/h (62mph). It caught those on the shore waiting to escape. They died huddled together, and were soon entombed in 20m (65ft) of ash. This is how they were discovered by excavators in 1982.

Those who had stayed in Pompeii spent a terrible night of anguish. The bejewelled mistress of the House of the Faun died when the roof collapsed under the weight of the ash and pumice which was now 2.4m (8ft) deep in the streets. The first three nuées ardentes did not enter Pompeii. At 07.30, the fourth nuée swept rooftops and upper storeys away completely, burning and suffocating everyone still sheltering in the town. The nuée ardente caught some as they struggled to escape: a slave bent double under a sack of food, a woman with her handkerchief in her mouth, two boys, holding hands, trying to protect themselves with a roof-tile, a priest clutching the treasure of a Temple of Isis, a doctor with his surgical instruments, an athlete with his bottle of body-oil, a noblewoman with her gladiator lover, and a dog on its chain. At 07.35 no-one was left alive in Pompeii. A fifth nuée completed the devastation of the town. The sixth, at 08.00, was the largest of all. It spread southwards as far as Stabiae and killed Pliny the Elder on the shore. It then spread westwards as far as Misenum where it lost its momentum, 32km (20km) away, in front of the eyes of Pliny the Younger.

Forgotten for 1,600 years, excavations began in the 18th Century, mainly for antiquities. More scientific excavations began after the unification of Italy in 1861. It was at this time that Giuseppe Fiorelli revealed the bodies of those who had died during the eruption. The fine dry ash from Vesuvius had encased the victims where they died. Over the years their bodies had decayed leaving a hollow encased by the ash. As soon as the excavators found one of these hollows, Fiorelli poured liquid plaster of Paris into it. When the plaster had set, the excavators scraped away the encasing ash to reveal a model of the victim, which often showed clearly their last expression as they tried desperately to keep the glowing ash from their eyes and lungs.

Excavations are still continuing because a quarter of Pompeii, two-thirds of Herculaneum, and nearly all of Oplontis and Stabiae, have still to be revealed.

key features

Plinian eruptions are characterized by:

- huge eruptive column
- repeated, devastating nuées ardentes travelling at speeds of up to 500km/h (311mph)
- ash and pumice falls covering wide areas
- enormous calderas created by explosions
- large-scale, wide-reaching effects
- viscous lava produced only in final stages of eruption
- dust and acid aerosols causing climatic changes

secondary effects of volcanic eruptions

VOLCANIC MUDFLOWS AND TSUNAMIS ARE THE TWO CHIEF SECONDARY EFFECTS OF VIOLENT – AND PARTICULARLY PLINIAN – ERUPTIONS.

Volcanic mudflows

Volcanic mudflows are produced when huge volumes of volcanic fragments mix with water derived from melting summit ice-caps, crater-lakes, or even torrential rainstorms, and they therefore tend to be a feature of powerful eruptions on large volcanoes. Indonesia is particularly badly affected: since 1586 eleven major mudflows have killed about 30,000 people, and the Indonesian word 'lahar' has been adopted by scientists as the term for mudflows.

Nevado del Ruiz, 1985

On 13 November 1985, the mudflows that raced from the summit of Nevado del Ruiz in Colombia killed more people than any eruption since 1902. The Plinian eruption was relatively small and the volcano, although large (5,389m (17,680ft) high), was a long way from any settlements. The mudflows produced by the eruption travelled 60km (37 miles) to the east, destroying the small agricultural town of Armero in the valley of River Magdalena, and killing 23,000 people altogether.

There was plenty of warning of the impending eruption. Volcanic earthquakes and steam-blast eruptions shook the mountain for 51 weeks before the great catastrophe, producing columns of steam and ash and scattering cool fragments as much as 10km (6¼ miles) from the summit. The crater was located on the north-eastern edge of the ice-cap, just above the valley of the River Lagunillas and its main tributary, the River Azufrado. It was clear that this would be the route a mudflow from the volcano would take, but unfortunately maps of likely threats to the area were not widely available.

In addition geologists were not able to agree over the likely extent of the area that would be affected by an eruption. Some said a large eruption would only affect an area of about 10km² (4 square miles) around the volcano. Other visiting experts, however, affirmed that a larger eruption was imminent and finally convinced local geologists of its dangers. In October, a group of Italian experts recommended that evacuation plans be prepared and safe refuges designated. Several towns drew up well-planned contingency arrangements but no refuges were set up.

The eruption finally began at 15.06 on 13 November 1985. Ash started falling on Armero at 17.00 and soon turned into muddy rain. Ruiz erupted molten fragments for the first time at 21.08. Very little molten rock erupted, but this was enough to melt one tenth of the

Ice structures such as this one around the summit of Nevado del Ruiz were melted by the eruption in 1985 causing devastating mudflows

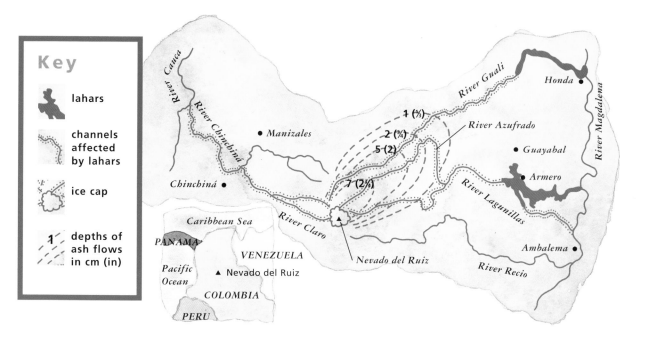

Key

- lahars
- channels affected by lahars
- ice cap
- 1 depths of ash flows in cm (in)

River Cauca
River Chinchiná
River Guali
Honda
River Magdalena
Manizales
1 (⅜)
2 (¾)
River Azufrado
5 (2)
Guayabal
Chinchiná
7 (2⅜)
Armero
River Lagunillas
River Claro
Nevado del Ruiz
Ambalema
River Recio

Caribbean Sea
PANAMA
VENEZUELA
Pacific Ocean
▲ Nevado del Ruiz
COLOMBIA
PERU

ice-cap, and form mudflows that picked up everything in their path. One of the flows raced west down the River Cauca. Immediately an order was given to evacuate Chinchiná, 50km (31 miles) downstream, but the mudflow arrived at 22.30, before the evacuation could be completed, and 1,927 people died.

The most lethal mudflow gathered impetus in the steep River Azufrado valley about 21.30. It was 30m (98ft) high and was travelling at 36km/h (22mph). This time, however, no evacuation order was given.

What happened when the mudflow finally reached Armero is unclear, but when it finally abated, it became apparent that it had damaged or destroyed two hospitals, 50 schools, 58 industrial plants, 343 commercial premises, 5,092 houses, 60 per cent of the livestock and 30 per cent of the area's rice crop. About 23,000 people and 15,000 animals died. Only 100 out of 5,000 houses in Armero remained intact, but the cemetery survived unscathed.

Arenas, the main active crater of Nevado del Ruiz

INTERVIEW

ARMERO, COLOMBIA, 1985

Dr Juan Gaitan

In November 1985 Juan Gaitan, a doctor who had been working overseas, was enjoying a vacation with his family in Armero, Colombia.

 'It was about 4.30 in the afternoon and ash started to fall ... I asked my father ... what was happening, and he explained to me ... that the Nevado del Ruiz was erupting and it was throwing ash and the wind was bringing it here. This was happening around four, five in the afternoon and it started to go dark and it started to rain, so the ash was mixing with the rain, so something like mud was forming.'

At about 20.30 Juan went to bed. He can remember the noise of the rain on the roof, part of which was made from corrugated iron. At 23.00 Juan's brother phoned to see if they knew what was happening. Shortly afterwards the lights went out and Juan, his wife, father and mother, took a torch out into the street to investigate.

 'What attracted my attention was the water that was coming down, as Armero is on an incline. The water that was passing through the street was black. Normally when it rains the water is brown ...'

They went back inside and were just lifting the living room rug to save it from flood damage when they heard something.

 'Suddenly we heard a huge noise and we turned to look at the front of the house when it shattered and at that moment something came into the house, neither hot nor cold ... then I felt something fall through the roof ... the level kept on rising, rising, rising ... forcing me against the ceiling when suddenly, I don't know how, I came through the roof of the house.'

 'At that moment ... we started going down through the town. We'd get to walls and the same pressure would knock them down ... I remember that we went past the dome of the church. I was able to see the dome of the church and calculate that it measures 20–30m [66–98ft] ... we fell on the main park of the town. We were going to crash and I remember the colour – I don't know why I remember the

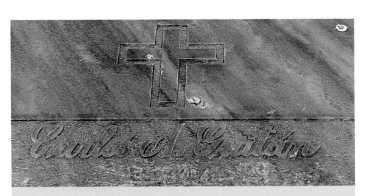

This grave is dedicated to the members of Juan Gaitan's family that died in the mudflow in 1985

colour – a grey wall ... it fell on me and I was trapped underneath ... I started to hold my breath ... I remember that something was squeezing my head ... and there came a point when I couldn't hold on any more ... I started to swallow that water ... there was some buzzing in my head and I saw some yellow stars and I lost consciousness ... In a little while I was breathing again ... we started again in that same wave that took us down through the whole town ...'

One of four views of Armero in a memorial dedicated to all those who died

During his terrifying journey down the hill Juan had been stabbed by a pole, but in spite of this, when he finally came to a standstill he began straight away to look around for some way to pull himself out.

 '... suddenly I saw the shadow of someone ... I lifted my arm and said "Here I am, help me out" ... The man pulled me and I got to where the man was, which was on a corrugated iron roof, and the man sat me down ... After a few minutes we began to talk. I asked him what his name was. He said "My name is Alfonso" and I told him "My name is Juan Gaitan ... I'm a doctor". "Yes" he said, "I know you are a doctor ... because I was a patient of yours when you were working here."'

Now he was out of the mud Juan became aware of the full extent of his injuries; the pole that had stabbed him was still embedded in his chest. Between them Juan and Alfonso managed to remove it. The deafening roar of the mud had given way to silence. Then people began to shout. Some were crying out in pain, others wanted to shout messages to loved ones, and find out the identities of those around them. Hours passed and the weather grew colder. Juan began

to throw mud on himself to try to keep warm. He also put mud inside his wound to try and stem the flow of blood. As the sun rose they became aware of the full extent of the damage.

 'As the dawn came we saw that the mountain was full of people ... We started to see around us and everything was grey, only grey ... And we could see around us that there were pieces of houses, of walls ... [I said] "Well we're sitting on what's left of Armero."'

It was many more hours before help arrived for Juan and the other survivors. Planes flew tantalizingly close but no rescuers appeared. Passers-by were too frightened to help. Many people died from their terrible injuries. Juan reflects on what it has taught him.

The memorial that houses the four views of Armero (see above left)

 'One learns to really live ... for the small things ... the real privilege of health, of your children, of the family ... these are good things that I learned from all these bad things that happened.'

tsunamis

Tsunamis are produced by violent eruptions that occur on volcanic islands or in coastal areas. Since many 'violent' volcanoes are located on or near the coast, particularly on the subduction zones around the Pacific Ocean, volcanic tsunamis can be frequent. Eruptions, however, cause only 5 per cent of all tsunamis.

The biggest and most frequent volcanic tsunamis occur when calderas and debris avalanches collapse into the sea. Those caused by nuées ardentes are smaller and less common, while mudflows and glacier-bursts produce the smallest and rarest of all. The largest tsunamis can be detected by equipment all over the world, whereas the smallest are noticed only within a localized area. The tsunami produced by Krakatau in 1883, for example, registered on tidal gauges in the English Channel, but the mudflow from Montagne Pelée caused a tsunami only 5m (16½ft) high. Volcanic tsunamis have long, imperceptible wave-lengths as they sweep across the deep oceans. In shallow water, the wave-length shortens, its height increases, and it curls over and crashes onto the shore at 80km/h (50mph) in a wall of water 30m (98ft) high.

One volcanic tsunami has been accused of destroying a civilization. The Bronze Age Minoan civilization in Crete came to an abrupt end c.1450 BC, when all but one of its palaces were destroyed. The Greek archaeologist, Marinatos, proposed that the Plinian eruption of Santorini, 125km (78 miles) to the north, was to blame. He suggested that a tsunami, generated when the great caldera collapsed, could have destroyed the palaces and towns. Although this theory initially attracted a lot of support, it became apparent that the eruption occurred about 50 years before the fall of the Cretan civilization. It also seems unlikely that a tsunami generated to the north of Crete could have destroyed palaces standing 200m (656ft) above its southern coast.

Anak Krakatau ('son of Krakatau'), the new cone that has grown up inside the water-filled caldera of Krakatau since the eruption of 1883

The eruption of Krakatau, 1883

Before it erupted, Krakatau was a small, uninhabited island, comprising three volcanoes, rising just 822m (2,697ft) out of sea. The events of 26 August, however, were shattering. The explosions were heard on Rodriguez Island, in the Indian Ocean, 4,653km (2,890 miles) away. Darkness fell for two days in southern Sumatra and western Java. Dust and acid aerosols circled the world for several years, reducing temperatures and producing brilliant sunsets and blue moons. Explosions and avalanches created a huge caldera and generated huge tsunamis which crashed onto the shores of Java and Sumatra. Falling ash and nuées ardentes

The *Berouw* was picked up by the tsunami and washed 2.6km (1½ miles) upriver in Teloeq Betoeng, southern Sumatra, killing all 28 crew members. The ship is still there today

claimed relatively few lives: most of the victims drowned 40km (25 miles) from Krakatau.

By the evening a huge column of ash and gas rose over 36km (22 miles) above Krakatau. Ash was falling thickly and explosions were shaking the ground. The first, small, tsunami (2m, 6½ft high), was recorded around 18.00. Gradually the waves became larger and began to travel further.

Monday, 27 August dawned clear. At 06.30 at Anjer, on the western coast of Java, telegraph-master Schruit was looking across the Sunda

Straits to Krakatau. Suddenly he saw 'an enormous wave … like a mountain' rushing towards the town. 'Never have I run so fast in my life … death was at my heels … I fell, utterly exhausted … and, to my amazement, I saw the wave retreating'. The tsunami destroyed practically everything below 25m (82ft) above sea-level and many thousands were drowned. Moments later, probably the same tsunami smashed onto Semangka Bay and Teloeq Betoeng in southern Sumatra. All the low-lying areas were smashed and sucked into the sea.

For the next few hours, the waves in the Straits were mountainous, whipped up by hurricane-force winds and a series of enormous explosions from Krakatau. Another great tsunami was unleashed about 10.30 in the pitch darkness on Monday morning. Again it smashed the coasts of western Java and Sumatra.

One of the survivors was a rice-grower, working in the paddy-fields 8km (5 miles) inland from Merak in western Java, at 10.30 that morning.

'We saw a great black thing, a long way off, coming towards us. It was very high … and we soon saw that it was water. Trees and houses were washed away … Not far off was some steep, sloping ground. We all ran towards it and tried to climb out of the way of the water. It was too quick for most of them, and many were drowned at my side.'

In the Sunda Straits the population was decimated. Below the great tidemarks left by the tsunamis, about 30m (98ft) high, the coastal areas were a tangle of smashed houses, trees, animal carcasses and human bodies. In Java and Sumatra, 132 villages were damaged and 165 were completely destroyed. 36,417 people were killed. Smaller waves were registered on tidal gauges as far away as Britain and America.

chapter **4**

FORECASTING

forecasting and predicting earthquakes

MAKING SHORT-TERM PREDICTIONS STEMS FROM LONG-TERM FORECASTS WHICH ARE, IN TURN, DERIVED FROM A STUDY OF THE PAST BEHAVIOUR OF THE EARTH'S CRUST. EACH YEAR THERE ARE ABOUT 1 MILLION EARTHQUAKES, MOST OF THEM VERY SMALL. WHAT IS IMPORTANT, HOWEVER, IS THE ABILITY TO PREDICT HIGH MAGNITUDE EARTHQUAKES THAT MAY HIT HIGHLY POPULATED AREAS. SUCH EVENTS ARE MUCH LESS COMMON AND THEIR WARNING SIGNALS ARE MORE DIFFICULT TO DISTINGUISH.

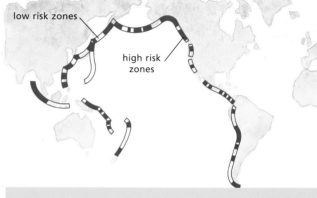

Segments representing seismic gaps around the subduction zones of the Pacific Ocean

In general terms the subduction zones and areas of active horizontal displacement, such as parts of China and California, are the areas in which earthquakes are most likely to occur. However, plate movements are far from continuous from a human point of view; some segments of a fault or subduction zone move, whilst others stay still for decades or even centuries. Immobile segments of faults, or seismic gaps, represent zones that have not experienced earthquakes for abnormally long time compared to segments nearby.

These seismic gaps are the places to look for future earthquakes in the mobile zones of the globe. Unfortunately there are a large number of them. About half the subduction zones around the Pacific Ocean, for example, comprise seismic gaps. Those situated in highly populated areas, such as California, south-eastern Japan, and Java, tend to attract the most attention, and are the areas in which accurate prediction of an impending earthquake would be the most valuable. Five earthquakes exceeding magnitude 8.5, have struck the United States Pacific coast north of Cape Mendocino in the past 1,700 years, with time intervals ranging from 90–560 years. It has been calculated that the last great earthquake occurred on 26 January 1700. Now the area is rising by 4mm (⅙in), and contracting by a significant amount each year. The crust is therefore being squeezed continuously and is bound to crack sooner or later.

Seismic gaps should reveal the areas where big earthquakes are possible, or likely, within several decades. Unfortunately scientists do not always know exactly what to look for. As earthquakes are caused when rocks crack

Tokyo, Japan is still a high risk zone

along a fault, in response to strains that have built up over many years, it would be logical to expect some precursory signs before an earthquake takes place. However, just because one particular sort of change is recorded before an earthquake, this does not necessarily mean that it is a warning sign. The Romans, for example, believed earthquakes occurred when the wind came from a certain direction.

Because of these doubts, experts measure as many changes as possible. This systematic, empirical method proved very successful in the prediction of an earthquake at Haicheng, China. A modified version of this system is also being used in Kanto and Tokai provinces in Japan, and at the Parkfield pilot site on the San Andreas Fault in California. There has been considerable investment in measuring all kinds of ground deformations – based on repeated surveys accurate to 1mm (¹⁄₂₅in) or less – that might show the minute effects of stresses and strains before the rupture.

Changes in ground-water levels and content seem to be more significant than changes in rocks at the present time. Ground-water aquifers delicately reflect the state of underground fissures or other conditions and, therefore, reveal

The Kobe earthquake of 1995 devastated many areas of the city. It lay outside the official high-risk area designated by the Japanese authorities

changes in such factors as temperature, pH value, and particularly radon content. Radioactive decay of uranium in the rocks produces the gas radon-222 which reaches the ground-water. Radon is itself radioactive but it decays within a few days. Therefore changes in radon concentrations give a good, quick picture of the varying amounts of water entering an aquifer. These changes may be caused when fissures open or close as stresses alter in the rocks. These variations can be relayed to laboratories and recorded at once. radon-222 changes can, therefore, indicate an imminent earthquake. They are measured widely in Japan. At Kobe the radon increased fourfold between the end of October and the end of December 1994. By 8 January 1995, there was ten times as much Radon present as in October. On 17 January 1995 the earthquake hit Kobe (see pp.74–75). It has also been discovered since that mineral water taken from thermal springs near the epicentre of that earthquake showed great increases in chlorine and sulphur ions between August 1994 and January 1995.

An ancient Chinese seismometer: a tremor would make a ball fall into a frog's mouth

prediction and prevention of tsunamis

NEAR THEIR SOURCE AREAS TSUNAMIS OCCUR WITHIN ABOUT 15 MINS OF THE EARTHQUAKE OR ERUPTION FROM WHICH THEY ORIGINATED. WITHOUT PREDICTING THE CAUSE, IT IS IMPOSSIBLE TO GIVE ADEQUATE WARNING OF THE TSUNAMI NEAR ITS SOURCE. LONG-DISTANCE TSUNAMIS MAY TAKE UP TO 22 HRS TO CROSS THE PACIFIC OCEAN GIVING SUFFICIENT TIME TO TAKE EVASIVE ACTION. FOR EXAMPLE A TSUNAMI COULD REACH SAN FRANCISCO FROM JAPAN, 8,000KM (4,970 MILES) AWAY, IN ABOUT 10 HOURS. BUT THERE MAY BE MUCH LESS TIME AVAILABLE.

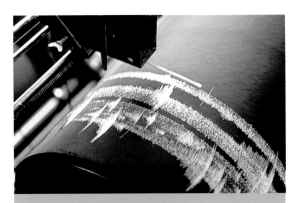

This smoke drum seismic record records earth tremors in the Hawaii Volcanoes National Park on the east rift of Kilauea

The Pacific Ocean experiences the most dangerous tsunamis and it is also fringed by some of the world's most densely-populated coastal plains. Hawaii is particularly at risk as tsunamis can reach the islands from all over the Pacific Ocean: about 100 have been recorded since 1813, and they often cause great coastal damage.

The Pacific Tsunami Warning System (PTSW) is an attempt to combat the potential destruction by quickly detecting earthquakes or eruptions that might produce tsunamis, and estimating their height and time of arrival at vulnerable places. The original American system was developed after a tsunami generated in the Aleutian Islands on 1 April 1946, swept away a 30m (98ft) lighthouse on Unimak Island and severely damaged Hilo in Hawaii a few hours later. It became an international organization after a powerful tsunami generated in Chile in May 1960 devastated Hawaii and Japan. There are now 23 member states, concentrated around the Pacific Ocean. The system is based on a network of 69 earthquake stations and 65 tide-stations to plot the course and likely size of the tsunamis, all co-ordinated from the Pacific Tsunami Warning Centre at Honolulu in Hawaii.

Tsunami, Hawaii 1957. This sequence of photographs shows the arrival of the Oahu tsunami at Laie Point, 9 March 1957. It was triggered by an earthquake in Alaska on this date

For example, the alert is raised after a magnitude 7.0 earthquake, the epicentre of which can be located in about 15 mins. If a tsunami develops, the warning is sent as quickly as possible to the threatened areas. By this time, however, the coastal fringes near the source of the tsunami would already have been inundated.

Under these circumstances, the safest place to be is onboard ship, and vessels should ideally be as far out to sea as possible (where the water depth is at a maximum). For those on land, if the sea starts to retreat after an earthquake, the most sensible places to head for are hills and valley sides at least 30m (98ft) above the old sea-level.

an earthquake and tsunami reaction timetable

19 September 1985

07.18	Earthquake, magnitude 8.1, strikes Michoacán, Mexico
07.19	Seismic waves reach Mexico City; eventually felt by 20 million people
07.19–c.07.24	412 buildings in Mexico City collapse, 3124 more badly damaged. Communication systems and Public Utility Systems put out of action, 30,000 injured, 9,500 (possibly up to 35,000) deaths and 100,000 left homeless in Mexico City. Estimated damage: US$3,000 million
07.23	Short-period alarms set off at National Earthquake Information Center (Golden, Colorado)
07.25	Interpretation of seismograms at NEIC begins
07.27	P-wave arrives at Honolulu
07.28	Surface wave arrives at NEIC in Golden
07.30	P-waves arrive in France and Italy
07.35	Preliminary estimate of epicentre: 17.8°N, 102.3°W
07.48	Pacific Tsunami Warning Center contacted. Estimated magnitude 7.8
07.49	U.S. National Warning Center notified of site and magnitude
07.52	Surface wave arrives at Shemya Island, Aleutian Islands
08.00	News Services informed
08.05	PTWC issues tsunami watch for Pacific region
08.18	World Organizations informed: eg. UN Disaster Relief Organisation; European-Mediterranean Seismological Centre in Strasbourg, France
08.20	Additional data received from Istituto Nazionale di Geofisica in Italy
08.30–Noon	Data exchanges with Seismic Stations in Central and South America
10.20	PTWC cancels tsunami watch: no dangerous tsunami
Noon	Additional data allows revision of site of earthquake: 18.13°N, 102.31°W

INTERVIEW

HAWAII, 1946

Marsue McShane

At 01.59 on 1 April 1946 the inhabitants of the north-east coast of Hawaii were unaware of the implications of an earthquake happening deep below sea-level, 3,700km (2,300) miles away. The earthquake took place on the ocean floor, on the northern slope of the Aleutian trench, off the coast of Alaska. Within 20 mins a lighthouse on Unimak Island, 96km (60 miles) to the northwest, was destroyed by waves 35m (115ft) high. At the same time, waves from the Aleutians were also heading south, towards Hawaii.

Marsue McShane arrived in Hawaii in 1945.

 'Before I came here I lived in Ohio, Cincinnati, and my first job was at Laupahoehoe ... I knew nothing about Hawaii but I wanted to teach around the world so I came here and I met my fellow teachers ... and the four of us shared a cottage ... and we couldn't believe the beauty of the place ... it was just an idyllic life.'

The waves caused by the earthquake took less than five hours to reach the capital of Hawaii, Honolulu, on the island of Oahu. They reached

Laupahoehoe about 30 mins later. Marsue remembers:

 '... we were not quite up ... we were still in our bathrobes and things ... Danny Axiona ... knocked on our door and said "Come and see the tidal wave" ... first we ... couldn't see any tidal wave, but there was a place to observe the cove, and we went up to look and we were standing in our pyjamas and slippers and everything ... and the water sort of sucked out like you were emptying a bath tub, and went a little bit beyond where it is usually at low tide, and then it slowly came back in and up a bit higher than high tide ...'

This process was repeated a second time, and by the third, a large amount of debris, sand and fish from the ocean floor was deposited on the sea front where Marsue's school's athletics field was situated. The mood at this stage was almost light-hearted: some children were trying to catch the fish that had been stranded on the playing field, another group of students was being taught about tidal waves by one of the science teachers. Marsue hurried back to the house to dress and to fetch her camera.

A memorial to all those who died in the tsunami overlooks the harbour today

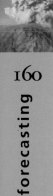

'[I] focused the camera on the waves [and thought] "I hope it's a big one this time" ... Then it got bigger and bigger and never did dissolve and go back – and that was the first time it occurred to anybody that it was danger ... I dropped the camera and tried to run ... the cottage just dissolved ... the roof went "Boom" and so ... I crawled up and sat on the corner of the roof, and it sucked way in up to where the school was ... and then began to suck out again.'

Marsue and her friends decided they would try to run as far as they could before the wave returned, but it caught up with them, and they were pulled underneath the water and out to sea. Huge walls of water continued to crash over the shoreline. Although a strong swimmer Marsue was unable to battle against the huge power of the waves.

'... I came up a second time and my head was right by [a] lighthouse, the light was sticking up and there I was facing the light on the lighthouse'.

When she emerged for a third time it took Marsue a few moments before she realized she was still alive:

'... I thought well nothing's broken, I can move ... my shoes were gone, my socks were gone, my blue jeans were gone.'

She now tried to get away from the cliffs. It was very difficult to move through the water as it was full of rubbish but eventually she managed to find a door to hold on to. She realized that it may be sometime before she was rescued and willed herself to remain calm until help arrived.

'Finally I saw an airplane circling, he never buzzed his motor to let me know he saw me ... but finally he dropped a rubber raft, but now the sea was too rough and it was too far for me to get there with my door ... but then he dropped another one, and it was

ABOVE Marsue with her class, 1946
BELOW The teachers at Laupahoehoe 1946, some of whom died in the tsunami

now 5.30pm, starting to turn dark ... and I swam over to this rubber raft ... and I got into it ... then that's when the rescue boat came out.'

Marsue was one of the lucky ones; 159 people were killed by the 1946 tsunami, including 21 people in the tiny settlement of Laupahoehoe, and 96 in the neighbouring village Hilo. Almost 500 homes or businesses were completely destroyed and 1,000 more were badly damaged. If modern alarm systems had been in place in 1946 it is likely that nobody would have died. With 30 mins warning there should be plenty of time for people to move to high ground away from the shore. There are now sirens to let people know that a tsunami is approaching.

success and failure in China

SEISMIC ACTIVITY IN CHINA IS DUE TO THE NORTHWARD PRESSURE OF THE INDIAN SUB-CONTINENT THAT IS SQUEEZING ASIA, AND PUSHING CHINA SIDEWAYS TOWARDS THE EAST. EARTHQUAKES PRODUCED BY SUCH MOVEMENTS ARE VIOLENT. THE AREA OF THE NORTH CHINA PLAIN, AROUND THE GULF OF CHIHLI EAST OF BEIJING, IS DENSELY POPULATED, AND ACCURATE PREDICTION OF EARTHQUAKES IN SUCH AN AREA IS VITAL.

In 1966 two earthquakes within as many weeks prompted the government to establish an earthquake bureau to investigate the possibility of prediction. Areas known to be prone to earthquakes were selected for intensive study, and 20,000 scientists and over 100,000 amateur assistants, were sent there. At the same time a public awareness and education programme was implemented.

As the general problem of prediction worldwide was a lack of knowledge of the vital signals of earthquakes, this labour-intensive, time-consuming, empirical method had undoubted merits. Local faults, tremors, ground tilt, changes in water levels in springs and wells, radon contents, magnetic field variations and unusual behaviour by animals, were all recorded. At the same time scientists mapped and analyzed faults and carried out precise levelling, gravity and magnetic studies.

By 1973 it was clear that the plain around the Gulf of Chihli was swelling, and that earth tremors had increased five times in the past year, and seemed to be moving north towards the Haicheng area. A major earthquake seemed likely but a more precise prediction was still needed. A network of seismic stations was set up in 1974. A 50 km- (31 mile-) long coastal area between Haicheng and Yingkow was the focus of 'abnormal features': water was seen shooting from the ground and animals were restless.

Around Haicheng in 1975, the water level began to alter in wells, implying that the ground might be starting to fissure in response

The focus of the earthquake in 1976 was directly under Tangshan and the epicentre was therefore in the town itself

forecasting

to the strains. In January 1975 experts said that an earthquake was imminent. A magnitude 4.8 earthquake struck the area 70km (43½ miles) north of Haicheng but this was not the high-magnitude earthquake they were expecting.

During the first three days of February 1975 over 500 tremors shook the area between Haicheng and Yingkow. On the morning of 4 February the tremors suddenly stopped. The scientists told the provincial government, who, at 10.00 issued the prediction that an earthquake of magnitude 6.0 would soon occur.

Tangled wreckage such as this proved lethal for most of those trapped inside

That Tuesday evening, a magnitude 7.5 earthquake devastated the Haicheng region. Thousands of buildings collapsed, but the people were already waiting outside, and a relatively small number were killed: 1,328. This was the first accurate short-term prediction of an earthquake based on scientific methods – albeit at enormous cost in man-hours.

Data collection continued and early in 1976 scientists forecast that the area between Haicheng and Beijing, where 'abnormal phenomena' had been apparent, would suffer a large earthquake at some time in the next five years. This was significant as the area included the large industrial city of Tangshan, 200km (124 miles) east of Beijing. However, there was no apparent major fault threatening the region and the city had not experienced an earthquake since records began. Magnetic and water level measurements varied slightly from their usual levels, but other than this, Tangshan seemed no more threatened than many other cities.

But if an earthquake were to happen, Tangshan was in a high-risk category as it was built on thick, silty sediment. The sediment was to have a two-fold effect in the disaster that hit the city: it obscured a major fault, and when the fault slipped, the sediment liquefied. Given the lack of apparent evidence of an impending earthquake, however, a decision was made not to evacuate the city.

The fault slipped for a length of 150km (93 miles), with a sideways dislocation of about 3m (9³/₄ft). The focus of the earthquake, with a magnitude of 7.6 or 7.9, was directly beneath Tangshan, and its epicentre was therefore in the city. It struck Tangshan at 03.43 on 28 July 1976. Half the brick buildings of more than one storey collapsed, only four remained undamaged. Roads and bridges in the area were shattered. The silts underlying the city had liquefied. In the wake of this disaster the official death toll was 240,000, but others have estimated fatalities at anywhere between 500,000 and 850,000.

Buildings near the epicentre of the earthquake were reduced to piles of rubble within seconds

INTERVIEW

TANGSHAN, 1976

Miner Wang Shu Bin was admitted to Kailuan Hospital in Tangshan on July 27 1976. The doctors decided to keep him in over night, he was put on a drip due to dehydration and his wife stayed to keep him company.

Wang Shu Bin

Wang Shu Bin and his family before the earthquake. Sadly his wife was killed

Wang Shu Bin had in fact experienced the most lethal earthquake of the 20th Century.

 'After the building collapsed there were 19 of us in the ward including doctors and patients ... I was trapped in the bed by a large piece of concrete ... The concrete above me was so close I could touch it just by stretching up ... A lot of people were crying for help, many people were still alive. After the building collapsed there was not even a chink of light.'

Wang Shu Bin's wife had been asleep on an empty hospital bed when the earthquake struck. Afterwards they were able to carry on a conversation. His wife was badly injured – crushed below the waist by a fallen piece of concrete. Wang Shu Bin tried to extricate himself from the tangle of metal, concrete and rubble.

 'At 3.42 in the morning my head was especially clear, and from the room I could see outside. There was lightning ... Lots of lightning ... I thought it was going to rain. The weather that day was ... very

The hospital in which Wang Shu Bin was being treated at the time of the earthquake

muggy, very hot. Gloomy and heavy. At that moment I saw the fluorescent light on the ceiling swinging violently ... I did not realize it was an earthquake. In the blink of an eye, around five seconds later, the whole building collapsed.'

 '... I used all my strength to push myself out with my feet and to pull out my hand that was trapped in the rubble ... After I pulled it out my wife was ... crying out, a lot of other people were calling for help. I felt that I was not injured very much and once I had saved myself I had to rescue my wife.'

In spite of what he believed Wang Shu Bin was quite badly hurt: his wounds were serious if superficial, but the dangers of infection were high; many people were already dead or dying. It is difficult to comprehend his painstaking progress as he first worked to free himself and then worked his way towards his wife.

 'From on my bed to under my bed [took] about two days. My hand was totally trapped. My leg was crushed – it felt like a wooden plank was on top of me. I felt later and realized it was a dead body.'

It took him another day to reach the concrete block that was the last obstacle separating him from his wife. This was to prove impossible to overcome. Only able to touch her fingertips, Wang Shu Bin and his wife talked about their family and their life together until she no longer responded. Wang Shu Bin remained underneath the rubble for a further four days as he dug his way out.

 'During that four days a lot of people were still crying out ... I touched a lot of dead bodies on the way digging myself out. Later when I got out, 19 people were in there, only I came out alive ... no matter what I did I couldn't find a way out ... big concrete pillars and blocks, and big bricks. Finally I found a bottle of glucose ... and a pillow stuffed with husks of grain ... Whenever I was hungry on my way out this was my food.'

Digging through the rubble to reach the outside was extremely hazardous work but the building skills Wang Shu Bin had learned as a miner helped to save his life.

 'I was crawling on my stomach through the filth, I had a lot of cuts on my body and the smell made me choke ... On the way digging myself out I ... ignored the pain. I

barely slept. I didn't rest ... I would stop and shore up my tunnel ... I reinforced the walls with pieces of brick, supporting the roof ... I dug a tunnel 12m [39ft] long.

Damaged roads and bridges made it difficult for rescue teams to move around the area

Finally, after seven days he collapsed, exhausted. And as he lay in the cramped tunnel he began to feel that perhaps it would be better to die with his wife in the rubble. Then he realized that he could hear noise from the road outside. He shouted to try to alert rescuers to his presence.

 '... I suddenly heard voices ... It was a military medical team from Shenyang. They were short of medicine and were looking for medicine in the ruins of this ... hospital ... I shouted upwards ... then they heard my shouts.'

 'They found me on August 4 at 9am, finally, at 6.50pm they got me out. It was very difficult. Then, when I saw the first beam of light it was like the first shaft of sunlight in my life ... The first thing I set eyes on was a blue sky and the big leaves of a tree and the face of the person that saved me ... I was very emotional. I clung to their heads and cried because I had been so lonely for the last eight days ... I couldn't believe that I was saved.'

Wang Shu Bin lost nine of his family in the Tangshan earthquake. He still mourns for all those that died, the people who were 'lost in a moment'.

handling earthquakes in Japan

JAPAN PROBABLY SUFFERS MORE NATURAL DISASTERS EVEN THAN CHINA. THE AREA AROUND TOKYO, IN KANTO AND TOKAI PROVINCES, IS ONE OF THE MOST VULNERABLE IN THE WHOLE COUNTRY, BECAUSE IT IS THE FOCUS OF TWO SUBDUCTION ZONES. JUST TO THE SOUTH-EAST OF THE CAPITAL, THE PACIFIC PLATE IS PLUNGING BOTH BENEATH JAPAN, ALONG THE JAPAN TRENCH, AND ALSO BENEATH THE PHILIPPINE PLATE, ALONG THE IZU-BONIN TRENCH. IN TURN, THE NORTHERNMOST POINT OF THE PHILIPPINE PLATE IS ALSO PLUNGING UNDER JAPAN AROUND THE IZU PENINSULA, WHICH IS IN FACT AN ISLAND ON THE PHILIPPINE PLATE THAT HAS BEEN CARRIED INTO COLLISION WITH THE REST OF JAPAN.

In addition, some scientists believe that Hokkaido Island and eastern Honshu belong to the American Plate rather than the Eurasian Plate, and this multiplicity of plate margins thereby increases the chances of violent earthquakes. About 12 million people live in the Tokyo conurbation. Kanto and Tokai provinces have experienced nine earthquakes exceeding magnitude 7.9 in the past 300 years and several earthquakes of over magnitude 6.0 hit the area every year.

The Seismological Society had already gathered together many historical records when an earthquake on 1 September 1923 devastated Tokyo and much of Kanto province. The earthquake started a huge fire, kindled by open hearths and wooden buildings. About 40 per cent of Tokyo was destroyed and 142,807 people died. Damage caused by the earthquake cost 7 per cent of GNP. The geological community was spurred into action.

In 1925, the world's first Earthquake Research Institute was founded, which studied the effects of earthquakes all over the world. The creation of the world-wide seismological station network and the formulation of the theory of

Kanto earthquake 1923. View from the roof of the Imperial Hotel, Tokyo. One of the few buildings in the

plate tectonics in the 1960s provided a boost, and a committee for predicting earthquakes was also established. The national threat to Japan from seismic activity means that, unlike in many other countries, there is a united political will to achieve accurate prediction, and a general recognition of the value of such a policy.

The Kanto earthquake, 1923

This initiative produced an early success: scientists discovered a seismic gap in the subduction zone along the Kuril Trench east of Hokkaido Island, in which one segment had remained still, whilst all its neighbours had produced major earthquakes since 1900. Accurate surveys then showed that eastern Hokkaido was contracting as if stresses were building up in the quiet segment. An earthquake was forecast, although not an exact date, and it duly arrived in 1973. Suitably encouraged, in 1978, the government designated eight highly-populated earthquake-prone areas for special monitoring, and two others – in Kanto and Tokai provinces – for the closest possible attention.

The most modern surveillance methods have been applied to the particularly vulnerable area of the Izu Peninsula, 100km (62 miles) south-west of Tokyo, which is still colliding with the rest of Japan. After 44 years of relative inactivity, a magnitude 6.9 earthquake shook the southern

end of Izu in 1974. From 1974–78, the eastern part of Izu swelled up by as much as 15cm (6in), accompanied by a swarm of earth tremors. In 1978, the radon content changed for five days, earth tremors increased for 15 hours, and then stopped dead. Three hours later there was a magnitude 7.0 earthquake offshore near Izu Island. Unfortunately, the monitoring network was not dense enough to predict this earthquake accurately. Conversely there were no such warning signs prior to a magnitude 6.7 earthquake off Izu in 1980.

West of Izu, the Philippine Plate is plunging under Tokai, producing magnitude 8.0 earthquakes every 100–150 years. There is a seismic gap, however, in the trench in Suruga Bay, west of Izu, which has not moved during the present century. The subducting Philippine Plate must, therefore, have built up stresses that should soon dislocate the rocks. There is some evidence of these stresses: the coast of Tokai has sunk by 60cm (23½in) since 1900 and Suruga Bay has narrowed by 1m (3¼ft). There are also not many earth tremors near the Bay but plenty around it and this so-called 'doughnut pattern' sometimes heralds a major earthquake. The whole area is now criss-crossed with monitoring equipment, and the hope is that, if all goes well, the experts may be able to issue a few days' warning of a future disaster.

city to remain standing, the hotel had been specially designed by American architect Frank Lloyd Wright

predictions on the San Andreas fault system

THERE ARE FOUR MAIN, AND A NUMBER OF MINOR, SEGMENTS ALONG THE SAN ANDREAS FAULT SYSTEM. THESE WILL ALL BREAK AT DIFFERENT TIMES IN RESPONSE TO DIFFERENT DEGREES OF STRAIN THAT BUILD UP AND, THEREFORE, THE FULL LENGTH OF EACH SEGMENT ONLY RARELY MOVES DURING ANY ONE EARTHQUAKE.

segment that slipped in the 1989 Loma Prieta earthquake

The northern, and longest, segment stretches about 480km (298 miles) from Cape Mendocino to Hollister, and appears to move once every 250 years, but not to the same extent along its whole length. During the San Francisco earthquake of 1906, the southern section moved much less than the northern section, and the southern section still has some ground to make up, even following the Loma Prieta earthquake in 1989. Between San Francisco Bay and Hollister there are three active branches of the fault system: the San Andreas fault proper going through San Francisco; the Hayward fault passing through Oakland on the east of the Bay; and the Calaveras fault, running alongside it, further inland. Each branch has moved independently in the past 160 years but magnitudes only exceeded 6.8 at San Francisco in 1906. On the Hayward and San Andreas branches, scientists believe that there is a 20 per cent chance of a magnitude 7.0 earthquake in the next 30 years.

A USGS scientist operates a two-colour laser geodimeter at a station near Parkfield

From Hollister to Parkfield, 150km (93 miles) south-east, the segment moves gradually, causing medium magnitude earthquakes asbout every 22 years. Between Parkfield and San Bernadino, north of Los Angeles, the fault system jerks more intensely, and at intervals of about 150 years. The southernmost segment of the San Andreas fault system, from San Bernadino south-east into Mexico, has been quiet over the past 250 years, but neighbouring faults have produced earthquakes of high magnitude.

Scientists have constructed a diagram of the probability of earthquakes occurring along the San Andreas system. The probability of a magnitude 7.5–8.0 earthquake within the next 30 years, in the southern segments of the fault, varies between 10 and 40 per cent. Los Angeles has a 60 per cent chance, and San Francisco a 50 per cent chance, of being shaken by a large earthquake in the next 30 years.

The Parkfield prediction

In 1985 the US Geological Survey predicted that 'an earthquake of about magnitude 6.0 would occur before 1993 on the San Andreas Fault near Parkfield [California] ...' Never before had the time, place and magnitude of an earthquake been so precisely predicted on a scientific basis. The project has had a great deal of support, and has been funded by US$1 million from Californian state authorities and US$1 million from the Federal Government. The aim was to find out if specific, measurable, recognizable changes occurred just before an earthquake. Such observations could then be tested further at Parkfield, and may be applicable to earthquake zones elsewhere in the world.

The village of Parkfield is packed full of highly sensitive equipment. The scientists register seismicity, strain, water levels, water chemistry, heat flow, geomagnetism, ground acceleration, seismic velocities and animal behaviour. The data are transmitted to and monitored at Menlo Park, the western headquarters of the US Geological Survey. Parkfield was chosen because it has suffered fairly frequent, but relatively minor, magnitude 6.0 earthquakes: in 1881, 1901, 1922, 1934 and 1966. The average interlude is 22 years, with a five year margin for error on either side. The next quake could be due any time.

San Francisco: a 50 per cent chance of a high magnitude earthquake in the next 30 years

Duane Hamann

Duane Hamann is a the only teacher at the small primary school in Parkfield, California. He also has another, very important, part-time job: he checks ground deformation using laser equipment as part of the United States Geological Survey's Parkfield Experiment.

'... about 13 years ago Al Lindh (see p.39) from the USGS came by my house one day and he said "Would you like another part-time job?"'

Although Duane had no formal training there were many reasons why USGS geologist, Allan Lindh, thought he was the right man for the job. First, he had the necessary time each day to devote to reading and adjusting the instruments. Second, he had already worked for the USGS prior to the introduction of specialist laser equipment. Third, the new equipment was being installed on land that had been owned by Duane's family for the past 100 years and he was involved with helping to set it up.

The machine he works with is known as a two-coloured geodimeter which is aimed at 19 different points on the horizon.

'The two-coloured geodimeter operates on the principle of how fast light travels ... we send a beam of light out and actually in this case we use two colours of light ... red and blue ... on the other end of the line that I'm measuring there's a reflector ... We send this beam of light out ... and it hits the reflector and it is returned to the instrument, and the amount of time that it takes ... in simple terms is how we get our measurement ... I can actually get an accurate measurement on a line that is (5.6km) 3½ miles away to within a fraction of a millimetre ...'

INTERVIEW

EARTHQUAKE 'SENSITIVES'

Many people and animals are able to feel or 'sense' when earthquakes are about to happen. Strange behaviour by domestic pets is particularly noticeable and people may experience headaches, electric shocks and ground movement.

Linda Curtis is a seismological secretary at the United States Geological Survey in Pasadena, California. She takes calls from people who feel earthquakes coming but do not know what to do with their information. There is no funded research into sensitivity at present and so the scientists themselves are busy with other projects. Linda makes notes and keeps files on Rodolex cards on everyone that calls.

'We receive lots of calls, for example, here is one from a woman who has a Japanese Love Fish named Richter. He likes to jump out of his aquarium right before earthquakes ... another guy whose house creaks before it quakes ... another gentleman has a TV that gets interference right before earthquakes ... a miniature dachshund that does circles ... an African Grey Parrot called Dorian that likes to pick feathers out of his chest several weeks to a month prior to an earthquake... and a Rottweiler named King who makes circles right before earthquakes.'

The 1994 Northridge earthquake caused this landslide at Pacific Palisades

King's owner is Dan Farell, a dog trainer and police dog handler from Whittier, California. The first example of King's sensitive behaviour occurred in June 1992:

The Northridge earthquake also seriously damaged many roads and bridges. This is a

'... At 1 o'clock in the morning, just getting ready to go to sleep ... and my dog starts going really crazy ... he starts running around in circles in the house, running circles in the room, barking at me, jumping on the bed. Finally, I got him calmed down five or ten minutes after that, not knowing what the heck is going on with him. About 6am the next morning my dog ... starts jumping on my chest, barking at me, doing all sorts of crazy things, about five minutes after that an earthquake hit ... About five minutes after that, he starts barking at me again, to let me know another one's coming ... [we] got inside of a doorway and we had a very nice-sized after-shock after that.'

Since 1992 King's sensitive behaviour has continued, particularly when there are 'swarms' of small, repeated earthquakes.

'When we start getting swarms of earthquakes King will actually look at the ground, he'll go in circles, he'll growl at it, he'll bark at the ground ... King really is a pretty happy-go-lucky dog.'

Linda knows there are a large number of people and their pets who sense something before earthquakes occur, and although she believes they all have something interesting to

collapsed span from a southbound intersection of Interstate 5

contribute, their information is not a priority for the scientists who are hard at work on quantitative research projects. Allan Lindh is a geologist with the USGS.

'I've had a lot of people call me or talk to me over the years about whether or not they can sense earthquakes, and some of them have been very convincing, and it's very hard for me to dismiss their stories altogether. But all efforts to treat it as a scientific phenomenon have proven fruitless ... if a few people can sense something in the earth, before earthquakes, some of the time, that doesn't help you predict earthquakes, especially if it's not a stable feature of those people's make-up ... I wouldn't be surprised if things as strange as that someday might prove to be true, but scientifically the only way to approach it is to find things you can measure ...'

An unreinforced building in Santa Monica, Los Angeles, damaged in 1994

'If people can sense something before earthquakes I think it ... has to do with some emotional state so that it is not repeatable. Science is based on repeatability. It is very hard to repeat experiments with earthquakes in the first place, if you throw in an additional variable like how people feel ... there's no evidence that it has come to anything trying to study that directly. I have over the years, asked people who believed they could predict earthquakes, to write down in a notebook every day ... I have told that to hundreds of people. Not one of them has ever brought me a log. So if people feel they can predict earthquakes they should write it down, keep a record, and we'll compare it to the list of earthquakes and see if they can.'

Linda Curtis also believes there are many more people able to sense earthquakes than are listed in her Rodolex.

'I think there's a lot more than I hear from. I think maybe for every call I get there could possibly be maybe 50 or 100 more people that are 'earthquake sensitives'. I know there's a whole network of sensitives that talk with each other and communicate with each other about sensing earthquakes on the World Wide Web.'

the Sicilian earthquakes of 1693 and 1968

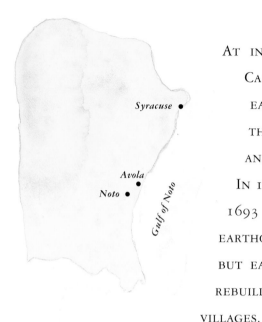

AT INTERVALS OF 90–125 YEARS EASTERN SICILY AND CALABRIA EXPERIENCE SOME OF THE MOST INTENSE EARTHQUAKES IN THE WORLD. IN 1908 THE FOCUS OF THE EARTHQUAKE LAY BETWEEN MESSINA IN SICILY, AND REGGIO IN CALABRIA IN THE STRAITS OF MESSINA. IN 1783, THE FOCUS WAS SITUATED IN CALABRIA, AND IN 1693 IT WAS WEST OF SYRACUSE, IN SICILY. THESE EARTHQUAKES ALWAYS CAUSED A GREAT DEAL OF DAMAGE BUT EACH TIME THE INHABITANTS WOULD ALWAYS BEGIN REBUILDING ON TOP OF THE RUINS OF THEIR TOWNS AND VILLAGES.

In 1693, however, a particularly severe earthquake killed over 60,000 people, destroyed 49 towns and numerous villages. This time the citizens of the Sicilian town of Noto decided to transfer their whole settlement to what they hoped would be a safer place.

One of the survivors, a monk called Tortora, described what had happened in Noto. 'On 9 January, at 4 o'clock in the night [four hours after sunset, 22.00], a sharp earthquake was felt which destroyed a great number of structures and caused the death of over 200 persons. The following day, everyone went to the open spaces, both within and without the town, and they stayed there throughout the Saturday night, fearing lest such a great scourge should be repeated ... As soon as the twenty-first hour struck on Sunday [15.00 on 11 January], and 40 hours, therefore, having elapsed, there was such a terrifying and horrible earthquake that the ground swayed up and down like the sea, the mountains tottered and fell down, and the whole town crumbled piteously, bringing about the death of about 1,000 people'.

Noto was a mass of ruins. The survivors held a mass meeting, and decided to rebuild their

Palazzo Astuto, Noto. A splendid example of 18th-Century Baroque architecture

town about 16km (10 miles) away, on the plateau overlooking the coastal plain. The rebuilding took 50 years but is now one of the most beautiful small Baroque towns in the world. Built in a rich honey-coloured stone, and recently restored, it is an operatic succession of squares, mansions and churches, with elegant façades, porticoes and balconies. Thankfully this jewel of the Mediterranean has not been hit by an earthquake since.

The original cathedral in Noto was destroyed by the earthquake. This replacement is one of the town's centrepieces

Ruderi di Gibellina to Gibellina Nuova

The worst earthquake to hit Sicily since 1908 devastated the villages in the Belice valley in the rugged western mountains in January 1968. Most of the people were made homeless and were forced to sleep out in the open until aid agencies were able to provide wooden huts as temporary accommodation. A decade later the huts were still the only homes available.

Like the citizens of Noto nearly 300 years before, the villagers of Gibellina decided to rebuild their settlement 20km (12½ miles) away, on the plain, near the motorway and the railway. The result is Gibellina Nuova the vision of the mayor Ludovico Corrao. Built to limit casualties in any future calamity, Gibellina Nuova has wide streets, with buildings only two storeys high. The most talented artists in Italy contributed sculptures decorating practically every junction. Squares are enormous whilst shops and cafés seem rare. This is a long way from the close-knit intimacy, hubbub and twisting alleys of the old Gibellina, now called Ruderi di Gibellina – the 'wreckage of Gibellina', but it will be safer.

The earthquake needed two attempts to destroy Old Gibellina. The first quake killed about 200 people and the survivors fled to the safety of the open hills. Three days later, the second quake threw the tottering ruins to the ground, killing the policemen who were on guard.

The mayor decided that the Ruderi should be preserved forever in a great tomb of concrete, with furrows marking the old pattern of the streets. Only a few larger ruins that stayed upright now rise above the white blocks that are a memorial to the old village.

The remains of Old Gibellina. Concrete covers the damaged houses and trenches have been left along the old streets

forecasting and predicting volcanic eruptions

VOLCANIC ERUPTIONS ARE SLIGHTLY EASIER TO FORECAST THAN EARTHQUAKES BECAUSE THERE IS USUALLY MORE WARNING. SIGNS, HOWEVER, CAN BE AMBIGUOUS OR DIFFICULT TO INTERPRET, AND IN SOME CASES, MAY SIMPLY PROVE TO BE FALSE ALARMS.

Children around Mt Unzen, Japan, wear protective clothing

The situation is further complicated by the fact that the distinction between volcanoes that are active, dormant or extinct is not always straightforward. Active volcanoes might erupt fairly often but eruptions are rarely continuous. Etna, for instance, is active: the emission of gas and steam from the main summit is relatively constant; ash and cinders explode regularly from a crater at the base of the main cone; and lavas spew out every few years from fissures on its flanks. Vesuvius was active in every decade from 1631–1944, but has not erupted since, and could now be described as dormant. Mount St Helens on the other hand was dormant from 1857 until its great outburst in 1980. Its most recent eruption, a very mild one, took place in 1986. The question that scientists need to answer, therefore, is whether it is still active or has become dormant once again.

There are also many volcanoes that are clearly active and probably dangerous enough to merit scientific attention. In fact, there are more potentially dangerous volcanoes in the world than scientists to monitor them, or funds available to buy the equipment needed. Therefore, the volcanoes that seem most likely to pose a real threat are selected for special monitoring. The geological and historical records show up the most dangerous candidates. Only about 50 of the 89 selected volcanoes are already under this intensive care. Some are located in remote, unpopulated areas and therefore present little threat to the human population. Amongst these are the many active volcanoes bordering the northern Pacific Ocean from the Aleutian Islands through the Kuril Islands to Kamchatka. Others pose a direct threat to large cities. In Japan, volcanic bomb shelters have been built around Sakurajima, to provide shelter from volcanic bombs. Also in Japan, the town of Shimbara lies at the foot of Unzen, a volcano that caused the deaths of 14,524 people in 1792, and killed three geologists and over 30 journalists in 1991. About 1 million people in and around Naples could be in grave danger if Vesuvius were to erupt violently again. Volcanoes such as these have to be watched very carefully, and both are amongst those selected for special monitoring.

Shelters have been built around Sakurajima in Japan to prevent injuries from volcanic bombs

Dangers posed by volcanoes

The monitoring of volcanoes takes on many varied and increasingly sophisticated forms. When the magma is rising towards the surface it causes earthquakes of increasing magnitude. It will sometimes heat the surrounding rocks and will almost always increase the amount of gas and steam expelled. Once it enters the body of the volcano the magma can also sometimes deform the shape of the cone. The earthquakes are frequent, usually of fairly low magnitudes, and have a shallow focus near the volcano. Generally, but unfortunately not always, the earthquakes occur more often as the magma nears the crater. Volcanic earthquakes increased in number before Pinatubo erupted in 1991, but not before the eruption of Mount St Helens in 1980.

Lava-flows from Etna in 1971 engulfed this house in Fornazzo, Sicily, on the east flanks of the volcano

When the magma rises closer to the surface, some of the gases trapped within it can escape without exploding and form fumaroles and solfataras on the volcano which are collected and analyzed. The most significant changes are increases in temperature and especially in emissions of gases common in magma, such as hydrogen sulphide, carbon dioxide and sulphur dioxide: Nevado del Ruiz was producing considerable amounts of sulphur dioxide from October 1985 until it erupted in November. Teide and Vulcano, however, have been emitting sulphurous gases for years at varying rates without bursting into violent activity.

Once the magma has entered the volcano, it can sometimes cause the cone to swell or bulge outwards. These swellings can be measured by tiltmeters, arranged in a triangle, to indicate changes in different directions. Kilauea in Hawaii swells by about 1m (3¼ft) before it erupts. Unzen in Japan, bulged by about 50m (164ft) during the last three days before it erupted on 24 May 1991. There were even more

disastrous results when the magma rose off-centre at Mount St Helens and caused a bulge on its north face that was clearly visible. On this occasion, however, the rate of bulging was not increasing when the earthquake precipitated the landslide on 18 May 1980. On a broader scale, the satellite-based Global Positioning System is now used to monitor all kinds of changes of level and lateral displacements on volcanoes that have no thick network of monitoring devices set up either on or near them. Similarly, satellites can be used to monitor the most sensitive of heat changes on volcanoes where magma is rising towards the surface. These can give early indications of eruptions that are especially valuable on remote, or even unknown, volcanoes.

All these methods of monitoring are useful, but are best used together rather than in isolation, because individual indicators may prove unreliable. This degree of co-ordination requires teamwork and is costly, but, if it works well, an eruption could be forecast to within a week or so, and subsequently predicted to within a matter of days. In the case of volcanoes however, it is not simply the knowledge of when the eruption is to take place that is important. It is also necessary to know the type of eruption that is likely to occur, and what materials will be emitted, so that appropriate action can be taken.

damage limitation in Sicily

ALTHOUGH IT IS IMPOSSIBLE TO STOP VOLCANIC ERUPTIONS, HISTORY CAN ILLUSTRATE MANY ATTEMPTS TO DO SO, USING BOTH NATURAL AND SUPERNATURAL MEANS. IN CENTRAL AMERICA ONE TRIBE USED TO OFFER HUMAN SACRIFICES TO THE CRATER OF MASAYA TO STOP ITS ERUPTIONS. THE NEAPOLITANS USED TO PARADE THE HEAD OF THEIR PATRON SAINT, ST JANUARIUS, IN FRONT OF THE TERRIFYING OUTBURSTS OF VESUVIUS. THE CATANIANS USED TO MEET THE ADVANCING LAVAS OF ETNA WITH THE VEIL OF THEIR OWN PATRON SAINT, ST AGATHA. THE VILLAGERS OF PARÍCUTIN, IN MEXICO, KNELT IN PRAYER IN FRONT OF THE ADVANCING LAVA-FLOW IN 1943 AND 1944. ATTEMPTS TO DIVERT LAVA-FLOWS FROM ETNA HAVE PRODUCED MIXED RESULTS.

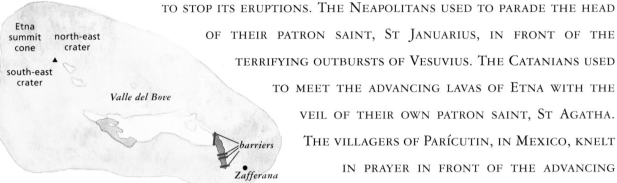

Etna summit cone
north-east crater
▲
south-east crater
Valle del Bove
barriers
• *Zafferana*

Key

☐ lavas extending first barrier 1992

▨ lava overflowed from first barrier 1992

▩ lavas diverted on upper flow from 29 May 1992

Catania 1669

On 30 April 1669, when the lava-flow from the flanks of Etna threatened the walls of Catania and started to invade the city, most Catanians thought that the city would be swamped. Diego Pappalardo, priest of Pedara, had the idea of trying to divert the flow near its source, where it would have the greatest effect. He decided to make a hole in the solid wall of the flow to encourage the molten lava to flow out sideways, take up a new course, and starve the snout that was advancing into Catania, thus bringing it to a halt.

He chose 50 men and, on 6 May 1669, took them up to the edge of the flow near the newly-buried village of Malpasso. The solidified sidewall of the flow was thin enough to be opened up, but still strong enough not to give way and drown everyone in molten lava at 1000°C. Armed with sledge-hammers, iron crow-bars and hooks, and protected against the heat with wet animal skins, they then lined up and took turns to run up to the lava-wall and hit it as hard as they could. Little by little, they knocked a hole in the sidewall of the flow and revealed the molten lava within. Then came the most difficult part of all: causing the molten lava to leave its old course and

During the eruption of Etna in 1992 helicopters dropped concrete blocks to slow down lava-flows

begin to flow out sideways without engulfing anyone. Amazingly they succeeded; some were burnt and singed, but nobody was killed. The molten lava began to trickle, and then gush, sideways. Diego Pappalardo then directed his men to block the old molten channel with boulders as best they could. They also succeeded in this Herculean task. Most of the lava started to flow out westwards. Rumours of the success spread like wildfire to Catania. The news also spread to the town of Paternò whose citizens noticed that the flow was now making straight for their own town. A group of enraged citizens rode off up to the new diversion, threatened Diego Pappalardo and his men with instant death, and drove them away from the scene. Left to its own devices, the diverted branch solidified, and the molten lavas resumed their previous course. They soon started to feed the snout again that was advancing slowly through western Catania. Paternò was saved. In the event, most of Catania was saved too, initially because much of the lava flowed into the sea, and then because the eruption stopped before it could overwhelm the eastern part of the city. Following this attempt to interfere with the lava's natural course, such activities were then banned until 1983.

Etna 1983

In 1983, the solidified walls of the lava-flow were blown apart by explosives. The molten lava then began to flow sideways out from the breach. At the same time, bulldozers and lorries were used to pile up ramparts of ash and cinders to contain the flow and direct it into a harmless course away from seven villages that it had been threatening. It was a vast task and could only have been done out of the way of farms and settlements on a mountain the size of Etna. As it was, it took seven weeks to move 750,000m³ (26½ million ft³) of ash and cinders into place.

Zafferana 1992

A bigger eruption on Etna, starting on 14 December 1991, seemed likely to swamp the town of Zafferana. A rampart of ash and cinders,

21m (69ft) high, was thrown across the valley where the lavas were advancing. They poured over it on 7 April 1992. Three other dams were built lower down, and the lava destroyed every one. In early May, the advancing snout was within 700m (2,296ft) of Zafferana. Faced with

Earthen barriers comprising bulldozed cinders and lava blocks were also used to slow down the flows

the increasing emergency, the experts decided to take more practical measures, this time near the source of the flow, 8km (5 miles) up valley from Zafferana. Helicopters dropped concrete blocks onto the molten lava four times. Each time the bombardment slowed down the snout's advance on Zafferana, but, each time, it started to move forward again. More drastic measures had to be tried. On 29 May 1992, the Pappalardo technique was used again. The solidified walls of the flow were blasted open, and most of the molten lava entered a newly-dug channel alongside it. Then the original channel was blocked with boulders, which cut off the supply of molten lava to the snout threatening Zafferana. Next, they channelled the diverted flow back onto the solidified old flow so that it would do no collateral damage. This new flow was advancing 6,000m (19,685ft), rather than 600m (1,968ft) from Zafferana, giving many weeks in which to prepare further efforts to save the town. In the event they were not needed. The eruption declined suddenly in June 1992 and lava emerged only fitfully until it stopped altogether in March 1993. Zafferana was saved.

damage limitation
in Iceland

THE VESTMANN ISLANDS IN ICELAND WERE JOINED BY A NEW MEMBER WHEN SURTSEY ERUPTED IN 1963. ON 23 JANUARY 1973 THE OLDEST AND LARGEST ISLAND IN THE GROUP, HEIMAEY, BURST INTO ACTIVITY. THIS POSED A REAL THREAT TO VESTMANNAEYJAR, THE MAIN TOWN ON THE ISLAND, WITH 5,300 INHABITANTS AND AN IMPORTANT FISHING PORT, LYING JUST 1KM (⅔ MILE) TO THE NORTH.

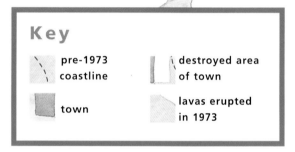

narrowed harbour entrance

Vestmannaeyjar

Eldfell ₛ

Helgafell ₛ

The authorities responded to the eruption first by evacuating the people and almost every moveable object of value from the town, and then by controlling the lava-flow advancing upon the harbour. These operations were aided by three factors. First, the fishing boats were in port sheltering from a storm, and were all therefore available for the evacuation. Second, the intensity of the eruption waned markedly after the first month, making its effects easier to control. Third, the eruption was a moderate Strombolian type: an outburst 1km (⅔ mile) further north on the same fissure would have caused a vigorous Surtseyan eruption in the harbour itself, that would have probably

Key

- ┄┄ pre-1973 coastline
- ▨ town
- ▨ destroyed area of town
- ▨ lavas erupted in 1973

destroyed the ships, the port and the town. The eruption was, however, a significant threat, and the action taken against it represents one of the very few successful operations ever accomplished against volcanic activity.

About 30 hours of increasing earthquakes warned everyone to prepare. At 01.55 on 23

The harbour at Vestmannaeyjar. Piles of volcanic ash reached 5m (16½ft) high in the eastern part of the town nearest to the volcano. Ash buried or burnt 80 houses in the area

January, an orange curtain of lava, 200m (656ft) high, appeared from a fissure stretching 1,800m (5,900ft) from the old volcano, Helgafell. Within a couple of days, activity had concentrated on one chimney exploding ash and cinders, and oozing lava eastward into the sea. On 30 January, the new cone, named Eldfell, had reached 185m (607ft) high, the lava-flow had added 1km² (⅖ square mile) to the eastern coast, and hot ash had crushed and set fire to some of the wooden houses in Vestmannaeyjar. By this time, however, the inhabitants had long been evacuated.

Lava-flows engulf this house located near to the volcano

The evacuation was a victory for contingency planning and efficient organization. Seventy-seven fishing boats in Vestmannaeyjar harbour took most of the people to the mainland; the old and infirm were taken by air. Within seven hours, most of the 5,300 inhabitants had been installed in temporary accommodation. Only the police and those with special skills likely to be useful in the emergency stayed behind. They then evacuated the animal livestock, cars, deep-frozen fish, administrative files, and the cash in the bank. A seven-person committee directed operations.

In late January and early February 1973, those who had stayed on Heimaey continually fought the hot ash piling up as much as 5m (16½ft) deep in the eastern part of Vestmannaeyjar. Metal sheets were nailed over the windows to stop them from being broken by volcanic bombs and large cinders. They

At night lava from the volcano illuminates the sky over Vestmannaeyjar

shovelled ash from the roofs to stop it crushing houses or setting them on fire. It was necessary to wear gas masks in the lower-lying areas and in cellars to guard against the dense, invisible and deadly carbon dioxide that sometimes erupted with the ash. No-one was killed. In spite of these efforts, ash buried or burnt about 80 houses, mainly in eastern Vestmannaeyjar, nearest the volcano. From mid-February, the explosions began to decline.

Then a new problem loomed: part of the crater wall of the new cone collapsed. The lavas were now free to flow northwards to Vestmannaeyjar harbour, instead of harmlessly eastwards. Officials considered the options. Bombing the crater might succeed, but there was always the

danger that the west wall of the crater would also collapse, and direct even more lava straight onto the town. As the lava-flow could not be safely diverted near its source, volunteers began pouring seawater onto its snout, to make the flow solidify faster and slow down. As soon as it became apparent that this method was working the Icelandic government, and then the United States sent ships with powerful pumps to quench the lavas more effectively. Soon, 20,000m³ (706,300ft³) of lava was solidifing every hour and, at the same time, ash barriers were bulldozed up around the flow to protect the rest of Vestmannaeyjar.

In spite of these heroic efforts the lava flows still cut the electricity supply from the mainland and destroyed three fish-processing factories and over 300 houses before they were brought to a halt. Disaster was averted but at huge cost in terms of time and money.

damage limitation in the Philippines

South China Sea

LUZON

Zambales Range

Pinatubo
● *Clark Air Force Base*
● *Manila*

FORECASTING A VOLCANIC ERUPTION DEPENDS NOT ONLY ON VOLCANIC STUDIES AND ASSESSMENTS, COMMUNICATION, AND A CORRECT PERCEPTION OF THE DANGERS POSED, IT ALSO REQUIRES ACTION. THE ERUPTION OF MT PINATUBO IN 1991 CLEARLY SHOWS THE RESULTS OF AN EFFECTIVE OPERATION IN TERMS OF MONITORING, ASSESSING THE THREAT, AND THEN COMMUNICATING AND ACTING UPON THE DANGER.

On 1 April 1991 Mt Pinatubo, a volcano in the Zambales Range, 80km (50 miles) north of Manila, capital of the Philippines, was thought to be 'dormant' as there had been no eruptions in recorded history. About 500,000 people lived on the plains around Pinatubo and about 15,000 semi-nomadic Aeta people, growing coffee, bananas and root crops, lived on the thickly forested slopes. There were also some 16,000 US personnel at Clark Air Force Base nearby.

In the afternoon of 2 April 1991 the villagers of Patal Pinto saw ash and steam explode, 500m (1,640ft) high, from a crack on the upper northern slopes of Pinatubo. On 4 April the first report of this activity was made to the headquarters of the Philippine Institute of Volcanology and Seismology (PHIVOLCS). Five thousand people were immediately evacuated from the vulnerable area within 10km (6¼ miles) of the summit. Surveillance was set up, and 40–178 volcanic earthquakes were recorded per day. Close contact was established with the US Geological Survey and Clark Air Force Base.

In early May geological field studies were undertaken which revealed a history of violent eruptions stretching back 1 million years, with the latest outburst about 400–600 years ago. There had been frequent ash-falls, volcanic mudflows and nuées ardentes, which had spread 20km (12½ miles) from the crest. On 23 May a hazard map was published, showing the likely spread of ash-falls, volcanic mudflows, and nuées ardentes. The National Disaster Organizations distributed the map to all national and local civil and military authorities.

Over the next week Alert Levels assigned to the increasing possibility of a major eruption were issued. On 8 June molten rock reached the surface and formed a dome of viscous lava, north-west of the crest. On 9 June the first nuées ardentes erupted at 14.55, and raced 4km (2½ miles) down the valley. PHIVOLCS issued Alert Level 5 ('eruption in progress') at 15.15. About 25,000 people were evacuated from an area within 20km (12½ miles) of Pinatubo.

The climax of the eruption occurred between 12–15 June. A Plinian eruption at 08.51 on 12 June generated a column 19km (12 miles) high in 19 minutes. Several other outbursts followed. Nuées ardentes raced down the main valleys, devastating some villages already evacuated. There was a general evacuation of all within 30km (18½ miles) of the crest, making a total of 58,000 evacuees. The climax of the eruption on 15 June 1991 formed a column up to 40km (25 miles) high. Earthquakes caused the summit to collapse into a caldera, 2km (1¼ miles) across.

Pinatubo quickly calmed down from 16 June and Alert Levels were gradually reduced. Two cities and 61 municipalities were declared calamity areas. About 860km² (332 square miles) of agricultural land was covered in thick ash. The

forecasting

Mudflows from Pinatubo as viewed from space. The abandoned Clark Air Force Base that housed 16,000 US personnel prior to the eruption is towards the upper left corner of the photograph

Key

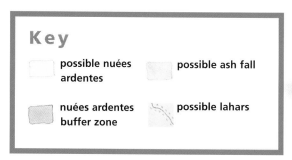

possible nuées ardentes	possible ash fall
nuées ardentes buffer zone	possible lahars

Aeta tribes lost nearly all of their traditional homeland. The Office of Civil Defence listed 847 dead, 184 injured and 23 missing. Of these, 537 died from diseases caught at the evacuation centres, 29 were victims of volcanic mudflows, and 281 were killed when roofs collapsed under the weight of ash drenched by typhoon rains. Thus, deaths caused by the eruption itself were effectively minimized. Efficient organization and communication and prompt evacuation saved thousands of lives.

Hazard map published before the eruption

Areas affected following eruption

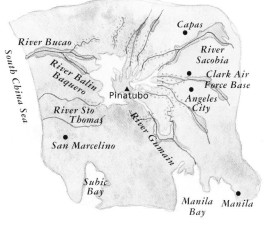

Key

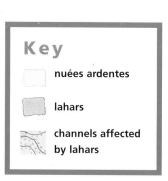

	nuées ardentes
	lahars
	channels affected by lahars

the future

IN SPITE OF ALL THE DIFFICULTIES FACED BY SCIENTISTS AND THE AUTHORITIES WHEN THEY ARE CONFRONTED BY THE THREAT OF EARTHQUAKES OR ERUPTIONS, CONTINUED EFFORTS TOWARDS ACCURATE PREDICTION AND DAMAGE LIMITATION ARE ESSENTIAL.

There are several basic lessons to be learned from past events. First, we should try to avoid living in the most dangerous spots, such as valleys draining from violent active volcanoes, or on weak sands and clays along active fault-lines. Second, we should endeavour to construct the strongest possible buildings, which is costly, but not as costly as the damage that can otherwise ensue. Third, danger spots should be monitored so that real warning signals can be detected, predictions can be made, and threatened areas can be evacuated in time. Fourth, there should be adequate, clearly designated refuges and organized practice-evacuations, so that the people recognize the danger and know exactly what to do when the danger threatens.

In reality, not all these lessons can be applied: Tokyo, Los Angeles and San Francisco, for instance, cannot be moved, and are growing increasingly crowded and therefore more vulnerable to earthquakes. Thousands of houses have been built higher and higher up the slopes of Vesuvius, on ground devastated by eruptions in the past few centuries. Japan and the United States do, however, have the resources to fund extensive monitoring and to make use of costly building techniques. Less developed and/or less politically stable countries are unable to afford such schemes, and are also ill-equipped to organise and implement emergency plans in the event of a disaster.

There is always the hope, however, that scientific advances will produce increasingly accurate predictions thereby minimizing the number of casualties and the amount of damage caused. Nevertheless, even if a successful prediction can be made, it has no practical value in the absence of appropriate action. In recognition of both of past failures, and the inability of many countries to cope with the effects of natural disasters, the United Nations has named the 1990s the International Decade for Natural Disaster Reduction. It was calculated that, between 1970 and 1990, natural disasters in the world, ranging from floods and hurricanes to volcanic eruptions and earthquakes, had cost 2.8 million lives and billions of US dollars. The problem is exacerbated in developing countries, where population, industrialization and city crowding have expanded so fast, that increasingly lethal natural disasters are inevitable unless new measures are adopted. In 1985, the mudflow from Nevado del Ruiz killed 23,000 people, primarily because damage-limitation procedures were not properly implemented. In 1991, orderly evacuations from the zone of much greater danger around Pinatubo saved at least twice that number of lives. In 1988, the Armenian earthquake buried 25,000 people when badly-constructed buildings collapsed heaps of rubble, but an earthquake of a roughly similar magnitude at Northridge, California, in 1992 claimed only 57 lives.

If the examples given in this book tell us anything it is that we cannot attempt to contain our savage Earth. The tasks for the future are to discover more about it, learn how to live with it, and above all to respect it. Be warned and beware.

forecasting

From top to bottom: Anak Krakatau, Indonesia; Nevado del Ruiz, Colombia; the cell of Sylbaris, St Pierre, Martinique; Tokyo at night

glossary

ash
Pulverized volcanic rock exploded violently from a vent in small fragments. It can form cones, widespread blankets on land, and the finest particles may remain in the stratosphere for years.

basalt
A dark, pasty-grey volcanic rock, poor in silica (about 50 per cent or less by weight) and relatively rich in iron, calcium and magnesium. By far the most common volcanic rock, forming the bulk of the ocean floors, and on land it occurs in many lava-flows, cinder cones, shield volcanoes and volcanic plateaux. On eruption it is usually hot and fluid, and flows 10km (6¼ miles) are common. It is chiefly erupted in effusive emissions without violent explosions, from fissures as well as single vents.

caldera
A large almost circular or horse-shoe shaped hollow, several kilometres across, formed mainly by collapse into the magma reservoir, but also by great volcanic explosions. Usually bounded by steep enclosing walls and formed most often on strato-volcanoes. The term is derived from the Spanish word for cauldron. The Portuguese spelling, 'caldeira', is sometimes used.

cinder cone
A steep conical hill, usually less than 250m (820ft) high, with straight slopes at the angle of rest of the loose materials composing the cone. Formed when moderate repeated explosions accumulate layers of cinders, lapilli and ash.

collision
Occurs when two plates carrying continental masses are pushed together, causing many faults and folds in the rocks and long, high mountain ranges in the continents.

convergent boundary
A boundary between two plates where they are moving together with the result that one plunges beneath the other and becomes assimilated into the mantle. This type of interaction can occur between two continental plates, two oceanic plates, or a continental and an oceanic plate.

crater
A bowl-shaped hollow in the summit of a volcano which lies directly above the vent from which fragments are ejected.

crust
The solid but brittle outer layer of the Earth forming the upper part of the lithosphere. It comprises continental crust composed of granitic types of rock, and oceanic crust, composed of denser, basaltic types of rock. The continental crust occupies relatively small areas resting on the continuous oceanic crust below.

divergent boundary
A boundary between two plates that are moving or rifting apart where volcanic activity creates new continental or oceanic crust.

earthquake
A sudden shaking of the Earth caused when a dislocation occurs along a fault. The pent-up energy released reverberates in waves from the point of dislocation.

earthquake epicentre
The point on the Earth's surface that is situated directly above the focus of an earthquake.

earthquake focus
The exact place in the Earth's crust where the dislocation causing an earthquake first occurs.

earthquake intensity
A scale of 12 degrees (I–XII), developed by Mercalli, and later modified, that describes the various amounts of surface damage caused by earthquakes.

earthquake magnitude
A scale developed by Richter, and later modified, designed to measure the energy released by an earthquake at its focus.

earthquake waves
Waves of energy that spread out through the Earth's crust from the focus of an earthquake. There are two types of body waves (P-waves and S-waves) that travel through the Earth, and two types of surface waves (Rayleigh waves and Love waves) that travel just beneath the Earth's surface.

elastic rebound
A sudden release of energy stored in rocks subjected to stresses and strains resulting in movement along a fault.

eruption
The way in which volcanic materials – gases, liquids and solids – are expelled onto the Earth's surface from a volcano.

fault
A crack in the Earth's crust caused

when the stresses and strains derived from plate movements dislocate the brittle rocks. Faults can be 'normal', 'reverse', or 'horizontal', depending on the direction of the dislocation. 'Blind' or 'masked' faults are covered by sediments and are thus invisible at the Earth's surface.

fault scarp
A cliff created by movement along a fault, representing the exposed surface of the fault before it is altered by weathering etc.

fissure
A crack, fault, fracture, or cluster of joints, cutting deep into the Earth's crust, up which magma may rise. Usually produces lava-flows with some cinder cones.

forecast
An informed estimate that an earthquake or eruption is most likely to take place within a period of several years, decades, or centuries.

fumarole
A vent giving off gases or steam and often surrounded by fragile precipitated crystals. Occurs on active and dormant volcanoes.

geological time
The entire history of the Earth, stretching back 4,600 million years, that is revealed by study of the rocks composing the crust.

geyser
A fountain of water, heated by volcanic activity, that spurts from the ground at intervals.

granite
A coarse-grained crystalline rock composed chiefly of quartz and feldspars. It forms when rhyolitic magma solidifies and crystallizes below the Earth's surface, and is only exposed by erosion.

historic time
The period during which events have been recorded by observers. It varies from about 3,000 years around the Mediterranean and in China, and 200 years in parts of the Americas.

hotspot
A stationary plume of rising mantle which generates chains of volcanoes as the plates move over it.

island arc
A gently curving chain of volcanic islands rising above sea-level from the ocean floor, formed when an oceanic plate is subducted beneath another. Volcanic chains are their equivalent on land.

landslide
A sudden, massive movement of rocks downslope under the influence of gravity, caused when earthquakes or eruptions make the bedrock unstable.

lava
Derived directly from magma, lava reaches the surface as molten rock or magma, but it soon cools and solidifies as flows, domes on land, and pillows under the sea. When shattered by gas explosions, it also forms fragments ranging in size from dust to blocks that are thrown through the air.

liquefaction
The invasion of rocks, sands and alluvium by groundwater when violent earthquakes greatly increase water pressure.

lithosphere
The brittle, solid outer shell of the Earth comprising both the crust and the solid upper part of the mantle. Broken up into plates, it is very thin at the mid-ocean ridges and thickest under the continents.

magma
Hot rock material formed by partial melting of the mantle below the lithosphere, usually at depths of 70–200km (43½–124 miles). It is a viscous liquid containing both gases and solid crystals. When it erupts on the Earth's surface, the gases explode and the molten materials form flows and fragments of lava.

magma reservoir
A large zone of ill defined fissures and cavities in the lithosphere where rising magma halts for varying lengths of time. Usually 2–50km (1¼–31 miles) deep.

mantle
The hot, but not wholly mobile layer of Earth situated below the Earth's crust and which envelops the Earth's core.

mid-ocean ridge
A large ridge on the ocean floor, where volcanic eruptions generate new oceanic crust, and where two plates diverge.

mudflow (lahar)
Fast-flowing and highly destructive currents of water, mud, sand, boulders or masonry, commonly formed when a volcanic eruption melts part of an ice-cap or disturbs a crater lake.

nuée ardente
A French term used to describe an incandescent cloud or glowing avalanche of hot gas and fragments

of all sizes, including ash, pumice rock debris in an aerosol-like emulsion expelled by explosive eruptions, which travels across the ground at very high speeds and gives off glowing, billowing clouds. It is, perhaps the most dangerous of all the forms of volcanic eruptions.

phreatic eruption

A sudden, violent eruption, chiefly of steam, that emits newly shattered fragments of older, solid rocks. Phreatic eruptions are caused when rising new magma meets water percolating downwards.

plate

Large, usually rigid slabs into which the lithosphere is broken. Their edges are the main zones where eruptions and earthquakes may occur, as the plates constantly diverge or converge, collide or plunge, or slide past each other.

prediction

An informed estimate that an earthquake or eruption is most likely to take place within a period of several hours or days.

rift

A long zone where the lithosphere is stretched, thinned and eventually broken so that areas on either side of it diverge. Rifting gives rise to faults, earthquakes and eruptions.

seamount

A volcanic mountain found below sea-level, and especially common in the Pacific Ocean. They often rise 2,000m (6,560ft) from the ocean floor. Active seamounts are being built up at present by submarine eruptions and could eventually form new volcanic islands. They may also be extinct, submerged remains of old volcanoes.

seismic gap

A sector of an earthquake-prone area where no earthquakes have taken place for an abnormally long time compared with sectors nearby. Such an area is deemed likely to experience an earthquake in the near future.

shield

A large, gently sloping volcano composed mainly of fluid basaltic lava-flows emitted from clustered vents, with relatively few fragmented layers.

silica

The molecule formed of silicon and oxygen (SiO_2) that is a fundamental component of volcanic rocks, and the most important factor in controlling the fluidity of magma. In general, the higher the silica content of a magma, the greater its viscosity.

solfatara

An Italian word used to describe the quiet emission of sulphurous gases from a fumarole.

strato-volcano

A large, often steep-sided volcanic cone composed of stratified, bedded layers of lava fragments and flows as well as many other volcanic products.

subduction zone

Where two plates converge and one sinks at an angle beneath the other into the mantle. The subducted slab stimulates melting in the mantle above it and helps form volcanoes. The slab's plunging action also generates violent earthquakes.

transform boundary

A boundary where two plates slide past one another without affecting the lithosphere

tsunami

A Japanese term used to describe huge, rapidly moving sea-waves generated by violent eruptions or earthquakes. Imperceptible in the open sea, tsunamis crash onto the shore at 80km/h (50mph) in waves reaching 30m (98ft) above sea-level. They are particularly common and dangerous in the Pacific Ocean.

vent

The conduit or pipe through which volcanic material travels through the crust to the Earth's surface.

volcanic chain

A series of volcanoes, arranged in a curve or straight line, erupted on the continents as a result of subduction. They are the land equivalents of island arcs.

volcanic fragments

Ash bombs, cinders, lapilli or pumice shattered by explosions during an eruption. They are the main constituent of cinder cones and many strato-volcanoes.

volcanic gas

Contained in small proportions within magma and commonly comprising, for example, steam, sulphur dioxide and carbon dioxide. As the magma closely approaches the Earth's surface, the gases are exsolved and can become a major factor in the violence of eruptions. Because several such gases are toxic, they can also be important contributors to volcanic death tolls.

volcano

A hill or mountain formed around and above a vent by accumulations of erupted materials, such as ash, pumice, cinders or lava-flows. The term refers both to the chimney or vent itself and to the often cone-shaped accumulation above it.

glossary

further reading

General

Levy, M. and Salvadori, M. (1995) *Why the Earth Quakes*. W.W. Norton & Company, New York, United States

Press, F. and Siever, R. (1986) *Earth*. W.H. Freeman, San Francisco, United States

Ritchie, D. (1994) *The Encyclopedia of Earthquakes and Volcanoes*. Facts on File, New York, United States

Tarbuck, Edward J. and Lutgens, Frederick K. (1996) *Earth: An Introduction to Physical Geology*. Prentice Hall, New Jersey, United States

Earthquakes

Aki, K. and Richard, P.G. (1981) *Quantitative Seismology*. W.H. Freeman, San Francisco, United States

Bolt, B.A. (1988) *Earthquakes*. W.H. Freeman, San Francisco, United States

Bolt, B.A. (1993) *Earthquakes and Geological Discovery*. Scientific American, New York, United States

Richter, C. (1958) *Elementary Seismology*. California Inst. of Technology, San Francisco, United States

Scholtz, C.M. (1980) *The Mechanics of Earthquakes and Faulting*. Cambridge University Press, Cambridge, United Kingdom

Yeats, R.S., Allen, C.R. and Sieh, K. (1996) *Geology of Earthquakes*. Oxford University Press, New York, United States

Volcanoes

Bullard, F.M. (1984) *Volcanoes of the Earth*. University of Texas Press, Austin, United States

Decker, R.W. and Decker, B.B. (1997) *Volcanoes*. W.H. Freeman, San Francisco, United States

Decker, R.W. and Decker, B.B. (1991) *Mountains of Fire*. Cambridge University Press, Cambridge, United Kingdom

Eyewitness Guide (1997) *Volcano*. Dorling Kindersley, London, United Kingdom

Fisher, R.V., Heiken, G. and Hulen, J.B. (1997) *Volcanoes: Crucibles of Change*. Princeton University Press, United States

Francis, P. (1976) *Volcanoes*. Penguin, United Kingdom

Green, J. and Short, N.M. (Eds) (1971) *Volcanic Landforms and Surface Features*. Springer, New York

Johnson, C. and Weisel, D. (1994) *Fire on the Mountain*. Chronicle Press, San Francisco, United States

Luhr, J.F. and Simkin, T. (Eds) (1993) *Parícutin: The Volcano Born in a Mexican Cornfield*. Geoscience Press, United States

Macdonald, G.A. (1972) *Volcanoes*. Prentice Hall, New Jersey, United States

Scarpa, R. and Tilling, R.I. (Eds) (1996) *Monitoring and Mitigation of Volcano Hazards*. Springer, Berlin, Germany

Scarth, A. (1994) *Volcanoes: An Introduction*. UCL Press, London, United Kingdom; Texas A. and M. University Press, Texas, United States

Simkin, T. and Siebert, L. (1994) *Volcanoes of the World*. Geoscience Press, United States

Periodicals and magazines

Fact Sheets, special reports and internet services are published by the Hazards Programs of the United States Geological Survey.

Also published by the United States Geological Survey, the periodical *Earthquakes & Volcanoes* was discontinued in 1995, but may still be held by some libraries.

Accessible articles may also occasionally appear in *Scientific American*, *Geographical Magazine* and *National Geographic*.

index

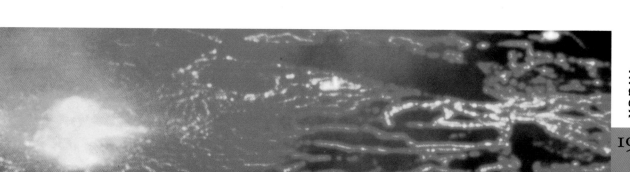

picture credits

Copyright in the photographs belongs to:
p.1 FLPA, R. Holcomb. p.2 t FLPA, Mex; b FLPA, S. Jonassan. p.3 t USGS, J.D. Griggs; b Northridge Collection, EERC, University of California, Berkeley, B. Stojadinovic. pp.4–5 t NASA; tc FLPA, S. McCutcheon; bc FLPA, M. Newman; b USGS/CVO, M.P. Doukas. p.6 cl USGS, J.P. Lockwood; cr USGS, J.D. Griggs; bl FLPA, S. Jonassan; br USGS, D.E. Wieprecht. p.10 tl USGS, W.C. Mendenhall; br USGS/CVO, L. Topinka. p.11 FLPA, D. Hosking. p.12 tl USGS, J.P. Lockwood; b FLPA, USGS/C. pp.14–15 t NASA; c USGS, R.E. Wallace; b FLPA/Panda Photo, S. Nardulli. Chapter motif pp.16–31 NASA. p.17 tl USGS, G. Tribble. pp.18–19 from Tarbuck, E.J. and Lutgens, F.K. *Earth*. p.27 b 19 FLPA, C. Mullen. p.29 FLPA/Panda Photo, G. Tomarchio. p.31 t NASA; bl USGS, R.E. Wallace; br FLPA, W. Wisniewski. pp.32–33 t USGS, M. Celebi; c FLPA, S. McCutcheon; b FLPA, Mex. Chapter motif pp.34–93 FLPA, S. McCutcheon. pp.35–37 Mary Evans Picture Library. p.39 cl USGS, California Earthquake 15; tr Granada Television. p.41 USGS, R.E. Wallace. p.42 br from Tarbuck, E.J. and Lutgens, F.K. *Earth*. p.43 t from Levy, M. and Salvadori, M. *Why the Earth Quakes*. p.45 USGS, J.K. Nakata. p.46 FLPA, Mex. p.47 FLPA, S. McCutcheon. p.48–49 USGS, W.C. Mendenhall. p.49 t USGS, W.C. Mendenhall; b USGS, G.K. Gilbert. p.50 tr USGS, M. Celebi; bl USGS, C.E. Meyer. p.51 USGS, Guatemalan Earthquake 25. p.52 USGS, Peruvian Earthquake 11. p.53 USGS, J.K. Nakata. p.54 bl USGS, Peruvian Earthquake 5; br USGS, Alaska Earthquake 238. p.55 bl USGS, Alaska Earthquake; br USGS, G.A. Lang Collection. p.56 USGS, Alaska Earthquake. p.57 FLPA, S. McCutcheon. p.58 FLPA, Mex. p.59 tl FLPA, Mex; br USGS, Alaska Earthquake. pp.60–61 USGS, J.K. Hilliers. p.63 t from Tarbuck, E.J. and Lutgens, F.K. *Earth*. p.64–65 Hulton Getty. p.66 b USGS, H.G. Wilshire. p.67 tl USGS, C.E. Meyer; tr USGS, J.K. Nakata. p.68 tl USGS, C.E. Meyer; tr Granada Television. p.69 USGS, J.K. Nakata. p.70 USGS, Alaska Earthquake. p.71 t USGS, Alaska Earthquake; b FLPA, S. McCutcheon. p.72 l © Bolt, B.A. *Earthquakes*; cr FLPA, S. McCutcheon. p.73 t FLPA, S. McCutcheon; b USGS, Alaska Earthquake. pp.74–77 Kobe Newspaper Company. p.78 tl Granada Television; b Kobe Newspaper Company. p.79 Kobe Newspaper Company. pp.80–83 Northridge Collection, EERC, University of California, Berkeley. p.80 R. Reitherman. p.81 br R. Reitherman. p.82 tr L. Lowes. p.83 tr, b B. Stojadinovic. p.84 bl Mary Evans Picture Library. p.85 tl, br Mary Evans Picture Library. p.86 b FLPA, Mex. p.87

tl FLPA, Mex; r FLPA, S. Harrison. p.88–89 FLPA, Mex. p.88 tl Granada Television. p.89 FLPA, Mex. p.90 tl, c, Mary Evans Picture Library. p.91 USGS/CVO, J. Valance. p.92 FLPA/Panda Photos, F. Parlato. p.93 Mary Evans Picture Library. pp.94–95 t FLPA, US National Parks Service; c FLPA, M. Newman; b FLPA, USGS, R Tilling. Chapter motif pp.96–153 FLPA, M. Newman. pp.98–99 USGS, J.D. Griggs. p.98 tl, tr USGS, J.D. Griggs; b USGS, J.P. Lockwood. p.99 USGS, J.D. Griggs. p.100 t USGS, J. Settle; tc FLPA/Panda Photo, J.C. Munoi; bc FLPA/Panda Photo, G. Prola; b FLPA/Panda Photo, A. Nardi. p.102 c, b USGS, D.E. Wieprecht. p.103 t FLPA/Panda Photo, G. Cammereini; b USGS, D.E. Wieprecht. p.104 FLPA, S. Jonasson. p.105 tr FLPA, Dr Guest; b FLPA/USGS, R. Tilling. p.106 FLPA, US National Parks Service. p.107 FLPA/Panda Photo, S. Nardulli. p.108 Mary Evans Picture Library. p.109 J-C Tanguy. p.110 FLPA, US National Parks Service. p.112 USGS, G. Tribble. p.114 tl USGS, J.P. Lockwood; bl FLPA, US National Parks Service. p.115 FLPA, M. Newman. pp.116–117. USGS, J.D. Griggs. p.116 tl Granada Television. p.117 tr USGS, J.D. Griggs. p.118 tl Granada Television; b USGS, J. Settle. p.119 FLPA, T. Micek. p.121 A. Scarth. p.123 tl, br FLPA/Panda Photo, L. Vigliotti. pp.125–127 FLPA, S. Jonasson. p.128 tr from LeGuern, F. *et al* 'Witness accounts of the catastrophic event of August 1986 at Lake Nyos (Cameroon)'; br USGS, M. Tuttle. p.129 b J-C Tanguy. p.130 bl FLPA, US National Parks Service. p.131 b USGS/CVO, D.A. Swanson. p.132 cr USGS/CVO, R.P. Hoblitt. p.133 r USGS/CVO, M.P. Doukas. p.134–135 t USGS/CVO, J. Vallance. p.134 c USGS/CVO, D. Dzurisin; b USGS/CVO, L. Topinka. p.135 c USGS/CVO, L. Topinka; b USGS/WRD, P. Carpenter. p.136 tl Granada Television bl D.A. Swanson. p.137 tl USGS/CVO H. Glicken; br USGS/CVO, T.J. Casadevall. p.138 t Mary Evans Picture Library. p.139 t A. Scarth; b Mary Evans Picture Library. p.140 Underwood & Underwood. Library of Congress. p.141 tl Mary Evans Picture Library; bl A. Scarth. pp.143 'Lancaster Sands' J.M.W. Turner, Birmingham Museums and Art Gallery. p.144 cl FLPA/Panda Photo, A. Nardi; br Mary Evans Picture Library. p.145 b Mary Evans Picture Library. p.146 A. Scarth. p.147 FLPA, US National Parks Service. pp.148–149 FLPA/Panda Photo, G. Cammereini. p.149 t from Sigurdsson, H. *et al* 'Pre-eruption compositional gradients and mixing of andesite and dacite magma erupted from Nevado del Ruiz volcano, Colombia in 1985'. p.152 b Granada Television. p.153 c

Mary Evans Picture Library. pp.154–155 t FLPA/Panda Photo, A. Nardi; c FLPA/Panda Photo, R. Massoli Novelli; b FLPA/Silvestris, J. Kuchelbauer. Chapter motif pp.156–183 USGS/CVO, M.P. Doukas. p.156 FLPA, H. Hautala. p.157 tr Kobe Newspaper Company; bl The Natural History Museum, London. p.158 t USGS/HVO; b USGS. p.160 tl; br Granada Television. p.161 M. McShane. pp.162–163 Institute of Geology, China. p.164 cl, tr Granada Television; b Institute of Geology, China. p.165 tr Institute of Geology, China. p.166–167 USGS, G.A. Lang Collection. p.168 USGS. p.169 FLPA/Silvestris, J. Kuchelbauer. pp.170–171 Northridge Collection, EERC, University of California, Berkeley. p.170 cr M. Aschheim. p.172 J-L Renaud. p.173 t FLPA/Panda Photo, A. Bardi; b J-L Renaud. pp.174–175 J-C Tanguy. p.176 tl from Barberi, F. *et al* 'The control of lava flow during the 1991–1992 eruption of Mount Etna; br FLPA/Panda Photo, G. Tomarchio. p.177 J-C Tanguy. pp.178–179 FLPA, S. Jonasson. p.181 t NASA; br from Wolfe, E.W. 'The 1991 eruptions of Mount Pinatubo, Philippines'. p.183 t Granada Television; tc FLPA/Panda Photo, G. Cammereini; bc A. Scarth; b FLPA, H Hautala. pp.184–185 NASA. pp.186–187 FLPA/Silvestris, J. Kuchelbauer. pp.188–189 M. Aschheim, Northridge Collection, EERC, University of California, Berkeley. pp.190–191 FLPA, R. Tilling. p.192 USGS, R.E. Wallace

Maps by: Neil Bulpitt. Artwork by: Roger Locke and Elaine Leggett at Oxford Illustrators; Raymond Turvey; Simon Williams

Thanks to: Julie Francis; the SAVAGE EARTH team at Granada Television

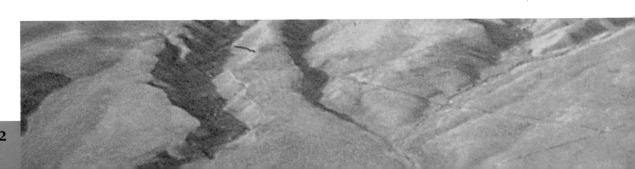